CULTURE

A Survival Guide to Customs and Etiquette

SHANGHAI

Rebecca Weiner
Angie Eagan
Xu Jun

Marshall Cavendish
Editions

Photo Credits:
All photos from Xu Jun except page xii (Lonely Planet Images). ▪ Cover
photo: Masterfile/Albert Normandin

All illustrations by TRIGG

First published in 2003
Copyright © 2005 Marshall Cavendish International (Asia) Private Limited

Published by Marshall Cavendish Editions
An imprint of Marshall Cavendish International
1 New Industrial Road, Singapore 536196

Other Marshall Cavendish Offices:
Marshall Cavendish Ltd. 119 Wardour Street, London W1F 0UW, UK ▪ Marshall
Cavendish Corporation. 99 White Plains Road, Tarrytown NY 10591-9001, USA
▪ Marshall Cavendish Beijing. D31A, Huatingjiayuan, No. 6, Beisihuanzhonglu,
Chaoyang District, Beijing, The People's Republic of China, 100029 ▪ Marshall
Cavendish International (Thailand) Co Ltd. 253 Asoke, 12th Flr, Sukhumvit 21
Road, Klongtoey Nua, Wattana, Bangkok 10110, Thailand ▪ Marshall Cavendish
(Malaysia) Sdn Bhd, Times Subang, Lot 46, Subang Hi-Tech Industrial Park,
Batu Tiga, 40000 Shah Alam, Selangor Darul Ehsan, Malaysia

Marshall Cavendish is a trademark of Times Publishing Limited

National Library Board Singapore Cataloguing in Publication Data
Weiner, Rebecca.
CultureShock! : Shanghai / Rebecca Weiner, Angie Eagan, Xu Jun. –
Singapore : Marshall Cavendish Editions, 2005.
p. cm. – (CultureShock!)
ISBN : 981-261-130-4
1. Etiquette – China – Shanghai . 2. Shanghai (China) – Social life and
customs. I. Eagan, Angie. II. Xu, Jun. III. Title. IV. Series: CultureShock!
DS721
951.132 -- dc21   SLS2005034521

Printed in Singapore by Times Graphics Pte Ltd

ABOUT THE SERIES

Culture shock is a state of disorientation that can come over anyone who has been thrust into unknown surroundings, away from one's comfort zone. *CultureShock!* is a series of trusted and reputed guides which has, for decades, been helping expatriates and long-term visitors to cushion the impact of culture shock whenever they move to a new country.

Written by people who have lived in the country and experienced culture shock themselves, the authors share all the information necessary for anyone to cope with these feelings of disorientation more effectively. The guides are written in a style that is easy to read and covers a range of topics that will arm readers with enough advice, hints and tips to make their lives as normal as possible again.

Each book is structured in the same manner. It begins with the first impressions that visitors will have of that city or country. To understand a culture, one must first understand the people—where they came from, who they are, the values and traditions they live by, as well as their customs and etiquette. This is covered in the first half of the book

Then on with the practical aspects—how to settle in with the greatest of ease. Authors walk readers through how to find accommodation, get the utilities and telecommunications up and running, enrol the children in school and keep in the pink of health. But that's not all. Once the essentials are out of the way, venture out and try the food, enjoy more of the culture and travel to other areas. Then be immersed in the language of the country before discovering more about the business side of things.

To round off, snippets of basic information are offered before readers are 'tested' on customs and etiquette of the country. Useful words and phrases, a comprehensive resource guide and list of books for further research are also included for easy reference.

CONTENTS

Introduction vii

Acknowledgements viii

Map of China x

Map of Shanghai xi

Chapter 1
First Impressions 1

Chapter 2
The Pearl of the Orient Lives! 5

Geography is Destiny:
The City on the Sea 6

Treaty Port
and Entrepôt 8

And Yet... And Yet... 10

The Jazz Age 11

The Chaos Years 12

The New Jazz Age 13

New Shanghai 14

Chapter 3
Shanghai's People 17

Shanghai Sojourners:
The Famously Famous 18

Shanghailanders
and Shanghainese 22

Shanghailanders and
Shanghailanders 24

The Newly
Famous of Shanghai 27

The 'Shanghai Gang'
in Beijing 27

Of Tossed Salads and
Melting Pots, Layer-Cakes
and Stir-fries 28

Chapter 4
Shanghai Life Cycles 35

Shanghai Culture Tips 36

The Wheel of
the Shanghai Year 43

Cycles of Life 47

Chapter 5
Settling In 54

A Bit of History... 56

Living the High Life:
Serviced Apartments 58

High Rise at Lower Cost:
Non-serviced Apartments 60

Downtown Garden Villas 62

Shanghai's Suburbs:
'Shangurbia' 64

Other Interesting
Housing Options 67

Buying Your Home
Away from Home
in Shanghai 69

For Kids and Families 70

Baby-sitter Bonanza:
Shanghai with
Small Children 72

Baby Supplies 73

Reading, Writing
and 'Rithmetic 74

Sticker Shock 75

Extra-curricular Activities 76

Family Fun Time 77

Teenagers 83

Mommy Needs a Break...
the All Important Ayi 84

Adult Education 86

Shopping Till You Drop 89

Hong Kong Pricey or
Xiang Yang Dicey:
Spotting Fakes 90

Custom Tailoring 91

Osh Kosh... My Gosh!
Suiting your Little Emperor
in Shanghai 93

Toys 93

A Book is Like a Garden
Carried in the Pocket
(Chinese Proverb) 95

Antiques and 'Antiques'—
DongTai Lu, Hu & Hu, etc. 95

Stocking the Fridge 96

Sundries and Necessaries 98

Money, Banking and Credit Cards	99
Health Care in Shanghai	101
Shanghai's Health Care System: Options for Foreigners	102
Health Insurance	105
Other Health Concerns	106
Tips For a Healthy Stay	108
Subways to Bike Lanes: Shanghai's Transportation	110
Taxis	111
Long-term Car Hire/ Car Purchase	112
Subway and Buses	113
Bicycles	115
Getting a Shanghai Driver's Licence and Car	116
Feet	118
Logistics, Formalities and Safety	118
Visa Matters	119
Household Goods Relocation	120
Telecommunications	123
Safety & Security	124

Chapter 6
Eating Your Way Around Shanghai
128

Eating In	129
Preparing for Guests	130
Protocol for Entertaining Traditional Chinese Guests	131
Eating Your Way Round the World	132
Chinese Cooking in China	133
The Many Cuisines of China—in Shanghai	134
A Short List of Long-Time Favourites	137
Shanghai Dim-sim and Snacks	152
International Cuisine	154
Fusion Food	156

Chapter 7
Enjoying Life
159

Sports and Outdoor Activities	161
Intellectual Clubs	163
Taking to the Street	165
Massage	165
'High Culture'	166
Late Night Prowling	167
Competitive Karaoke	173
Recreational Guides	173
Festivals	174
Beyond the Bund: Shanghai's Many Neighbourhoods	176
Old City	178
The Bund	181
Fuzhou Lu and Renmin Square	182
Jing'ansi and Nanjing Road	188
The Guesthouse District	191
The French Connection: Lu Wan District	194
Xujiahui and Longhua: Martyrs Christian and Communist	199
Hongqiao: Mistressville and the Suburbs of the West	202
Jewish History and the Hongkou 'Ghetto'	203
Pudong	209
Past City Limits	212
Day Trips	213
Weekend Excursions	217
Volunteering	220
Charitable Giving in China	222
Charitable Due Diligence in China	224
Charitable Organisations that Welcome Foreign Involvement	225
Additional Ways to Get Involved	232

Chapter 8

Learning Shanghainese
234

Origins of Shanghainese	235
Shanghainese and 'Immigrant Chinese'	236
Shanghainese Today	237
Pronunciation	238
Common Phrases	240
Non-verbal Communication	243

Chapter 9

Business Unusual
244

Think Local: Be Aware of Shanghai's 'Special Status'	245
Be Flexible, in this City of Rapid Change	249
Maintaining a Clear Channel with HQ	257
Building Strong Cross-cultural Teams in Shanghai	262

Think Broadly: Consider All Your Markets and Audiences	266
Keep a Tight Lid on Costs	268
Think Globally: Help Shanghai Move to Globally-Accepted Norms	270

Chapter 10

Fast Facts about Shanghai
54

Culture Quiz	280
Do's and Don'ts	291
Glossary	293
Resource Guide	299
Further Reading	322
About the Authors	327
Index	330

Why Shanghai?

Well, if you've picked up this book, you probably already know some of the attractions of this fast-growing metropolis. You're taking an expatriate position with one of the estimated 100,000-plus foreign-invested firms in the city. You're planning to teach or study at one of Shanghai's 50-plus universities, or research in one of the specialised institutes powering further growth, or perform or display works in one of the city's thousands of art spaces. Or you are a diplomat, or are accompanying a spouse to a position in Shanghai, and want a meaningful life there in your own right. You want to make the most of your time in Shanghai, and this book was written to help you.

The authors are all seasoned Shanghai business-people who, like well over 60 per cent of city residents (Chinese and foreign), were not born there. We all had to adjust to life in this mega-metropolis, and have come to love the place, and are happy to share some of what we have learned, in the hope you will love your time in Shanghai too.

ACKNOWLEDGEMENTS

We all met working for Burson-Marsteller, the world's (and China's) largest public affairs and public relations consultancy, and have shared the challenges and triumphs of helping firms succeed in East China's complex business climate. Our Burson-Marsteller experience informs all these pages, especially the Chapter 9: Business Unusual. The authors are grateful to Susan Tomsett, Chief Operating Officer, Burson-Marsteller/China, for permission to reprint here some case studies originally developed for the firm. For more information on Burson in China, see http://www.bm.com.

We are also enormously grateful for the assistance of several area experts who have donated time and energy to write some of our sections. These are:

- Sam Crispin, of Crispin Property Consultants (samcrispin@sipin.net), for writing the section on finding the right home for yourself (pages 55–70)
- Susan Schleu Schulman: Mom, expat wife, and part-time employee of AmCham for contributing both the sections, 'For Kids And Families' (pages 69–87) and 'Shopping Till You Drop' (pages 87–96).
- Andrea Phillips, Director of Marketing and Client Services, Shanghai World Link Health Centres, and Governor, AmCham, for both the sections, 'Health Care in Shanghai' (pages 96–103) and 'Volunteering: A Place For Your Heart' (pages 216–228)
- The wife/husband team of Helen Yan, former Burson colleague, and Josh Perlman of Groove Street for the section 'Logistics, Formalities and Safety' (pages 107–116).
- Seth Kaplan, Shanghai Jewish organiser/educator,for contributing the section on Hongkou and Jewish History (pages 201–207)
- We also thank Grant Xia, Burson colleague and Shanghai native, for reviewing Chapter 4: Shanghai Life Cycles (pages 36–53); Louise Leonard, Marketing Consultant/community organiser, for reviewing the section 'Past City Limits' (pages 210–215); and Susan Tomsett for reviewing Chapter 9: Business Unusual (pages 245–274).
- We thank Carl Yiu for creating the subway map (page 114) for this book.

We also deeply thank Angie's super executive assistant Shu Ping, for invaluable help with maps, websites, fact-checking, and other support. Last but not least, the authors thank the editorial team at Marshall Cavendish for the opportunity to write this book, and for their stellar job in transforming manuscript to publication. The book has been made far stronger by the comments and contributions of all these experts. Any errors which remain are, of course, our own responsibility.

The Authors
August 2005

MAP OF CHINA

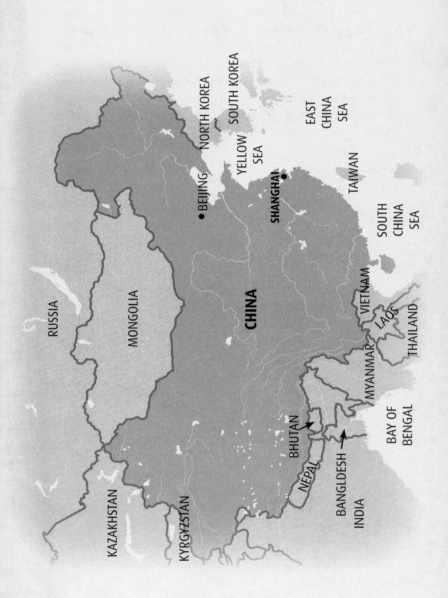

The hip and trendy in Shanghai.

FIRST IMPRESSIONS

CHAPTER 1

'The light of the city illuminates the soul.
The sunlight bouncing off glass and chrome, its heat
reflecting off the hot pavement, or cool-coloured neon at
night. The Chinese have a word *renao*... which literally
means warm and noisy. This is the essence of city light:
the heat of the crowd and excitement, noisy to the senses.'
—Vivienne Tam, *China Chic*

JUST WHAT IS THAT OVERWHELMING *RENAO*, the heated excitement with which Shanghai greets visitors and residents alike? It's a little different for us all.

Some new residents focus on the hustle-bustle excitement (and annoyance) of life in a perpetual construction zone. At the height of Shanghai's real estate boom, over 100 skyscrapers over 30 stories tall were going up at once, and rumour claimed the city housed some 25 per cent of the world's construction cranes. Chinese and global economic slowdowns have pruned things, but construction still proceeds at a pace that the most boosterish US and EU mayors must envy.

Others see Shanghai life as a cultural and social whirl, perhaps surrounding the grand museum invested in by city leaders eager to make marks on Asian and global cultural maps. Or the opera house, where performances range from Pavarotti to Andrew Lloyd Webber to Latin Salsa to Russian Ballet. Some focus on the jazz renaissance, the blues cafés of Maoming and Xintiandi, the Big Band on the Bund. Others love the wild nightlife: the strip-joints and transvestite shows, the bars and clubs of Julu Lu that get started at 2:00 am and end in bleary-eyed breakfasts at the 24-hour dumpling shop on Changshu Lu (*Lu* is Chinese for 'Road').

Then there's the academic Shanghai of Jiaotong and Fudan (and the city's 50 other colleges and universities), the financial Shanghai of stock exchange and banking empires centred

The Bund at night.

in Lujiazui, the industrial-muscle Shanghai of warehouses and factories and free trade zones. There's a Shanghai of incredible wealth, of graciously refurbished mansions in the tree-lined old French Concession, and soaring penthouses with river views. And there's (though less than there used to be) a Shanghai of abject poverty, of teeming alleys without running water where 'floating population' migrants return at night after shining shoes and sweeping construction sites for the better-off. There's even still a bit of old Shanghai, of shaded tea-houses and pretty parks where old men play elephant-chess while listening to caged songbirds and Kunju opera.

In other words, like all great metropolises, Shanghai is a universe unto itself. Its natives have the grandiose short-sightedness of all great urbanites, famously satirised in that cartoon 'New Yorker View of the World': Manhattan streets, a thin strip of New Jersey, the rest of America (some pimples labelled 'The Rockies'), and a few distant islands called 'China', 'Russia', 'Japan'. The Shanghai version would swoop from Pudong's futuristic Pearl TV Tower west over the old city to Hongqiao, then a strip of Jiangsu and Zhejiang Provinces, the rest of China (a pimple each for Huangshan and the Himalaya), then islands: 'Indian market', 'EU market', 'US market'. For true Shanghainese—bankers, tinkers, tailors, truckers—all those benighted souls Outside Town exist to buy their goods. It's a view that, soon enough, tends to influence new arrivals as well!

Feels Like Home

Rebecca (one of the co-authors) first saw Shanghai in 1985. She was teaching English in the then-sleepy coastal town of Qingdao, where her first car ride in from the airport, often at crawl speed behind bicycles and ox-carts, signalled that life had slowed down. In Qingdao, she learned much about Chinese culture, and enjoyed many new experiences (pig-ear dumplings, anyone?), but often felt more exotic than welcome. When she picnicked with students, Rebecca—one of only six foreigners then resident in Qingdao—drew gawking crowds by her mere presence.

Arriving by train to Shanghai for a long weekend visit, Rebecca found life suddenly speeding back up, becoming oddly and wonderfully familiar. More taxis than pedicabs swarmed the station; crowds bustled by, too busy to notice mere foreigners. Suddenly, Rebecca felt like the gawking bumpkin.

Dropping bags at a hostel, she walked up the Bund, its huge stone buildings and bustling crowds so like and unlike New York. Ending at the Peace Hotel, Rebecca sat in a proper café, at a table spread with a tablecloth, and ordered a coffee, croissant—and soymilk; like the city around her, a wonderful mix. Around her, both Chinese and foreigners from many countries spoke in a variety of languages. From across the lobby began to float the strains of jazz. Right then, Rebecca knew she would someday live in Shanghai; the place already felt like home.

Shanghai is, depending on your perspective, a feast for the senses, a mish-mash of cultures and experiences, or an overwhelming rush of *renao*. We hope in this book to introduce you to enough of her many faces and places to inspire you to continue with what could easily be a lifetime of exploration.

THE PEARL OF
THE ORIENT LIVES!

'shanghai (shâng-hi') v. To kidnap (a man) for
compulsory service aboard a ship, especially after
rendering him insensible.
Shanghai (shâng-hi'). A city of E. China.'
—*American Heritage Dictionary*

How can we summarise in a chapter the history and geography of a mega-metropolis so famous its name is a verb? The facts are easy enough. Shanghai, one of the world's largest and fastest growing cities, has an urban population topping 16,700,000 in an independent metropolitan district that has the status of a province. The central city covers some 340 sq km (131.3 sq miles) of flatlands where the Wusong River meets the Huangpu. That central city is core of a 'Greater Shanghai' of 6,300 sq km (2,432.4 sq miles) that sprawls across the whole rich river delta where the Changjiang (Yangtze) River, China's great 'water highway,' after its 6,400-km (3,976.8-mile) journey, meets the sea.

Thus, Shanghai is seaport, river-port and a major commercial and cultural entrepôt. It's also a birthplace of the revolution that led to modern China, and one of the engines of China's ongoing growth.

GEOGRAPHY IS DESTINY: THE CITY ON THE SEA

It all began with a few fisherman in the 7th century AD, setting up a mud-walled village here where the rivers turn salt (the Chinese characters for 'Shanghai' mean 'go up to the sea'). For centuries, locals netted shrimp and clams in the salt marshes of the delta, traded for rice and vegetables grown on fertile soils inland, and offered fresh water to seafaring junks that made it up the muddy estuary of the Huangpu. By

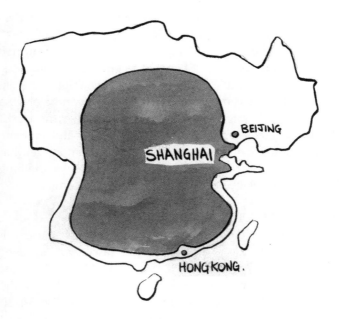

1265, the Mongol governors of the Yuan Dynasty established a Superintendency of Foreign Trade in what was already a key port of exchange with the newly formed nation of Japan; by 1292 Shanghai gained county-level status in the Yuan bureaucracy. In the 1420s, the Ming Dynasty Admiral Zheng He launched at least two of his massive armadas, en route to exploring sea-trade routes to India and Africa, from the Shanghai harbour of Liujiagang.

Of course, borderlands and trading ports are vulnerable to battles and blockades—and to politics. Shanghai's fortunes have 'waxed and waned with the amount of overseas trade and travel countenanced by the ruling power in Peking', writes historian Lynn Pan. In 1533, when the increasingly protectionist Ming Dynasty government banned foreign trade altogether, Shanghai merchants went bankrupt—or turned to piracy. The Ming fell and in the 1660s, the Qing government ordered the city evacuated, cordoning off coastal ports to block supplies to Ming loyalist rebels holed up on the island of Taiwan. As it is now, so it was then; there has long been a long, thin umbilical cord tying the wealth of Shanghai traders to the health of the markets in Taipei.

By the 1680s, Taiwan had (for the time being) returned to the Beijing fold, and Shanghai re-opened for business, growing rapidly with trade in the East China Sea: tea, silk, ivory and, increasingly, opium. Says Pan: 'even before the British flag was raised over it, Shanghai had become one of the world's greatest ports, with a forest of masts and a volume of trade equal to or greater than London's. It is not true what many foreigners have claimed, that the place was nothing but a sleepy village on a mudflat before they came.'

TREATY PORT AND ENTREPÔT

That foreigners did come, with their gunboats and extra-territorial laws, their bankers, lawyers, architects, soldiers, visionaries and missionaries, is a matter viewed almost schizophrenically in Shanghai. As the 'Opium Wars' of the 1840s wound down, leaving the trade world safe for British opium, Shanghai became a 'treaty port,' ceded in the 1842 Treaty of Nanking. The story is well-known: co-managed by British, French, American and (ultimately) Japanese governors, Shanghai was sliced into Chinese City, French Concession and International Settlement, concessions the foreign powers held until World War II. The Opium Wars were—and are—a symbol of China's humiliation. Charges that foreigners 'carved China up like a melon' became part of the war-cry that ultimately toppled the Qing dynasty, leading to Republican and then Communist China. It's no accident that the Chinese Communist Party (CCP) was founded in the ferment of anti-imperialist sentiment in foreign-controlled Shanghai.

Nor was the anti-imperialist sentiment limited to the Chinese; reform-minded foreigners also decried treaty port evils. Mark Twain wrote: 'these foreigner communities took it upon themselves to levy taxes on the Chinamen living in their so-called 'concessions'.... Perhaps these Chinamen were just as well governed as they would have been anywhere in China… but the principle was… taxation without representation—a policy which we [Americans] fought seven long years to overthrow'. Historian Hugh Deane notes that Twain was one of few Americans to support the Boxers, an anti-foreign movement in China that killed thousands in 1900, including in Shanghai. Twain called the Boxers 'patriots', writing to a friend that 'they have been villainously dealt with by the sceptered thieves of Europe, and I hope they will drive all foreigners out and keep them out for good'. In the end, Twain predicted, 'China will go free and save herself'.

Twain's description must have resonated still in the 1930s for Polish journalist and anti-opium crusader Ilona Ralf Sues, who preferred to: 'Let other people sing the praises of Shanghai. Granted it was a great modern city [like New York]… but New York's grandeur—the sweeping gesture of a giant sure of himself… was painfully absent from Shanghai. The city was cut up into several areas which hardly resembled one another…. But the atmosphere in all of them was identical. Cold, hard, conceited faces. Everybody seemed to despise everybody else'. That was the dark side of a Shanghai funded by gangs, drugs and slaves. That was how Shanghai became a verb.

Du Yueshen, Opium King

Ilona Ralf Sues was one of few journalists to personally interview Shanghai's opium boss Du Yueshen, 'a combination Al Capone and Rockefeller'. Du controlled an interlinked network of banks, factories, rural co-operatives, philanthropies, corrupt police, intelligence rackets and opium dens. He was also, rumours say, enslaved by his own top product. Sues described him as 'a gaunt, shoulderless figure with long, aimlessly swinging arms… receding forehead, no chin, huge, batlike ears, cold, cruel lips uncovering big, yellow, decayed teeth, the sickly complexion of an addict… [and] eyes so dark that they seemed to have no pupils, blurred and dull—dead, impenetrable eyes'.

Du was protected from arrest by patronage with 'Generalissimo' Chiang Kai Shek, head of the Nationalist Party (Kuomintang or KMT), the party the US backed in China's Civil War. Chiang earned the love of Shanghai's foreign bosses by slaughtering anti-imperialist Communists who threatened foreign rule. With Chiang's blessing, Du managed the 'Shanghai Opium Oppression Bureau', the ironically named monopoly by which Chiang and his brother-in-law, financier TV Soong, directed opium wealth into private pockets via shell firms like the (also ironically named) 'Farmer's Bank'.

Deane has described the climactic battle of April 1927 in which Chiang turned solidly into running-dog-of-imperialism. Before that, he'd co-operated with the fledgling CCP in a 'United Front' against Japanese aggression. But as United Front troops took Shanghai, supported by militant trade unions, foreign firms and residents feared losing property to radicals, so fighting the Japanese war machine took a back seat to fighting Communism. Writes Deane, 'The American Chamber of Commerce in Shanghai called for armed intervention by a concert of powers'. The powers responded. Soon 'forty-seven foreign warships were in the harbour', and 'reinforcing the Shanghai volunteer corps of armed foreigners were 9,500 British and 1,500 American troops'.

Chiang knew where his bread was buttered—or chopsticks laden. He 'turned on his Communist allies, and his troops and local gangsters began a massacre of unionists, students and all suspected Reds. The assembly of foreign armed forces found that its work was being done for it'. By the end of the slaughter (which went house to house through poor unionist neighbourhoods like Zhabei), historians estimate some 20,000 Chinese were dead; there were no known foreign casualties. Bodies were flung into a creek that ran stinking red till it was filled in and paved over (it's now Zhaojiabang Lu), and Chiang and TV Soong became darlings of the foreign community, entertained by admiralty aboard those warships. Within a few years, Japan occupied the area and the 'Rape of Nanjing' began.

AND YET... AND YET...

Unfair, unjust and corrupt as the treaty-port powers and their Chinese lackeys were, they also founded a society where cultural cross-fertilisation reached fusion intensity and created something new. 'Shanghai would not be Shanghai,' Lynn Pan admits, 'without the treaty port experience.' The foreigners brought administrative, legal and police systems, however self-serving, which influenced the city in positive ways—and are likely part of the reason why Shanghai government and businesses are still somewhat 'cleaner' than the rest of China. They built the banks and art-deco towers that make the stretch of grand Shanghai riverfront known as the Bund (itself an Anglo-Indian colonial word) such a symbol of wealth and power. If they turned a blind eye to the opium dens, prostitutes, taxi-dancers and filth in the city's poorer quarters, they also created—with elite Chinese—the glitterati that made jazz-era Shanghai the 'Pearl of the Orient'.

THE JAZZ AGE

'Consider,' Pan writes, 'the Club, the gaol and Courthouse, the racecourse, the amateur dramatic society…' Consider the Cathay (today the Peace Hotel), a monument of art-deco luxury where beautiful people danced all night in the private ballroom of builder Sir Victor Sassoon, and Noel Coward recovered from fever while writing *Private Lives*. It was an era of passion and fashion, when everyone loved the 'Shanghai Ladies', those sexy-kittenish calendar girls both slim and lush in their high-necked *cheongsam*, advertising everything from cigarettes to perfume to soap.

That glittering Shanghai—and the legal protections of the foreign enclaves—brought local immigrants flocking from all over China. The poor sought work, the wealthy opportunities, and Bohemian artists sought the cultural freedom of the concessions. Thus came what Pan calls the third of the 'fertile encounters' that created modern Shanghai: of land and sea, Chinese and foreign, and immigrant with immigrant. By 1880, only 15 per cent of the Chinese in Shanghai were born there. The rest came to the metropolis, adopted its ways, and learned its local patois (Shanghainese is to Mandarin Chinese—the official national dialect—as French is to Spanish: close, but not mutually intelligible without study). The question 'What defines a Shanghainese?' Pan writes, could only be answered 'by reference to abstract qualities such as cosmopolitanism and urbanity'.

As war engulfed the world, adventurers and refugees poured into Shanghai, one of few global havens for the stateless: nearly 25,000 European Jews, White Russians, gays and many others. Wartime Shanghai fascinated writers like Vicki Baum (whose pre-war success with *Grand Hotel* enabled her own family's escape from Hitler to Hollywood). Baum's novel *Shanghai '37* entwines the lives of coolies, spies, nurses, collaborators, Nazi refugees and others—and describes their deaths in a fictional version of an actual bombing that killed nearly 1,000 in the collapse of the Palace Hotel, next-door to the Cathay. *Shanghai '37* is a must-read. HJ Lethbridge called it an 'absorbing novel of a city where, for foreigners, the clocks stopped in 1941, and never chimed again'.

THE CHAOS YEARS

Well, not exactly. Lethbridge was describing the effects of World War II's Chinese aftermath—the Civil War the KMT lost, bringing the CCP to power. In the McCarthyist fervour of the 1950s, most foreigners abandoned Shanghai. Those that did stay were nearly all pushed out in 1966 when anti-foreign fervour rose again, in Frankenstein combination with an attack on Chinese tradition: the so-called Cultural Revolution. Not surprisingly, the infamous Gang of Four blamed for master-minding the Cultural Revolution all hailed from Shanghai—though, also typically, three weren't born there. Chairman Mao Zedong's wife—the failed actress Jiang Qing—and her Shanghai 'chicks' Zhang Chunqiao and Yao Wenyuan, all moved to Shanghai as adults. The fourth 'Gangster', former textile worker Wang Hongwen, grew up there. Writer Nien Cheng has described the horrors they helped create in *Life and Death in Shanghai*, her harrowing account of the 'ten years of chaos' in East China.

It wasn't till Mao died and the Gang of Four fell that Deng Xiaoping, in 1979, became midwife to a rebirth of trade and industry, the twin heroes of Shanghai growth, past and present. At first, the heroes grew slowly.

Double Shock
A Taiwanese matron of our acquaintance who'd been shocked into embarrassment at her own provincialism when 'beautiful, fashionable Shanghai Ladies' arrived in Taipei as war refugees in 1948, was shocked again when she visited Shanghai in 1980, and found all the ladies wearing Mao suits.

THE NEW JAZZ AGE

But life changed faster and faster. Within a decade, Shanghai was once again paying more taxes to the central government than any other city. By 1995, Shanghai per capita GDP was thrice national average and rising, Pierre Cardin and Louis Vuitton had brand-name boutiques on Huaihai Road (the fashionable former 'Avenue Joffre' of the old French Concession), and several ex-mayors were part of the 'Shanghai Gang' helping reform the leadership in Beijing. Today, with 1 per cent of China's population, Shanghai produces 5 per cent of the country's GDP and 10 per cent of its exports, leading to a per-capita GDP of US$ 4,180, in a country whose national urban per-capita GDP is just US$ 757 (and rural incomes much lower). It's easy to see why many Shanghainese, like an editor quoted by journalist Ian Buruma, 'want to connect today's Shanghai with the Shanghai of the 20's and 30's and cut out everything in between.'

Many jazz-era icons have revived; Lethbridge would goggle at the foreign throngs flocking to '30s-retro entertainment today. You can dance again to big-band jazz at special events in Sir Victor Sassoon's ballroom and, nightly downstairs, listen to a jazz band of oldsters, some of whom played when the Peace Hotel was still the Cathay. Art-deco has revived from the Bund to Hongqiao, and dinner-theatre restaurants like the Sunflower feature Shanghai showgirls in jazz-inspired extravaganzas. A whole subculture reigns, of '30s-retro bars and restaurants in dark wood and lush silks, hung with deco glass, tea pots, 'Shanghai Lady' cigarette and soap ads, cotton-mill spindles and opium pipes. Many of these items were hawked from blanket stalls along Fuyou Road in Old City until the Mayor's office, deeming the stalls unseemly, had them all moved to an indoor mall. Only Shanghai would have an indoor, air-conditioned '30's-retro flea market.

Shanghai's deservedly famous snack culture has also revived, from stalls in the Old City to whole restaurants dedicated to sampling smoked fish, sweet red bean cakes, soy-cured tofu and other traditional Shanghai snacks.

One recent census estimated over 30,000 restaurants, meaning in that area at least, Shanghai once again rivals New York.

Meantime, the sweet sauces, crisp vegetables and fresh seafood of Shanghai are served again with flourish in cheap eateries and gourmet settings city-wide.

NEW SHANGHAI

For Shanghai has always been too energetic and creative to survive for long on a culture that's derivative, even of its own history. So while jazz-era architecture and entertainment revives in traditional Shanghai, a whole new city has been rising. Maps from the 1930s show Shanghai limited to the compact territory on the west of the Huangpu's great curve, where it meets the Wusong. Today, Shanghai sprawls over (or has developed, depending on your perspective) basically the whole peninsula between the Yangtze's mouth in the north and Hangzhou Bay in the south, a vast swath sliced in half north to south by the Huangpu. The traditional city is now often referred to as Puxi—'west of the Huangpu River'—while the new city to the east is Pudong.

Pudong is as powerful a symbol of Shanghai's future as the Bund is of her past. Just a dozen years ago, most of Pudong was farmer's fields. Today, you can sit at Starbucks on the Pudong side of the river, with several of the world's tallest buildings at your back, and sip caramel machiato latte while gazing at the historic Bund. Among Pudong's highlights are the six-star Grand Hyatt and the gleaming towers of the Lujiazui financial district. Created by a combination of government fiat (the Customs House and Stock Exchange were moved there), tax incentives, real estate investments by state-owned firms and global trade, Lujiazui is testament to Shanghai's ability to reinvent itself. Within 15 years of getting tacit permission from Deng Xiaoping to establish a global financial centre, Shanghai created the hardware—and much of the human capital—of a district to rival Wall Street or Bond Street. Beyond Lujiazui, new industrial and residential districts (most also created by fiat, with forced relocations out of the crowded old city) stretch to the Yangtze and the bay.

A view of Pudong, with the futuristic Oriental Pearl TV Tower on the left.

Whatever the Shanghainese may have thought of the fiats, most enjoy the results. Once stinking Puxi tenements have been levelled for parks and shopping malls, and Pudong neighbourhoods have become livable, with their own markets and movie theatres and a bit more fresh air than downtown. Shanghai residents, formerly fearful of losing their Puxi cubbyholes, now often wait eagerly for THEIR turn to relocate to the new city.

To the occasional bemusement of foreigners, the great symbol of Pudong is the Oriental Pearl TV Tower, a futuristic complex of red and purple globe-shaped revolving restaurants and observation decks affixed to a silver needle 468 m (1,535.4 ft) high. The unkind have various nicknames for this somewhat startling piece of architecture, but it's a beloved sign of progress to most Shanghainese. Most Chinese tourists far prefer the shining obelisks of Lujiazui and the TV Tower as photo-op backdrop over the deco ranks of the Bund, so reminiscent of foreign domination.

Alien Attraction

One foreign teacher assigned her English-language students in Shanghai an essay on where on earth they'd take a group of space aliens to better understand earthlings, given a million-dollar travel budget. Half the class suggested not leaving Shanghai. Of those, the majority would stay in Pudong. Every one of the essayists planned to take their aliens up the Oriental Pearl.

Today, old and new city alike are alive with clubs, discos, art shows, fashion shops, restaurants, businesses, hawkers and street life. The recently expanded subway system and ring roads have relieved some of the congestion on downtown streets, so Shanghai seems to move faster all the time. As one long-time expat commented, 'Blink, and you'll miss something. Go away for a month, and you'll hardly recognise your neighbourhood when you get back.' Shanghai is a city still in the process of reinventing itself, of reclaiming its history and creating its future, and that makes it an exciting, confusing, frustrating, difficult and ultimately wonderful town to call home.

SHANGHAI'S PEOPLE

CHAPTER 3

'Every morning when I open my eyes I wonder what
I can do to make myself famous. It's become my ambition,
my raison d'être, to burst upon the city like fireworks.
This has a lot to do with the fact that I live in Shanghai.'
—Zhou Weihui ('Coco'), in *Shanghai Baby*

SHANGHAI: CITY OF ARTISTS AND REVOLUTION, city of whores and other businesspeople, city of cities, constantly calls on her people to invent themselves anew. It's a city of poseurs and posing, where everyone, on every topic, seems frequently called on to take a stand. Take Coco, for instance, whose quote starts this chapter: China's most famously public transsexual—though in the semi-autobiographical novel *Shanghai Baby*—s/he reinvents herself as straightforwardly a woman. In her extremeness, Coco perhaps most clearly illustrates a need that seems basic as air and water for many in Shanghai; the need to stand out. The need to be noticed in a city so notable for notedness that bright minds fear sliding below her murky surface and disappearing without a trace.

"A mystical fog envelops the city," Coco says, "mixed with continual rumours and an air of superiority, a hangover from the time of the *shili yangchang*, the foreign concessions. This hint of smugness affects me. I both love it and hate it." That 'mystical fog', that something about Shanghai's weight of traditional ambition, has pushed more than the city's share of natives and visitors to heights (and depths) of notoriety, for good or ill.

SHANGHAI SOJOURNERS: THE FAMOUSLY FAMOUS

That said, it's indicative of that hangover from the *shili yangchang* that the first thing one must ask is: famous according to whom?

Ask a foreign resident today to name the ten most famous people who've ever lived in Shanghai, and you'll likely hear of some of the colourful foreigners who ruled the city in the Treaty Port Era or the Jazz Age. You might hear, for instance, of Jewish opium tai-pans like Victor Sassoon, or his protegee Silas Hardoon (see the next section); of military men like General Stillwell; writers like Noel Coward; or the actress Marlene Dietrich (who prowled the city before making Shanghai Express in 1932).

The Sephardim of Shanghai

As you stroll the historic concessions, note how many architectural icons were built by Jews: Peace Hotel, Metropole, Marble Hall—not to mention synagogues, a hospital, school, clubs, and so on. (*For more details, see the section* 'Jewish History and the Hongkou 'Ghetto' ' *in* Chapter 7: Enjoying Life *on pages 203–208*.) These opulent residences and edifices came not from the refugees who sheltered in Shanghai through World War II, but from the wealthy Sephardic Jews who preceded them.

The first Jew documented as visiting Shanghai was a British soldier after the first Opium War in 1841. Three years later, with the new 'free trade' port firmly in foreign hands, wealthy Baghdad-born, Bombay-based Jewish trader Dawid (David) Sassoon sent his son Elias to scout Shanghai as a possible base for expanded operations.

Dawid liked what Elias saw and began dipping into the East China trade in tea, cotton, silks and opium (a legal trade then, of course, practised by houses like Jardine & Mathesons, and a cornerstone of the British East India Company). In 1850, David Sassoon & Sons opened major offices in Shanghai. As they had in several cities in India, they built synagogues and other infrastructure to attract other Jews, for the Sassoons were committed to Jewish traditions in their charities (and their operations—Sassoon employees had to learn the evening Minha and 'Arbith prayers in the Baghdadi style).

The Ezras, Hardoons, Kadoories: several other major Sephardic trading families with Baghdad and/or Bombay

The Marble Hall, once home to the Kadoories, is now the Shanghai Municpal Children's Palace.

connections followed the Sassoons to Shanghai, where they traded successfully. Upper-crust Anglo-American society may have sniffed at their accents (old Dawid never learned English; and his sons, while fluent English speakers, were better in Hebrew, Arabic, 'Amral, Punjabi and Hindustani). But it respected their success. By the 1920s, Sephardic Jews reportedly controlled some 40 per cent of the Shanghai stock exchange (*see* Chapter 7: Enjoying Life *for a tour of surviving landmarks on pages 203–209*).

Other Famous Foreigners

As like as not, some names mentioned will vary with the nationality of the speaker. Americans might talk of Mark Twain, or philosopher John Dewey, whose theories on idealism grew in part from watching Shanghai student protests in 1919. Or perhaps they'll remember Frederick Ward Townsend, who led the army of drunkards that defended Shanghai in 1860 from the Taiping 'Great Peace' rebels (that peasant-army, whose civil war left 20 million dead, followed a 'King of Great Peace' who claimed to be younger brother to Christ). Townsend had the dubious honour of being named a military hero by Tzu-hsi T'ai-hou, the infamous Dowager Empress of China's last dynasty, herself remembered for squandering China's naval budget on a marble yacht for her Summer Palace.

Japanese might mention Kanza Uchiyama, whose bookshop was so crucial to the intellectual growth of 'May Fourth' intellectual rebels; or cite the 'righteous consuls' whose refusal to comply with Hitler's deportation orders helped save 25,000 Jews from Hitler. The French might note how Jesuit fathers in their old concession brought modern meteorology and other Western sciences to China, or remind you that André Malraux drew on his Shanghai experience in writing *La Condition Humaine*.

An Englishman might explain that Captain George Balfour laid out much of the central city in 1843 (after helping win the war masterminded by British opium king William Jardine), or that Horatio Nelson Lay almost single-handedly brought a Western-style Customs service to China. Anyone Irish is sure to remind you, though, that Customs grew best under the masterful leadership of the Irishman Sir Robert Hart.

Even when foreigners name famous Chinese from Shanghai, the first names they think of still often come from the past. They'll remember the writer Lu Xun, that giant of Chinese literature (see the following section). They might mention Mao's wife Jiang Qing, the harpy everyone loves to hate, and joke how the Chaos Years might have gone easier had Shanghai sophisticate audiences not laughed at Jiang Qing's attempts as an actress. Perhaps they'll remember successful Shanghai film star *Ruan Lingyu*, whom Jiang bitterly envied, despite Ruan's tragic suicide at age 24.

Lu Xun and the Baihua Yundong

Born to a merchant family in Shaoxing, Lu Xun studied in Japan to be a doctor, but returned home fired with the idea that China, like Japan, needed modernisation—a healing of the soul—more urgently than physical medicine. Like many reformers, Lu saw China's hope in revolution, in throwing off the shackles of the dying Qing Dynasty. But Lu never believed

"Throughout the ages," Lu Xun wrote, "the Chinese have had only two ways of looking at foreigners; up to them as superior beings, or down on them as wild animals." Thus did the celebrated author of *The True Story of Ah Q*, *Kong Yiji*, *Diary of a Madman*, and other classics fire his shot across the bow of a China still moving downwind from opium-era humiliation by the West.

that the revolution alone was sufficient. Chinese, he believed, needed to liberate their minds—or remain the hapless peasants Lu parodied in *Ah Q*: humiliated over and over, then singing about being reborn as heroes.

Head of a talented circle of revolutionary writers, Lu became a standard-bearer of the 'Vernacular Movement' (Baihua Yundong), calling modern writers to shun the opaquely flowery language of Mandarins past in favour of simple, clear clarion calls the people would understand and be stirred by. Lu's writings were part of the intellectual ferment that led from the 1911 Revolution, to the May Fourth protests of 1919, and beyond.

A perennial outsider, Lu remained sceptical all his life of those drawn to political power, and never joined the CCP. He died (of consumption) in 1936, too early for his refusal to join to have become a political liability—and promptly became, after death, what he never was in his life: an icon for the ruling establishment. Simon Leys points out the irony of museum displays revering Lu Xun, often adorned with encomoniums from party toadies Lu scorned in life. He remains today, a revered symbol of nationalism and intellectual freedom for leaders and ordinary Chinese alike.

SHANGHAILANDERS AND SHANGHAINESE

For many foreigners, in other words, the Shanghai that's somehow clearest in focus is still often Shanghai of the past, of that strange era, now frozen in sparkling memory, when Westerners largely headed the Chinese city. It was an odd division of the world then, into 'Shanghailanders' (the foreign sojourners' title for themselves) and 'Shanghainese' (the natives). And it's indicative of an enduring oddness in the city's race relations that for many, that linguistic division persists. Quite a few Shanghai expats still call themselves 'Shanghailanders', most quite innocent of the curdled feelings that privileged title can evoke for the Shanghainese. "After all," one young local journalist sniffed to us, "Hemingway wasn't a 'Parislander'—he was an 'American in Paris'. What gives foreigners some special title here?"

What, indeed? What exactly is that 'hangover' from the concessions?

To understand it, we must peer closely at social life back in the old days (bad or good, based on perspective), when Shanghai was steeply hierarchical, organised around nationality. As one older matron puts it, 'society was like a layer cake with vanilla frosting: the white part was always on top.' And the sugar on top of the frosting was the British and American community—the founders and defenders of expatriate Shanghai.

Life at the Top

Life in that layer could be sweet indeed, full of amusing diversions. Popular guidebooks of the day lists 70-odd clubs and associations within the expatriate community, from Amateur Dramatics to the YMCA, via Baseball, Cricket, Fencing, Golf, Lawn Tennis, Midget Sailing, Rugby and Union Jack Yacht Club.

Typical is *The Upstairs Veranda*, the childhood memoirs of Norah Shaw, daughter of a British police constable in Shanghai's International Settlement and his former-nanny wife. Though not the wealthiest foreigners, on a constable's salary, the Shaws lived at a standard scarcely imaginable today. Norah describes a house graced with courtyards and verandas where five children had half again as many servants, including cooks who learned their favourite treats and tailors who made costumes for dress-up parties (we later learn Norah's childhood home today houses SEVEN Chinese families). For little Norah, life was a whirl of parades, picnics and outings, her greatest trouble a spanking if Mother discovered she'd sneaked into the neighbour's garden again.

At least until the Laozha Riots of 30 May 1925, which followed the death of a Chinese worker in a Japanese-owned factory. Student protestors surrounded police stations, and one Inspector Everson, an inexperienced young officer left in charge of Laozha Station while his commissioner went to the racecourse, panicked and ordered his men to open fire. Forty-four students died and within hours, 50,000 rioters took the streets, followed by 150,000 workers on strike. British troops and US gunboats restored foreign order for a time but it was, says historian Pan Ling, the 'beginning of the finale of Western imperial power in China... The foreign press thought it all a Bolshevik plot, but the more percipient foreign observers saw the groundswell for what it was, and in the distance heard the knell'.

Norah Shaw, with all her happy memories, was not among the percipient. Her memoirs briefly describe the Laozha riots as seen through the eyes of a five-year-old girl, then focus on the stirring aftermath—the 'arrival of a contingent of British troops,' whereon a 'surge of relief bordering on lightheadedness swept through the community'; one hardly need ask WHICH community. That odd perceptual double-standard appears throughout memoirs like these. Shaw seems sympathetic to the Chinese poor, but her greatest sympathies lay elsewhere—like with the pet rabbits she raised, only to be 'horrified' when a scarecrow-like Chinese beggar stole them to eat.

Double Standards

Witness, for instance, Shaw's description of the now-infamous Public Gardens on the Bund, where posted rules excluded both Chinese and dogs; Shaw understood that 'resentment smouldered amongst the Chinese, as they were the only nationals not permitted'. But she still loved those gardens. 'In spring hyacinths, tulips, snowdrops and other bulbs imported from Europe added fragrance and freshness to the magnolias... During hot summer evenings the Municipal Orchestra played...' For Shaw 'the most beautiful place in that garden was the smaller fountain under which two Victorian children in terracotta clung together beneath an umbrella... Little Nell, Oliver Twist... Fascinated by these pathetic waifs, unloved and unwanted, I always hurried to that spot, just to... assure them that I cared about them'. She displayed, alas, no equivalent concern for the real-life waifs among the beggar-children at the ragged edges of the Settlement.

SHANGHAILANDERS AND SHANGHAILANDERS

But then, glasses are often half-empty or half-full. The fact that 'the British were at the top of the heap... was an accepted circumstance' in the 1930s, remembers ex-Shanghailander Elfreida Read. 'As a classmate once said to me, 'The British don't have to be good at anything, they just need to be British'.... Just under them came the French and the Germans and the Scandinavians. Below these, and slightly suspect, were the Greeks and Italians and a sprinkling of central Europeans. Considerably lower on the scale we had the Japanese, though they were few at that time... closely followed by the jetsam and flotsam of society: the Jews, the immigrant Russians, the Eurasians, and, last of all, the Chinese.'

These tiers were not to be overcome with effort, merit or even money, Read says. 'There were extremely rich Jews and Eurasians and Chinese, but the stigma of racial differentiation clung fast.' As a child in Shanghai, Read struggled to rationalise her Estonian ancestry: "Estonians were close to Scandinavians, I reasoned. That brought me well up on the racial scale. I began to stress my Estonian ancestry. I was Estonian I told my new friends. Estonians were not Russians."

For the Russians were MOST disappointing to Old Shanghailanders when they arrived in droves after the Bolshevik revolution in 1919—stateless, homeless and not choosy about jobs. The White Russians 'showed up the entrenched Shanghailanders,' Pan Ling says, by making the 'native realise that the white man was not always so posh after all.' The other Europeans had kept their social circles successfully separate from the Chinese, 'believing themselves naturally to be the superior breed. To them the Russian émigrés were a disgrace: the way they let the side down and fraternised with the natives, selling their services to all buyers, Chinese and European alike—the men as riding instructors and bodyguards, the women as hairdressers, dance hostesses and whores.'

And then there were the Jews. As we've seen, a few famously wealthy Jews were among the leaders of expatriate Shanghai. Some in the crust of the upper-crust may have sniffed at Sir Victor Sassoon's religion, but most still danced in his ballroom.

In perhaps the most famous example, an entire religious school, the Mir Yeshiva, moved all 400 students and faculty from occupied Europe to Shanghai, and continued reading Talmud right through the war.

Most Jewish immigrants to Shanghai, though, came as refugees fleeing pogroms in Russia, rising anti-Semitism in Prussia and throughout Europe and, eventually, Hitler. "When all the civilised world closed its doors to Jewish refugees," historian Pan Guang proudly writes, "we in Shanghai provided a vital haven and every possible relief."

Between Shanghainese acceptance, assistance from settled Shanghailanders (especially Sephardic Jews), and self-help groups, Shanghai's refugee Jews were soon thriving. Life for most was materially poor (often several families to a room), but culturally rich, with synagogues, schools, women's groups, a hospital, burial societies, training classes for migration to Israel, even newspapers. Wartime Shanghai had 50 Jewish periodicals, in English, French, Chinese, German, Russian, Yiddish, Hebrew, Polish and Japanese—all despite restrictions imposed after Japan invaded in 1938.

The Japanese sent all but the wealthiest of Shanghai's then-30,000 Jews to the Hongkou ghetto, forced to register and use passes. To their honour, though, the Japanese dissembled and 'lost paperwork' rather than actually killing Jews. Even when Hitler dispatched Gestapo Colonel Josef Meisinger to supervise the Final Solution in Shanghai, the Japanese found excuses. Despite their many wartime sins, the then-rulers of Shanghai got to Armistice without shipping any Jews to death camps.

Jewish refugees understood the knife-edge odds that created their unlikely Asian refuge, and responded with affection for Shanghai and China that transcended the city's social layer-cake. Spurned by upper-crust Shanghailanders, many Shanghai Jews supported the Chinese resistance. Some even served in the Chinese army, like journalist Hans Shippe, surgeon Dr Jacob Rosenfeld (who became Medical Corps Commander to the Communist People's Liberation Army, and an advisor to Mao), and the colourful soldier-strategist Morris 'Two-Gun' Cohen.

For that service, some achieved the distinction—rare among Shanghailanders—of remaining honoured in the memories of Shanghainese. A statue (at a famous battle site in North China) commemorates Hans Shippe, and much writing celebrates Dr Rosenfeld. In their honour, the periodic reunions of Shanghai Jews that take place even today never fail to attract senior leadership attendance and approval. "Chinese people," Pan Guang says, "will never forget their great contribution to helping resist Japanese aggression and establish the People's Republic."

THE NEWLY FAMOUS OF SHANGHAI

That said, most Shanghainese now focus less on the yesterday of Shanghailanders, and more on today, and tomorrow. They may enjoy the frisson of the city's naughty history through visits to '30s-retro bars, but their key energies look forward—like our teacher friend's students who wanted to take space aliens up the Oriental Pearl. There's a sense among most Shanghainese that the future's more fully THEIRS than the past.

So when thinking about famous Shanghai people, for instance, a Shanghainese will less likely talk about the Jazz Age, than about the here and now. You may well hear about captains of industry like Xie Qihua, the entrepreneurial leader who turned around the Bao Steel Corporation; or Chen Xianglin, who guided Shanghai Automotive Industrial Corporation through negotiations bringing world-class car manufacturing technology to the city. Maybe you'll hear of top-ranking athletes like soccer star Fan Zhiyi, or three-time world-record-breaking high jumper Zhu Jianhua. You might hear about culture vultures like conductor Chen Xieyan, a guiding light of the Shanghai Opera; or pop-culture icons like film director Xie Jin, or the wonderfully self-promoting 'visionary artist' Chen Yifei.

THE 'SHANGHAI GANG' IN BEIJING

Any Shanghainese worth his soy-cured tofu will happily tell you about the many Beijing leaders who hail from Shanghai. Leading into the 16th Party Congress, Shanghai's role as training ground for central leadership was especially clear. Then-President Jiang Zemin and Premier Zhu Rongji were both ex-Shanghai Mayors, while then-Vice-Premier Wu Bangguo was a former Shanghai Party Secretary, and Minister of Education Chen Zhili did her training as a Deputy Party Secretary.

The 'Shanghai Gang' controlled Beijing leadership for so long that it became the stuff of legend—and jokes, many roasting the then-National People's Congress Chair Li Peng, a non-Shanghainese widely loathed both for his role in suppressing the Tiananmen protests in 1989, and for rumoured corruption.

On a Different Page

Shanghai jokesters claim Li Peng once went home so unhappy that his wife asked: "What happened today at the Politburo, dear?"

"Nothing," came Li's gruff reply.

"Nothing?" his wife asked, astonished, "Why, dear, how could our nation's greatest leaders meet all day, and have nothing happen?"

Still, Li insisted, nothing. Again she asked; again he evaded until, exasperated, Li Peng's wife said, "Darling, were you even at the meeting?"

At which point, Li slumped in his chair and admitted, "I was, but I couldn't understand a word. They all spoke Shanghainese."

As Zhu Rongji and Jiang Zemin retired and the 'Fourth Generation' leadership of President Hu Jintao and Premier Wen Jiabao emerged, the 'Shanghai Gang' seemed to slip from power somewhat. But Shanghai influence continues to be strong in the new line-up. Jiang Zemin and Wu Bangguo have retained much control, while former Shanghai Party Secretary Huang Ju has joined the Politburo. Shanghai is likely to remain a power behind the Beijing throne for a long time to come.

OF TOSSED SALADS AND MELTING POTS, LAYER-CAKES AND STIR-FRIES

Meantime, closer to home: how do all these communities—Shanghainese and foreigner, famous, infamous, and downright ridiculous—come together in Shanghai today?

The answer is reminiscent of a well-known quip on US society. The old analogy, the saying goes, was the 'melting pot,' where foreign identities melted after immigration into a rich, uniquely American soup. The more favoured analogy in recent years is the 'tossed salad', a new image for America at its best: allowing individual identities to remain crisply separate, while joining in a harmonious blend.

So, if the old analogy for Shanghai society was the 'layer-cake,' perhaps the new analogy should be a 'banquet of stir-fry dishes'. Shanghai society today is too large, varied, complex and multiply focused to imagine it on a single plate; nor is it by any means as clearly hierarchical as in Elfreida Read's day. And so, a banquet of dishes: some hot, some sweet, some salty, some pretty sour, but all laced with the saucy cosmopolitanism of Shanghai. And in this rich smorgasbord of social 'dishes', just about everyone can find a community of shared interests.

Specific clubs and associations are described in later chapters. As an overview, following are some key groupings within the Shanghai 'banquet' today:

The Busy Business Crowd

Whoever invented the word 'networking' could have been living in Shanghai, where expats and locals alike have raised business-related socialising to a high art. Chapter 9: Business Unusual (*page 245–274*) explores reasons for this (briefly: Asian preference for a personal touch in business, combined with relatively limited home/family obligations among expat businesspeople), and lists the best-known of the hundreds of networking associations in the city. Suffice it to say that a reasonably well-connected Shanghai businessperson, member of two to four active associations, could easily spend every breakfast, lunch, dinner and cocktail hour 'on the circuit', building the relationships that help cut the deals that make this most businesslike of cities tick.

The Athletes and Hobbyists

Given how hard Shanghai people work, it's unsurprising that they play hard too. There are sporting groups for casual

A statue of Buddha in the Chenghuang Miao Temple.

walkers and hard-core hikers, joggers and marathoners, practitioners of Shaolin sword and Taiqiquan 'shadow-boxings', racing cyclists and single-track fans, sailors and swimmers and speedboat drivers, and every imaginable sort of ball player. There are chess clubs and model rocket clubs, singing and dramatic societies. Many of these function as social groups too, offering classes and celebration dinners and even road trips meeting (and competing) with counterpart clubs elsewhere in China/Asia (*see* Chapter 7: Enjoying Life *on pages 163–164 for details*).

The Faithful

Religious organisations are many and varied. There are Jews again in today's Shanghai, meeting in rented hotel rooms for services and celebrations that, at times, include Shanghainese families who trace their Jewish heritage from 1930s intermarriages. Catholic masses are said again in the great cathedrals of Xujiahui (history's 'Siccawei') and Xiangshan, and Protestant services of many kinds meet in churches, halls and apartments. Several Buddhist temples have been restored, and a number of Muslim mosques have quietly restarted operations.

Religion is, for many reasons, a sensitive topic for China's still nominally Communist government. Rules limit both licensing of religious groups and freedom for Chinese to worship with foreign-funded groups. Nevertheless, many organisations thrive, and except during periodic crackdowns, Chinese-foreign mixing in a religious context remains quite common.

The Party Animals

In the clubs and discos, another sort of mixing goes on late into every night. The club scene ranges from the tame (darts and drafts at the Irish pubs) to the offbeat (punk clubs, gay clubs, techno clubs, trannie clubs). Then there's Shanghai the wicked—tamer than it once was, but still offering plenty of drugs and easy sex for those who want them. In clubs like those, the Shanghai showgirls of yesteryear have been reinvented as Shanghai *xiaojie* ('Young Misses'), in skin-tight minis, fishnet stockings, and see-through blouses. (*For details, see* Chapter 7: Enjoying Life *on pages 167–173.*)

The Family-focused

On the other hand, Shanghai can be a fine place to raise kids. There are great schools in both the Chinese and international communities (interestingly, kids from Chinese public schools who switch to international schools often find they are two to four years ahead in sciences and math). There are also family activities throughout the city, in parks, gardens, theatres, museums, children's palaces and hotels. (*For more on this, see the section* 'For Kids and Family' *in* Chapter 5: Settling In, *on pages 70–88.*)

Intellectuals and Arties

Around universities and art galleries, in cafés and literary salons, among diplomats and journalists and hangers-on, Shanghai maintains an intellectual life that's as rich and varied as Noel Coward found it; perhaps more so, given the porous lines now dividing expat from Chinese. For details of the many local schools that welcome expats to take or teach classes, as well as the art and literary salons that dot the city, see Chapter 5: Settling In (*pages 86–88*) and Chapter 7: Enjoying Life (*pages 163–164, 166–167*).

National Identity Fans

"A traveller," Edith Templeton has observed, "never so fervently represents her own country as when she is abroad." Many an American who would never attend a 4th of July party at home, many a Briton who has never before toasted the Queen's Birthday, have found themselves as expats drawn to the business and social clubs organised by their consulates/compatriots. Such groups give chances for the expat community to celebrate national holidays, and network in their 'own community'.

But Shanghai being Shanghai, as often as not, they also provide another venue for cross-cultural mixing. For instance, the American Chamber of Commerce (often shortened to AmCham; this is Shanghai's largest expat business association), has a membership that is less than 50 per cent American. The Irish have monthly mixers rotating between two popular pubs, supplemented by weekly 'practice sessions' in which every nationality is encouraged to have a touch of the Blarney. The Indian business community organises a lecture series around networking lunches for members—then invites speakers from throughout the Shanghai community. The British and Australian Balls are widely attended by all nationalities, and so it goes.

An Ironic Situation

So commonly assumed is such cross-cultural mixing that those few events limited to single nationalities can meet with sharp disapproval. During the security scare after NATO bombed China's Belgrade Consulate, for instance, Chinese members of AmCham arrived for a consular security briefing that was, it turned out, limited to US citizens. Consular guards apologised repeatedly as non-US AmCham members left in a huff. Citizen attendees spent the next quarter-hour discussing whether it was right to exclude non-US citizens from a security briefing in the US Consulate-General during what was considered a US security crisis in China. Had the situation not been so serious, the whole discussion would have been rather funny. It was one of those moments when it was clear just how far Shanghai has come from the Shanghailander days.

That Shanghai has come so far, that there is so much variety in social groupings, is much of what makes life there such a rich banquet. People pick and choose, or focus on one 'dish'. One busy Shanghai businessperson may also be an athlete and an art fan. Another may spend all his or her spare time with family. Yet another may find one club or social group to focus on and rise in, becoming Soccer Club President, leader of the Baptist Reading Group or Best Dancer Ever Seen in Maya Disco.

In other words, Shanghai today has many hierarchies, many more ways to stand out and be famous, more so than the layer-cake of yesteryear; nor is any one way universally 'best.' To be sure, many people care deeply about football matches, say, or elections for the Board of Directors of AmCham. But there is no universal agreement that it's better to be President of AmCham than of the Shanghai

Professional Women's Association, say (or, for that matter, of the Dramatic Society or the Volunteer Committee for the Shanghai Orphanage). As Calvin Trillin wrote of formerly elite clubs at Yale, today: 'those sorts of things seem to matter only to the sort of people who care about those sorts of things.' There are many routes to famousness in Shanghai now, and many more options for those who care less for famousness than for life balance.

Figuring a way to a happy, balanced life is a key challenge for all modern urbanites, and perhaps nowhere more so than in Shanghai. Helping expats find that balance sooner than later is the goal of the rest of this book.

SHANGHAI LIFE CYCLES

CHAPTER 4

'Shanghai may have changed radically since 1949,
but its atmosphere and populace still have something
unique and different about them—quite potent too...
China looks at Shanghai rather the way provincial and
puritan America looks at New York: as an urban monster
that drains the intelligence, dynamism and daring of the
whole nation, a fascinating and disquieting Babylon.'
—Simon Leys, *Chinese Shadows*

ONE OF THE FIRST THINGS TO THINK ABOUT when planning your life in Shanghai is the sort of relationships you hope for with Shanghainese. Many expatriates get through entire assignments with little awareness of the seasons and cycles that shape local lives. Such expats socialise with other expats, take vacations outside China, and never visit private local homes. They may as well be in Bangkok or Jakarta—or almost anywhere else.

It would be a shame to let that happen to you, for some involvement with Shanghainese will add immeasurably to the richness of your Shanghai experience, while total disconnection with local culture means missed opportunities. That includes missed chances for shared pleasures, for stronger relationships with colleagues that make for more productive work life, and for the possibility of new friendships.

With that in mind, we offer here a brief guide to the rhythms and cycles of local Shanghai, with special attention to the ways foreigners can tap into, share or otherwise become a part of them.

SHANGHAI CULTURE TIPS

Shanghainese culture is, of course, rooted in the larger Chinese culture. Such China-wide issues as concern over face, intensity of family and other key relationships, and the importance of consensus as part of decision-making are covered amply in many volumes on China, and we won't re-cross that ground here. Scott Seligman's *Dealing with the Chinese* is one particularly good source. Some other tips are also provided in Chapter 9: Business Unusual (pages 245–274). Here we list just a few particularities that distinguish life in Shanghai, and the views of Shanghainese, from what is typical elsewhere in China:

Multinationalism

Shanghai today is truly global. While the government does not release exact statistics, by many estimates it has well over half a million foreign residents, hailing from every part of the globe. And in Shanghai today, all nationalities mix freely, for perhaps the single greatest contrast between today's groupings and their 1920s counterparts is the fact that they are now multiracial.

To be sure, some individuals still prefer to associate mostly with 'their own kind', and sensitivities endure on both sides toward vestiges of the Shanghainese-Shanghailander divide. There are Chinese government and corporate positions that cannot be held by foreigners, and consular offices and foreign boardrooms that are rarely, if ever, entered by Chinese, and these facts still cause resentment.

But on a social level, mixing now occurs freely. Interracial friendships, dating and marriages are common (though foreign man-Chinese woman relationships are still far more common than the inverse). Business, athletic and other groups are as likely to have members from Beijing and Buenos Aires, Switzerland, Nigeria and Ningbo, as from Britain, the US or Shanghai. That cosmopolitanism is an exciting part of everyday life. True internationalism still perhaps sits less naturally than in Paris or New York. But it's far better than the 'cosmopolitan' old Shanghai that essentially excluded Shanghainese. Whatever oddness remains in Coco's 'hangover from the *shili yangchang*', progress has been made, and there's hope for more.

Cosmopolitanism and Pride

Shanghai is a great melting pot, for immigrants from across China and for expats. Recent Chinese immigrants may feel scorn from longer-term residents as they struggle with the rudiments of the Shanghai dialect but somehow, fairly soon after arrival, most start feeling more sophisticated than bumpkin cousins who have never known Shanghai. Stay long enough and they too feel like Old Shanghainese, scorning newer arrivals.

The bottom line is that Shanghainese are generally (justly) proud of their city, while also having the slightly jaded been-there-done-that cynicism common to New Yorkers, Parisians and other great urbanites. As an expat, you will more easily befriend and work with Shanghainese if you acknowledge both the cynicism and the pride.

Heavy Business Focus

Other Chinese often call Shanghainese 'clever', and not as a compliment. The word refers to Shanghai's hard-driving business intensity, which the more laid-back/socialist Chinese elsewhere often perceive as railroading. The truth is, for Shanghainese, doing business well is both game and point of pride. That sensibility underlies Shanghai's economic boom and helps makes Shanghainese good marketers. Businesspeople may appreciate that drive among employees, while at times being frustrated by it in negotiators across the table. The keys to success are recognising the strength of Shanghai 'cleverness', harnessing it within your team and learning to counter cleverness with cleverness when you negotiate. After all, games are more fun with two players and in Shanghai, you can practise negotiating every time you buy eggs!

Education and Opportunity

Shanghai's average educational level is stratospheric by China standards and, at this point, higher than most places. With many of China's top universities, best-paying jobs and most vibrant artistic and cultural associations, Shanghai attracts top talent. This causes some brain-drain in 'the provinces'—an issue Beijing attempts to combat via perks associated with 'develop the West' campaign. Shanghai also attracts disproportionate shares of 'returnees' from university studies throughout the globe—and of Overseas Chinese. Many Taiwanese are making a new home in Shanghai, with current counts edging towards half a million and growing. Hong Kongers and Taiwanese increasingly see Shanghai not only as a business venue, but also as a cosmopolitan and relatively affordable place to retire.

The upside of all this brainpower magnetism is a pool of local talent unmatched even, dare we say, in Beijing. This is a boon for business; it's no accident that high-tech firms like Alcatel and Intel are building labs and factories in Shanghai. Having well-educated, well-travelled local colleagues is also a great social boon for expats. "In Beijing," recalled one Australian, "I had Chinese employees. In Shanghai, I have Chinese peers—which makes it easier to have real Chinese friends."

The expatriate community is also generally experienced and well-travelled, for the cost of bringing expats to Shanghai forces careful resumé reviews. Most expats earn sky-high wages by local standards, most have domestic help and relatively few have extended families nearby. All this frees up lots of hours despite heavy work/networking. TV is also not a big leisure activity for most expats; Hong Kong satellite footprints bring sports and CNN, but there's nothing like the variety of English- or European-language programming available in the US or Europe. Thus Shanghai expats tend to have both high disposable income and relatively substantial free time, which leaves room for high-energy socialising.

> As one American said, "It's an elite community, and in that sense not very 'real'. It reminds me of Ivy League college days—everyone's pretty interesting to talk with and usually has time and money to pursue their interests. I wouldn't want to spend my life here; but for a few years, it's an awful lot of fun."

Strong Women

Shanghai society has long been tolerant of strong women. Historians tell us that women owned property and ran businesses in Shanghai more commonly and earlier than in many other parts of China, and Shanghai men seem to have been less likely than compatriots elsewhere to take multiple wives. From the chic-sexy Jazz Era 'Shanghai Ladies', to tragic-artist film stars like Ruan Lingyu, to revolutionaries like Qiu Jin (who cut her hair, dressed in pinstripe and led a 'battalion' of former seamstresses who dropped their sewing for military drills), Shanghai women stand out.

This history has not gone unnoticed elsewhere in China, where it's become fodder for traditional rivalries. One quip offers 'Shanghainese man' as a synonym for 'hen-pecked husband'. Another asks, "How did [Mao's dictatorial wife] Jiang Qing get so bad?" Answer: "How could anyone restrain her? She's a woman from Shanghai." But these snide asides perhaps mask a jealous awareness that Shanghai has achieved all it has in part by harnessing the energy of that half of the population whose talents are neglected or squashed elsewhere.

Qualifications in Relationships

The truth is, Shanghai men seem happy on the whole with their strong wives and enthralled with the children they help raise. One popular quip among English-speaking Shanghainese sums up these feelings, "Marriage is like graduating. You first earn your BA (Become Attached). If things go poorly, you degrade into MBA (Married But Available). But if all goes well, you end up as a PhD (a Person who Has a Daughter)." The pride Shanghainese take in calling themselves 'PhDs' says much about how far Shanghai's moms AND dads have come from parts of China where girls are selectively aborted. Expats should consider the joy Shanghainese take in their children and be careful about imposing on the personal time of employees with families.

Meantime, for male expats, both respect and caution are in order when dealing with those strong Shanghai ladies in your office. This includes respecting Shanghai women, who are unlikely to accept glass ceilings or perceived sexist comments as readily as their sisters in other Chinese cities; and caution with those who might be MBAs or seeking to earn their BA with you.

For female expats, traditional Shanghainese acceptance of female leaders has many upsides. Businesswomen regularly report easier acceptance of their roles by male counterparts in Shanghai than in other Chinese cities—or for that matter, than at home. Even women in the traditional role of trailing spouse often note an easier time dealing with everyone from household repairmen to male colleagues in community associations than elsewhere in China and Asia.

One downside sometimes discussed by expat women, though, is the difficulty of competing on 'style' with local women, should expats want to try. Traditional tolerance of strong women comes at a price for local 'dragon ladies' who are generally accepted only if they are also seen as feminine. Being strong and feminine at once is, of course, hard work—work that many Shanghai women are schooled in from birth.

Living Up to an Image

Designer/artist Vivienne Tam remembers '[growing] up with Shanghai Lady images', even after her parents moved to Hong Kong. "Mother used to buy a brand of cosmetics called Two Girls—white face powder, scented soaps, hair oil and a Florida water perfumed with peppermint and lavender." For Tam, Shanghai Ladies were 'idealised, exotic'. The *cheongsam*—the tight cut, high-neck dress Shanghai Ladies made famous—was both 'liberation' and 'a new kind of vulnerability—suddenly there was only a thin layer of silk between a woman's skin and the air and eyes around her'.

Today's Shanghai women retain a stylish focus that fuels multi-million dollar industries in fashion, cosmetics as well as exercise and diet aids. "Who can keep up?" asked one American woman of our acquaintance. "And who would want to? These Shanghai *xiaojie* weigh about an ounce and are thin as grass blades, and still live on broth and wrap themselves in Saran wrap and steam themselves to death to stay thin, then dress to kill just to go to the grocery store. I mean, I have no interest in living like that; but still, at home I feel reasonably attractive, and here I'm a fat old hag."

Shanghai can be unforgettable, but a dating paradise for single expat women over 'a certain age', it is not. There are exceptions of course, but by and large, as a German woman friend said, "You don't go to Shanghai to meet a guy." That said, as a self-styled 'charter member of the Sisters of Celibacy of Greater Shanghai', our German friend found the experience provided 'great creative energy; in that sense,

Freud was right'. While her career blossomed, she read books, went on trips, learned rock-climbing, danced her heart out and 'had more fun than in just about any other city'.

Alternative Lifestyles

As mentioned before, Shanghai offers a broad range of lifestyle alternatives. There is a large gay community, local and expat. There are artist's colonies. There are alternative music scenes. There are religious groups and orders. One of the best things about Shanghai, relative to almost any other Chinese city, is the variety of options—and the ability to pursue them without many others—in this busy, busy city, really having time or attention to care what you are up to. Recent issues of expat publications like *City Weekend* (*see* Chaper 7: Enjoying Life *on pages 173–174*) list many options and venues. Please note, though, that there are a few alternative lifestyle choices about which the government still does care a great deal, especially if engaged in by foreigners. Chief among these is open use by and especially dealing in illicit drugs; unless you are truly eager to explore the inside of Chinese jails, we strongly advise against.

Competition (and Stress)

The chief downside (or, depending on perspective, another upside) of Shanghai's business focus, education, opportunity and high-energy, is a lot of competition—both for expats and Shanghainese. The 'work hard, play hard' mentality infuses life and can bring a lot of excitement. The running and hiking and biking clubs always seem to be looking for more adventurous outings, each new restaurant or club seems wilder than the last. But constant competition can also create deep tension, leaving the unwary trapped in a world where every meal is a networking opportunity, every conversation a research project, every pick-up ball game a battleground.

Even for those who find competition exciting, too much causes stress. A British medical doctor in a Shanghai clinic once told us he had 'never before in a long medical career, outside of one stint in war-torn parts of Africa, seen the

variety or frequency of stress-related illnesses we see among expats in Shanghai'. His list sounded like the warning label on a bottle of caffeine pills: 'jitters, bad nerves, poor sleep, bad dreams, ulcers, stomach pains, neck pains, back pains, colds that won't clear up, wounds that won't heal…" It's enough to make the new expat want to turn around and head home.

Instead, we suggest you get involved with the community around you so you can find a comfortable place and ways to relax in the rhythms of Shanghai.

THE WHEEL OF THE SHANGHAI YEAR
Spring

Spring brings the Spring Festival (Chunjie), the traditional Chinese Lunar New Year, (sometime between January and March in the solar calendar). The pre-Chunjie calendar is packed with parties and celebrations. You should allot funds and time to at least send nice cards to all business contacts, and hold a small party for employees. Remember also that the Chunjie 'bonus' is not optional; employers who skimp there regret it later. If business warrants, give your team a budget and they'll happily plan lavish Chunjie events that

will position you well with employees, customers and clients. But plan ahead; book Chunjie parties early, avoiding those packed last few days before Chunjie Eve when employees are distracted by family obligations and senior guests can't commit, in case they get summoned to yet more senior parties elsewhere.

Once Chunjie hits, business essentially stops. It's a family-based holiday, refreshingly non-commercial, since the traditional emphasis is on home-cooked meals (rice and stir-fries, not the dumplings and noodles popular up north). Recent years have seen a new rage in eating out for Chunjie, with select restaurants offering family meals at lavish prices—and getting booked months in advance! But in general, from Chunjie Eve through the next several days, Shanghai shuts down; woe to the expat who tries to schedule a meeting or project then.

Even movement is tough, since transport clogs as everyone visits ancestral homes. Most expats take a vacation then, outside China, returning near the holiday 14 days after Chunjie ('15th of the 1st Lunar Month', or Yuanxiao 15), after which China gets back to work (officially vacation often ends earlier; in businesslike

Shanghai, real business can be done between Chunjie and Yuanxiao 15).

Enjoy the Celebrations

Even if you take some vacation between Chunjie and Yuanxiao 15, try to spend Chunjie Eve in Shanghai at least once, especially if you can snag an invitation to a family gathering. You will never eat better, and it's a great opportunity to share Shanghainese family joy, and watch the city light up with fireworks.

April brings Qingmingjie, the 'Clear-Bright', or Grave-Sweeping Festival, when families visit ancient gravesites or modern mausoleums to tidy up, and then have a family dinner. Then as spring turns to summer, the rainy season begins, a month of steady downpours that turn the city green. There are regular floods, and if you're not scrupulous about airing things out, leather will go bad in your closets. The Chinese expression is Mei Yu, which means, poetically, the 'Time of the Rain that brings Berries'. But that expression is infamous for homophony with another phrase that local wags claim is more accurate: the 'Time of the Rain that brings Mould'.

Summer

Soon enough, high summer comes, and the heat is extraordinary. Shanghainese eat ices, bring fans and mattresses out to balconies, and often wear light pajamas all day, a silly summer pleasure to see. Summer also brings Duanwujie, the Dragon-boat Festival. While not celebrated on the same scale as in southern China, Duanwujie is still an excuse for a Shanghai get-together, if possible on the river, maybe competing in Dragon-Boat races. It's worth renting a boat for a Duanwujie dinner cruise at least once in your Shanghai stay, and/or trying your hand at a Dragon-boat oar.

Summer is also the most common time for employee outings, team- and morale-building trips that are a key perk (many Chinese rate job opportunities in part based on the quality of outings). Westerners may rarely want to spend free time with work colleagues, but Chinese value these outings highly. It is worth allotting budget for employees to plan them, and important to attend and enjoy the outing yourself.

Autumn

Autumn means cooler weather, visits to Buddhist temples at Putuoshan to see the leaves turn colour, restaurants full of Shanghai's famous 'hairy crab', and mooncakes for the Zhongqiujie or Mid-Autumn Festival. Shanghainese take the exchange of mooncakes seriously. Make sure your office orders early and stocks up sufficiently for all key business contacts.

Winter

Then comes Winter, whose grip in Shanghai is not so much icy as chill with damp that can seep into your bones. Shanghainese fight it by eating the spiciest foods of the year, washed down with heated servings of *huangjiu*, the smooth local rice wine, sometimes steeped with cured plums for sweetness. Winter is a special time to visit the mountains, especially Huangshan. Bundle up and prepare carefully, as for any winter mountain trip; but the cable cars still run and heated lodges still welcome guests, and you will rarely see more stunning natural vistas than the crags of Huangshan sparkling with snow.

Christmas and the Western New Year are not traditional Chinese holidays, but are increasingly celebrated by Shanghainese, who are always up for a celebration. New Year's Day is now an official holiday. For most Shanghainese, Christmas is stripped of religious connotation, which can make for surprising displays: would you believe a giant neon shopping-mall Santa, holding a baby girl in the pose traditional for Baby Jesus, wearing fashion-plate clothes and pouring gold coins from her fist? Try not to be too startled, even if such sights may offend traditional Western sensibilities; take them in the spirit of Chinese pageantry they were designed to appeal to.

Most global firms have at least a short break for Christmas in addition to the New Year's holiday; again expats often use their vacation then. If you choose to stay in Shanghai and have a Christmas Eve or day dinner for your staff, you may find it both gives opportunity to share your feelings on the holiday, and reaps benefits in terms of morale and team cohesiveness.

CYCLES OF LIFE

The wise employer looks to life-cycle occasions as opportunities to show appreciation for employees, and to share the pleasures of being involved in local life.

Birth

Birth is always a major event, especially for most Shanghainese, for it will be the only child. Local law mandates 90 days of Maternity Leave (more for difficult labour and for new mothers older than 23) and three days of Paternity Leave; the wise employer always errs towards generosity in interpreting the law. Traditionally, Chinese mothers rest for weeks past child-birth, staying abed and eating foods considered 'healing' in traditional medicine, while friends and family crowd around to care for mother and baby. It's called in Chinese 'Zuoyuezi', literally the 'Seated Month'. The new baby is passed around and made much of, as auspicious things are said of his or her future health, wealth and joy.

It is very appropriate, once mother and baby are home from the hospital, to visit during the Zuoyuezi of an employee or spouse to offer compliments and token gifts such as baby clothes, toys or 'healing' foods for the mother. You should, as much as possible, cut slack in this period for new dads AND moms. And once baby is old enough to be brought into 'society' (usually three to six months), you should expect—and invite—a visit to the office. It's always a pleasure to see the wee ones dressed in their best, sometimes with traditional hand-embroidered caps and shoes, being shown off to the world.

> **Proper Scheduling**
> Try to schedule such visits away from urgent deadlines though, as
> the whole office inevitably stops work to crowd around and coo at
> the happy couple and their bundle of joy.

Most Shanghai moms take a fairly short time off work, arranging for childcare through parents, friends, play groups and/or *Ayis* ('aunties', hired help seen as quasi-family members; for details, see the section on '*For Kids and Families*' in *Chapter 5: Settling In* on pages 84–86). But don't expect intense work focus in the first year or so of a child's life. Remember, there will probably only be this one child, and good employees are worth keeping through distracted periods. More and more firms are formalising this distraction, by offering flexi-time.

Childhood and Beyond

Once children are old enough to start formal day care and then school, employees will likely return to a strong work focus, for school means long hours for Shanghai children. Even grade school can be competitive, with top kids vying for slots in advanced classes, and in limited-enrolment enrichment activities at the Children's Palaces, from music and dance to chess and sports to math and science clubs.

A girl practising her Chinese calligraphy in the park.

By middle school, classes become seriously competitive, as students prepare for the dreaded exams. Parents often choose apartments based on the relative fame of neighbourhood middle schools, and will use back-door pull to get kids into better classes. For at the end of middle school is a rigorous exam, the results of which (together with whatever 'pull' the parent can muster) determines which high school the student attends—a very serious matter among competitive Shanghainese.

At the end of high school come the dreaded college entrance exams, a three-day ordeal offered in spring and again in summer, the results of which (combined with back-door pull) determine which college the child attends. As in many countries, a child's alma mater may not, in the end, influence life overall as much as doting parents imagine. But most families still prepare for college exams as they would for a military campaign.

Doing Your Bit to Help

When an employee's child is preparing exams, particularly for college, you will want to cut the employee some slack if possible, for they will likely spend long hours coaching, and drilling exam material. You can also give big face by offering to visit the family, or inviting them to a restaurant or your home at some point in the preparation process, to help the student 'practise English'. The actual value of a session or two in your presence in helping the student ace the (required) English exam may be doubtful, but the positive effect of the gesture on employee relations is not.

Once in college, paradoxically, many students slack off a bit relative to the intense pre-exam push of high school. College thus becomes, among Chinese students, the time for silly teenaged exploration that Western students often get out of their systems in high school; this alone helps explain some of the excesses of Chinese student protests. Still, most Chinese students are serious learners. Though colleges are adding enrolment and new private colleges are springing

The Lecturing Circuit

This makes occasional lecturing an excellent opportunity for Shanghai-based firms. Sending appropriate team members to lecture on global business or the specialities of your discipline can help attract good employees down the road, position your firm as a good neighbour/partner of choice for China, and strengthen positive awareness of your position on any issue you choose to address. Lectures also offer good training in public speaking, in a fairly low-risk environment, for up-and-coming employees. For this reason many top global firms in Shanghai maintain a 'speaker's bureau' sending speakers regularly to local colleges and universities to address everything from environmental protection to strengthening rule of law.

up, as of today, less than 15 per cent of China's population gets a college education (much higher among Shanghainese). Most students are aware of their privilege and eager to learn.

In late college many students seek internships and part-time work, an excellent opportunity to recruit future employees. Best-and-brightest students from across China attend school in Shanghai, and a high percentage want to stay after graduation. A well-designed internship program can be a powerful recruitment tool.

As students graduate and make decisions on working life, they are often pulled between competing goals. Will they earn big bucks at foreign-invested firms? Or join local firms and help build home-grown pride? Or accept government jobs and help push forward reform? Or respond to the call of a Communist Party eager to attract next-generation members? And if so, how seriously will they take their Party obligations?

Don't be surprised if an employee seeks your advice on some of these questions, for themselves (with young employees), or on behalf of nearly-grown children. It is traditional in China to seek advice from employers and other authority figures, a ritual showing respect for you, as much as a genuine search for your wisdom. Show the employee respect in return by being attentive and offering your best advice.

More and more today, young employees also seek opportunities for continuing education, with everything from legal studies to MBAs. Many part-time 'executive MBA programmes' have sprouted up, catering to rising-star employees too valuable for employers to lose to traditional

MBA programmes. Many firms find that flexi-time and flexible tuition grants/loans allowing employees to attend such programs, in return for a pledge of service post-graduation, can be a powerful retention tool.

Marriage

Eventually the time will likely come for marriage, (although more and more young Shanghainese are eschewing that institution). Marriage is, if possible, surrounded by even more pomp than birth. The ceremony itself is generally limited, given that there's rarely a religious content; often it's only the couple and witnesses registering at a Civil Affairs Office. But most couples have events surrounding the ceremony, including a session at a photo studio where bride and groom wear rented finery from many eras and styles, and get photographed in a series of fun, romantic poses. Friends and colleagues will put on dinners; it would be highly appropriate for you to host one such gathering. And there's usually at least one large wedding banquet, inviting family and friends for food, drink, toasting and perhaps some mildly naughty games where close friends at the end of the banquet seek to gently embarrass the newlyweds.

If you're invited, and have never seen the Ang Lee film *Wedding Banquet*, watch it; it will give some sense of what you're in for. When invited to an employee's wedding, you should prepare a congratulatory toast (and someone to interpret it, unless you speak Mandarin), and a gift. The most traditional gift is cash, in a red envelope, with a card. Amounts vary, in part depending on how lavish the banquet is. A typical gift, as of this writing, is around Rmb 1,000–1,500 when invited to a fancy banquet. Check with local colleagues to be sure.

Increasingly in Shanghai, one key item young couples attend to after marriage is buying an apartment. Many companies find that creating housing funds or allowances, whereby the firm provides a down payment and/or mortgage guarantee in return for pledges of service, can be the ultimate retention tool.

Retirement

After years in the working world, most Shanghainese look forward to active retirement, funded through a combination of pensions and individual savings (China's Social Security system is still being developed). In addition to spending time with grandchildren and pursuing hobbies, Shanghai retirees have many options for keeping fit and active. A network of parks and community centres offering classes, clubs, exercise groups and part-time work opportunities make retirement a fulfilling time of life.

From the perspective of foreign employers, it is important to give face to retiring employees with an appropriate retirement party (as well, of course, as having arranged pension benefits all along). Afterward, retiree part-time consultants can be a great source of knowledge and connections, and retiree part-time workers can be a resource for innovative activities.

The Advantage of Experience

One insurance firm, for instance, gained positive awareness through funding a clean-up campaign, paying retired workers to do the cleaning and issuing special T-shirts. Several food and beverage firms, meantime, have found that small vendor carts staffed by retirees can get them into neighbourhoods they could not otherwise reach.

Death

Finally, though death is always sad, it is not always a tragedy. Chinese culture puts great premium on the cycles of life and family that maintain traditions over time. Death at the end of a long and full life, with children and grandchildren and perhaps great-grandchildren to carry traditions on, can be seen as fulfillment. From an employer's perspective, Chinese law mandates three days of Bereavement Leave for the death of a parent or child. The wise employer will cut slack when possible whenever a close family member is ill, and certainly during bereavement. It is also appropriate for the company to send a wreath of flowers to the funeral.

Funerals are generally fairly low-key and not religious, a time for appreciating the deceased's life, and consoling the family. Generally, a small gathering meets in a function room at one of the city's crematoria (all bodies are cremated by law in China, to save land that would otherwise go to gravesites; the only exceptions are minority groups like the Tibetans who have traditional religious ceremonies). If invited to attend, you may wish to say a few words of appreciation, even if you never met the deceased, as a way of giving face to the employee. Check with local colleagues for advice. Following the ceremony, ashes will most likely be deposited in one of the city mausoleums, which the family will later visit on each Grave-Sweeping Festival.

SETTLING IN

CHAPTER 5

'The landscape of a Chinese city isn't
so much botanical as human.'
—Vivienne Tam, *China Chic*

THE 'PIONEER' EXPATS WHO FIRST RETURNED TO SHANGHAI after economic reform had very little choice as to where they lived. They were either assigned housing if they worked for a Chinese organisation, or got on waiting lists for one of the relatively few places that accepted foreigners. This mirrored a housing shortage faced by all Chinese. After 1949, all land was nationalised and could only be allocated by the government, for instance, to enterprises which factored the land use as a unit of production. Housing of individuals and families was provided by work units that the people themselves were 'allocated' to, also as factors of production. There was almost no real estate available on the open market.

With economic reform, real estate for sale or lease became essential to attracting foreign investment—an issue that the leadership gradually came to understand. And so in 1988, the government revised China's constitution to allow the sale of 50-year and 99-year 'land-use rights' for property development, paving the way for a re-emerging real estate market.

There followed a building boom of epic proportions in China's more open cities. Shanghai led the pack and built some 5 million sq m (54 million sq ft) of office space between 1995 and 1999, about the same amount as was built in London between 1955 and 1965 in the post-war building boom.

The residential sector saw a similar flurry of new projects, even in outlying areas. Houses in 'Shangurbia' now compete for tenants with high-rise apartments and old houses in the former French Concession area. One thing is for sure, expats in Shanghai today are spoiled for choice when it comes to housing options.

The next section offers a bit of history of Shanghai architecture and residential infrastructure, then goes through several top residential options for expats today, discussing some pros and cons of each area, and providing sample prices that are current as at this writing. For up-to-the-minute information, consult a reputable rental agency or property consultant on your arrival in Shanghai.

A BIT OF HISTORY…

Few take the stroll along Shanghai's Bund without expressing wonder at the contrast between Classical architecture from days gone by on one side of the river, and the newest and boldest buildings on the other. In its heyday, though, the Bund itself showcased the newest and boldest the world had to offer. The 52 'Old Bund' buildings date from the late 1800s to the early 1900s, and accommodated everything from consulates, foreign banks and gentlemen's clubs

New apartment buildings in the Pudong area.

to insurance firms and news agencies. Shanghai's then-builders were not shy about experimentation, and if you look carefully, you'll note an eclectic range of styles among the 52 'Grandes Dames'.

You can see more such experimentation on Huaihai Lu, running east to west across Shanghai from the French Concession towards the River, much of it built in 1901. Many buildings along the road were influenced by Western styles (like 'Huaihai Fang', just off Huaihai Zhong Lu between Maoming Lu and Shanxi Nan Lu, built in 1927). Most detached houses were built for foreign businessman, and some have now been renovated to become sought-after residences.

The same boldness also applies to modern Shanghai, and for some of the same reasons. Continued rapid growth has created room and funding for both experimentation and collaboration. Extensive foreign expertise now supports the best in Chinese capabilities, supplying everything from architects to new materials to property management.

Between 1949 and 1988, Shanghai was barely touched by infrastructure works or new construction, reputedly a punishment for ill-gotten gains in 'pre-liberation' days. 1988 was the year that the Government launched a series of policies to re-open the city and attract foreign investment. With that, global expertise poured in.

One premier example of the result is Shanghai Centre, long the most prestigious comprehensive real estate project in the city, designed by Portman and Associates of Atlanta. Still a premier address about 11 years after completion, it is a fine example of what can be achieved by bringing in world-class expertise to support China's home-grown design and construction talents.

A more recent, but equally successful, fusion is Xintiandi. The master plan for the neighbourhood-wide renovation was completed by Wood and Zapata Inc, a Boston-based architectural firm specialising in adaptive re-use of old buildings, and by the Singapore office of Nikken Sekkei International Ltd. Project designers have carefully preserved the unique building architecture of Shanghai's Shikumen culture, and combined it with modern renovations, with results to rival London's Covent Garden or Sydney's Darling Harbour. New apartments have been built in the area to benefit from the newly found value of the location.

Looking back over the past decade, Shanghai has experienced astounding improvements in both infrastructure and the built environment. Bridges, tunnels, metro lines and a new airport have all been built to upgrade the transportation network, and world-class technology is being incorporated in everything from telecoms to Magnetic-Levitation trains. As Shanghai continues to position itself as a key world financial and economic centre, expect the world to continue to be seduced by this city for many years to come.

The next sections explore in turn each of the key housing options for expatriates.

LIVING THE HIGH LIFE: SERVICED APARTMENTS

Shanghai goes beyond expectations for business and tourist visitors alike. Businesses can lease a serviced apartment, serviced office, and car/driver in little more time than it takes to check into one of the city's array of fancy five-star hotels.

Serviced apartments provide fully furnished homes with housekeeping services, laundry, swimming pool and gym. Those that are part of a larger hotel complex also offer hotel services to tenants. Shanghai has a full range to choose from.

Luxury/serviced apartment projects tend to be located in central areas. Most provide a range of services, from full furnishings to hotel-style housekeeping and maids. Some serviced apartments are available for short-term leases, and these are in demand from people working in the city for short periods but tired of living in hotels, and from people who do not want to have to worry about housework.

Shanghai Centre was the first true serviced apartment project in modern Shanghai. Since 1998, a number of other major luxury and serviced apartment projects, including City Apartments, Shangri-La Residences, 41 Hengshan Road, Century Court, Royal Pavilion, The Ascott and Somerset Grand have come onto the market. In all of these projects, fixtures and finishes are of a high standard throughout.

According to the latest survey, a total of approximately 40,000 households lived in serviced apartments at the beginning of 2001. Tenants prefer to lease serviced apartments over hotels largely due to cost, comfort, range of services and privacy. Consequently, serviced apartments not only attract long-term tenants but also short-term tenants whose only alternative is to stay in a hotel.

In the past, serviced apartments were mostly concentrated in central areas, particularly in the Changning, Xuhui and Jing'an districts, and this is expected to continue. At the same time, as the city develops, new projects are rising in the Bund area, and especially on the Pudong side of the river.

Rents for serviced apartments are on an upward trend due to strong demand, limited new supply, improved facilities

Pros & Cons of Serviced Apartments

Pros
- Central location
- Full facilities
- English-speaking staff
- Laundry and housekeeping services
- Business facilities
- Fully equipped
- Cheaper than long-term hotel accommodation

Cons
- 'Detached' from the 'real' Shanghai
- 'Intrusive' service
- Costly in the longer term
- Not always possible to personalise

and services as well as much-improved infrastructure. A growing economy and increasing foreign investment are likely to keep rents on this trend for the next two to three years at least.

Selected Serviced Apartments in Downtown Shanghai		
Project	**Size (sq m)**	**Rent (US$ per month)**
41 Hengshan Road	87–550	2,350–11,500
Century Court	63–131	1,500–2,500
Chelsea	145–328	2,300–9000
City Apartments	156–305	3,000–7,500
Kerry Residence	76–396	2,000–13,000
Royal Pavilion	215–458	4,000–1,000
Shanghai Centre	50–270	1,600–9,800
Somerset Grand	83–233	1,800–6,000
		Source: Crispin Property Consultants

HIGH RISE AT LOWER COST: NON-SERVICED APARTMENTS

For longer-term residents on a budget who don't want to brave Shanghai's increasingly epic traffic jams to and from work each day, leasing a standard apartment is often the preferred option. Usually these come either furnished or unfurnished depending on the rent and the preference of the tenant.

It is often also possible to rent an unfurnished apartment, and negotiate a deal with the landlord to amortise the cost of furnishing it over the term of the lease, with furnishings you will leave there. That way you can have a fully furnished apartment, personalised to your preferences, paid for within a monthly rent that will unlikely break an expat housing budget. If you go for this option, however, be sure to itemise which pieces of furniture and decoration were purchased under the landlord's budget and which were not. This will help forestall landlord attempts, when your time comes to leave, to attach that fine painting or Ming cabinet you acquired during your stay.

Non-serviced apartments cover a wide range, from small renovated Jazz Era buildings, to modern high-rise towers. Most are wholly Chinese owned and operated, though some involve some foreign investment. On the whole they are cheaper (sometimes MUCH cheaper) than serviced apartments in terms of rent. Often they are inferior (sometimes MUCH inferior) to foreign-invested complexes in construction quality and service. Whether or not this is an issue for you depends on your tolerance for occasional problems with heat, electricity or noise from other apartments. The wise prospective tenant speaks with current tenants, and visits at various times of day and night, before signing a lease. In particular, look out for late night taxi queues beneath your bedroom window, a key source of irritation for residents.

Some non-serviced buildings are highly desired and, even in today's wide-open market, have waiting lists; like

Pros & Cons of Non-serviced Apartments

Pros
- Central location
- Generally fully or at least semi-furnished
- Most include some services, such as building security and cable TV
- Cheaper than fully serviced apartments and much cheaper than hotels
- Closer to local life, while remaining slightly 'above it all'
- More flexibility to personalise space than with serviced apartments
- Residents free to hire their own cleaning lady if desired

Cons
- Can be somewhat pricey compared to many 'Shangurbia' options
- Generally under local management, which means few English-speaking staff
- Sometimes 'too close' to local life
- Construction quality can be mixed

Huaihai Apartments, an Art Deco-era building with large, airy rooms that rent for surprisingly low rates. Some of the newest locally-built complexes, such as Villa Beau Rivage, are also quite popular, with services and quality at or near the level of the foreign-invested serviced apartments, at less cost.

Some older complexes, such as Aijian Towers in Longhua (built in the 1980s, managed by the China National Offshore Oil Corporation), have been surpassed by more popular areas, and regularly have vacancies. Those on a budget may want to look into these less fashionable complexes as, despite construction and other issues, they can offer surprisingly pleasant accommodations at a fraction of the cost of serviced apartment towers. In some cases, when expats spend far below their maximum allotted budget, companies will agree to pay for other amenities, such as extended vacation, golf or hardship allowances. For the independent-minded, it's an option worth considering.

Selected Non-serviced Apartments in Downtown Shanghai		
Project	Size (sq m)	Rent (US$ per month)
Huaihai Apartments	62–280	1,000–4,500
Palace Court	105–222	1,000–4,200
Villa Beau Rivage	128–171	1,800–4,500
Zhonghui Gardens	120–180	1,000–2,500

DOWNTOWN GARDEN VILLAS

The French Concession area offers the most attractive 1920s and 1930s colonial architecture in the city. Those with romantic notions of living in a downtown house with a garden like something from the smart inner suburbs of Paris or London will love the housing options in Shanghai's old French Concession.

Old houses on offer range from quaint 40-sq-m (430.6-sq-ft) studio apartments on one floor of a large old house, to 1,000-sq-m (10,764-sq-ft) multi-storey mansions or houses with private gardens of up to 2,000 sq m (21,528 sq ft). The demand for old properties with character invariably exceeds supply; quality properties only remain on the market anywhere from a few hours to a few weeks before being leased, making it a sellers market. Prices in this sector generally range from US$ 1,500–20,000 per month or more.

Pros and cons of this type of housing are outlined in the box below, but those that fall in love with the leafy streets of downtown Shanghai—as many do—will enjoy these houses immensely. Drafts and damp notwithstanding, the opportunity to be able to walk to work and have a garden may outweigh cons, especially when an employer is paying the rent and you can leave after a year if you decide it was a mistake.

Pros & Cons of Downtown Garden Villas

Pros
- Attractive historical architecture
- Central locations
- Gardens
- Immersed in local life: fun neighbourhood markets, local neighbours
- Walk-to-work possibilities

Cons
- Often lack modern conveniences
- 1920s construction, often with little upgrading
- Expensive, particularly relative to the facilities provided
- Immersed in local life: noise, poor security and sometimes nosy neighbours
- Damp and drafty
- Car parking difficulties
- Absentee landlords
- Poor power supply
- Subdivided houses

Most of these houses are owned by individual landlords, many of whom live overseas. The stubborn owner can be the greatest drawback with this type of housing, as many have unreasonable and irrational expectations of tenants. To be fair, there are plenty of friendly landlords, but be patient and do not rush into a lease. As more and more houses come on the market, there is greater choice. The best way to find a good one is by word of mouth, or through an agent who specialises in this kind of housing, rather than a generalist agency.

The main areas where downtown garden villas can be found are in the roads and alleys off Huaihai Lu, Hengshan Lu, Changle Lu, Jianguo Lu and others in Xuhui District. Many Shanghai guides have extensive introductions to the history of some of these properties.

SHANGHAI'S SUBURBS: 'SHANGURBIA'

Development of Shanghai's 'burbs' comes as an inevitable consequence of comprehensive improvement in road and rail systems, combined with growing wealth, increasing cost of downtown homes, cheaper cars and a booming property market. Anyone who has seen real estate advertising on local

TV will know that the sales these days is all about green grass, blue skies, children playing in the garden, a car in the garage and a house in the suburbs.

The Hongqiao area remains the most popular 'inner' suburb among expatriates, but Pudong is increasing in popularity all the time. Apart from several top quality villa projects like Tomson Golf Villas, Green Villas and the Four Seasons, Pudong also has three international schools (see the section 'For Kids And Family' [pages 74–75]) and excellent shopping (see 'Shopping Till You Drop' section [pages 89–99]).

Areas like Minhang, Songjiang and Kangqiao were originally developed to relocate residents from condemned city centre housing, as new highways carved up the city. With Metro Lines and the Outer Ring Road offering quick and easy access to downtown areas, Xinzhuang has now emerged as one of the more popular of Shanghai's 'burbs'. North of Xinzhuang, Shanghai Racquet Club and Apartments has successfully drawn expat residents further out of the city than would have been imaginable a couple of years ago. A tennis

Pros & Cons of 'Shangurbia'

Pros
- All modern construction
- Reasonable cost
- Facilities usually include swimming pool, gym and tennis court
- Secure compounds
- Open space
- Close to international schools

Cons
- Distance and traffic issues
- Often characterless modern architecture
- Local management in cheaper compounds
- Absentee landlords if houses individually sold to investors

club, the American School and regular shuttle bus services make it acceptable, even to those with offices in Pudong.

The push south-west doesn't stop at Xinzhuang. The farmland around the 'Shanghai Rockies' at Sheshan has all been sold and will be covered with surburban housing within three or four years. The only question is whether the new golf course comes before or after the housing.

The effects of new infrastructure is felt in many locations in Greater Shanghai—perhaps most spectacularly in Kangqiao in the south-east. This was a location unimaginable for expat residents before 2001, when new roads opened the area up. Even as at this writing, a semi-detached house with garden can still be bought for as little as US$ 100,000 in a project called Cambridge Forest New Town, which includes an International School and clubhouse. Since the completion of the Lupu Bridge in 2003, it will be possible to lease a house with garden for US$ 1,000 a month just 20 minutes (not counting traffic jams) from the main office areas in the city centre.

While housing is the most obvious form of suburban development, Shanghai's industrial parks are all experiencing a boom and expansion. Companies located in these parks provide employment for many of the residents, foreign and local, who are moving to suburban dwellings. The typical socialist urban planning model located factories downtown; in Shanghai, land reform has changed all that. In a fine example of 'socialist market economy', a virtuous circle has been created whereby money raised from the sale of central city industrial sites has been invested in new infrastructure in the suburbs. This raised land values, and enabling more land to be sold, the proceeds or which are used to finance more infrastructure, and so on.

Most factories have long since moved to orderly industrial parks. Minhang Development Zone is now home to 151 companies, including 28 Fortune 500 companies. Caohejing houses 16 per cent of all hi-tech firms in Shanghai, and Shanghai Business Park will soon provide R&D and office space for companies who realise the benefits of offices in the 'burbs, Songjiang has attracted US$ 3 billion-plus in investment since 1992; nearby a Taiwanese chip company is investing US$ 10 billion. Further south, Caojing Chemical Park had attracted some US$ 7 billion in contracted foreign investment by late 2002. Clearly, if you work in one of these complexes, you will want to look into living nearby.

Whatever else happens to Shanghai, the 'burbs' are here to stay. Just 15 years ago, areas like Hongqiao were mostly farmland. Within five years of the first land sales, it was the stage on which Shanghai's first post-war real estate bubble was set. As Hongqiao boomed, textile mills and run-down housing in Lujiazui were cleared to make way for the new Pudong Financial District. Once again now, the boundaries of Shanghai are pushing out. With real estate prices rising, developers are casting hungry eyes at green sites in Shanghai's new suburbs. A new lifestyle in Shangurbia is emerging.

OTHER INTERESTING HOUSING OPTIONS
Golf Course Living

It should come as no surprise that many like to live near a golf course; expats have been doing the same around the world for donkey's years. In Shanghai, golf course options are growing all the time. Appropriately enough, there are, at this writing, 18 golf courses in Shanghai, Kunshan and Suzhou.

One of the earliest golf villa projects is Tomson Golf Villas in central Pudong, by Zhangjiang Hi-tech Park. Tomson Golf Villas have been well received by the market since completion in 1997; nearly all Phases I and II units have been sold, and occupancy rates for Phases IV and V have reached 98 per cent. The project is considered one of the best in Shanghai, and houses many senior expatriates in multinational companies.

Shanghai Links, near Pudong International Airport, is planned as the largest high-grade residential development in Shanghai, offering 476 north-American-style low density homes, 315 apartment units and an 18-hole championship golf course on-site. The first 50 units were completed in 1998, and enjoy an 80 per cent-plus occupancy rate. Units are offered for lease only, with average rents at US$ 27 per sq m a month. Shanghai American School (Pudong branch) is located at Shanghai Links.

Tianma Golf Villas (on Tianma Golf Course in Songjiang Country) is 45 minutes, in normal traffic, from Shanghai, and has proved popular among Taiwanese and local buyers. Phase I comprises 63 villas, all almost fully sold out at a price of US$ 2,000 per sq m. Further phases are under construction. Grand City Golf Club comprises a nine-hole par 3 golf course, and is offering 49 villas at US$ 500,000 each; two blocks of apartments are also going up.

Of projects under construction, Sheshan International Golf Club is probably the most notable. Offering stunning views of Sheshan and US-designed houses for sale and lease, this is one of our tips for the future. The new elevated highway to Qingpu puts country living within range of downtown (though again, you will want to consider the hours you need to travel and average rush-hour traffic).

Downtown Renovations

Meanwhile, back in the city centre, something special is happening. It is rare, among the hundreds of real estate projects in the city, to find something that shows signs of much more imagination than wistful names and wishful thinking, but some projects have risen above the pack. The Xintiandi complex is today's hottest new address. Tomorrow's may well, according to many industry insiders, be Gaofuli, the first large-scale solely residential renovation project in the city.

Located at the corner of Ruijin Yi Lu and Changle Lu, Gaofuli will offer convenience for most parts of the city. A tranquil location at the heart of Shanghai, Gaofuli advertises modern materials and new buildings with all the character of Shanghai's famous 'stone gate' architecture. For details, see http://www. gaofuli.com.

Going forward, several other Puxi districts may experience similar renovations, and for those who want to combine the convenience of central living with the tranquility and comfort of the 'burbs, these new-old projects may offer the best of all possible worlds.

BUYING YOUR HOME AWAY FROM HOME IN SHANGHAI

Housing prices have fallen considerably since the mid 1990s (although they bounced back some 25 per cent from the bottom of the market at this writing). Quality of housing has also improved. New rules govern pre-sale, and improved overall design and layout, facilities and car parking have all been give much more consideration than before.

Renminbi-denominated mortgage availability for expatriates living and working in Shanghai is no longer an issue. Many foreign purchasers have bought for investment, and the number of newly-arriving expatriates is surpassing the number of those leaving the city, making leasing relatively easy for the right project.

Apart from house deposits, there are other costs involved including taxes, fees and the cost of decoration, since most new properties are sold as concrete shells. As a rule of thumb, allow Rmb 1,500–2,000 per sq m for renovation, including air conditioning and hot water. It will usually take two to three months to complete the work.

Consider carefully your reason for purchase. Houses are to be lived in, so first ask yourself where you would like to live. Small investors should buy properties they would be happy to live in themselves if need be. Whether buying for occupation or investment, it is smart to ask help from experienced valuers to ensure the price is reasonable and in line with the market. You can compare expert advice with what the vendor tells you and negotiate terms, remembering that while vendors may be unwilling to reduce price, they may be more flexible on payment terms and other incentives.

Be prepared to not necessarily find a tenant for your new house right away, although professional agents can help. It is usually better to secure a good tenant at a slightly lower rent than to leave places vacant in hopes of higher rents. Location is key. Check if the area has a sound track record of attracting good tenants.

Look for easy access, shopping, car parking, good facilities and property management, reputable developer and construction firm, and overall project quality. Visit at different times of the day, in different weather conditions, to check traffic, noise and rain penetration. Walk the surrounding area; if the developer says two minutes to the subway station, walk it yourself, and use the opportunity to check out other facilities like supermarkets, schools, parks or a hospital (ideally nearby, but not TOO nearby); and any new infrastructure under construction or being planned. Watch out for vacant land plots. Parks should add value to your property; additional buildings may affect your light or view, and brace yourself for noise during construction. Finally, check the specific unit you want to buy: unit size, price, layout, views, size of each room. There are many reasons for buying property in Shanghai, but whether you are buying for your own use or for investment, choose quality over quantity.

A reputable agent can help you through many of these processes, but the final decision is yours, so be wary of high-pressure tactics. The government is putting more effort into regulating the market, but it is still best to use a lawyer to avoid later disputes. Appendices can be added to the standard Shanghai property sales contract to boost protection in the areas that concern you most. Be careful, but be bold. It is worth it to have a place you can really call home.

FOR KIDS AND FAMILIES
Children

For businesspeople with a spouse and/or children, options for the family are major considerations in any expatriate assignment. Are there good schools and extra-curricular activities? Will trailing spouses find career options or other meaningful activities, and be able to make friends? These are crucial questions to explore. While the expat is busy with the new job, the spouse and/or kids need healthy involvements that give life abroad meaning for them as well. It is a truism among relocation agencies that more expatriate assignments fail due to family strife than for any other single reason, while families who find purpose and meaning via involvement in the new community add immeasurably to their overall experience, as well as to the expat's career.

Crossing the Cultural Barrier

Susan Schulman learned those lessons her first time in Shanghai—with her parents, in the mid-1980s. As dad worked as a real estate developer, mom found work teaching English and Susan became an exchange student at Fudan University. These involvements meant a happy stay for them, and Susan learned from the contrast with 'trailing families' that spent their days bored, waiting for vacations home.

Those lessons have served Susan well in expat assignments since, in London, Japan—and again in China. Susan returned to Shanghai with her husband David and cat Slate in 1995, working as Director of Public Relations for the Shanghai Centre. The Schulmans have lived in Shanghai more or less ever since, and their red-headed bilingual children—Jake and Stephanie—now think they are Shanghainese!

The good news is, Shanghai offers educational, recreational, vocational and other opportunities for families, giving them the chance to be involved in ways that provide trailing spouses with a sense of community and meaning, and teach Western children what it must be like to be a rock star! This next section focuses on educational, recreational and vocational opportunities for kids and families. (*For information about volunteering opportunities, see* Chapter 7: Enjoying Life *on pages 220–233.*)

BABY-SITTER BONANZA:
SHANGHAI WITH SMALL CHILDREN

Asked what special challenges she had met in Shanghai, new UK mother Sandy Jenkins said, "I wished I'd known before I arrived just how much adoration my baby son would receive from local people. This worried me for the first few weeks. If I had been more prepared I think I would have been pleased to have waitresses take him to the kitchen while I had lunch, instead of wondering if he had been kidnapped!"

Her experiences are common to many a Shanghai parent. The Chinese love children, perhaps even more than traditionally, now that most families are restricted to one child. The novelty of different skin and hair colours make Western babies particularly loved. Do not be surprised if strangers on the street stop to stare or blow kisses at, or even pet, pick up or play with your infant or small child. If you prefer strangers not touch your child, you will need to find a polite way of discouraging it, explaining cultural differences on that point, while recognising that the intent is positive.

And if you can get comfortable with the unrestrained joy the Chinese take in babies (at least in controlled situations like restaurants where you can see the door!), you will find it remarkably safe to allow this city of 17 million free babysitters to share the joy of your child. For many Shanghai-based parents, the real challenge is teaching the child more caution with strangers once the family repatriates home!

For longer-term child care, of course, you will not rely on strangers, especially if both parents work. Shanghai offers Montessori and other day care and pre-school options for children starting at age three (*see the* Resource Guide, *pages 304–306*). Given how inexpensive household help is in Shanghai, though, many parents choose instead to hire a full-time (sometimes even live-in) nanny. There are tips on pages 84–86 on choosing *Ayis* (the Chinese word means 'Auntie', which says a lot about how the Chinese view the relationship between family and hired help).

Given the Chinese love of kids, the low cost of household help and multiple day care options, you may well find, as one

Shanghai mom says, that "finding good babysitting care for small children is easier in Shanghai than at home."

BABY SUPPLIES

Some other areas offer greater difficulties. For nursing infants, most expat mothers, if they use formula at all, prefer to bring powders from home, given past scandals about quality issues with locally-produced formulas. Meantime, the La Leche League has a chapter in Shanghai, and many expats prefer to nurse their babies until they are old enough for solid foods and cow's milk.

Even then, Sandy Jenkins points out that many Chinese baby cereals are flavoured with fish, bone or other ingredients Chinese medicine consider 'strengthening', but Westerners find unusual. Western brands are available, but at highly inflated prices. You may want to consider shipping non-perishable baby foods with your household goods, unless you will be making your own (though, with inexpensive household help, home-preparation is an option many expats choose to go with).

The same holds true with disposable diapers. Chinese brands are available, but the quality varies, and Western brands are pricey. Again, you may want to either ship many boxes of disposables, or have household help manage sterilising reusable cottons.

Jenkins also notes that 'narrow and manoeuvrable strollers are crucial for negotiating crowded sidewalks and cramped supermarkets. Also make sure it folds up easily and quickly to shove in taxis'. And educate even the smallest children on traffic safety. "We had a few near misses before I realised that traffic lights mean nothing to bicyclists and motorcyclists, and pedestrian crossings mean nothing to anyone at all!"

Finally, the enticing green lawns in virtually every park in central Shanghai are for show only, off-limits to all pedestrians, including running children. While foreign children will unlikely be stopped, it does not improve race relations for Chinese kids restrained by their mothers to watch enviously as Western kids race the forbidden sward. Unless you live in 'Shangurbia' or have a garden villa, better keep your small child's grass exposure to the few parks and gardens that allow walking on the lawns. These include Xijiao, Longhua Martyr's Park, the Botanical Gardens and a few others. When in doubt, do as the locals do.

READING, WRITING AND 'RITHMETIC

School-aged children have plenty of choices in Shanghai. The most widely attended international schools are Concordia International, Shanghai American, Shanghai Community International, Shanghai French and German, Shanghai Japanese, Shanghai Singapore International and Yew Cheng Shanghai International. With a British school available and the Number One Shanghai High School offering an international division, families can choose between courses of schooling similar to what their children would have at home, or new curricula.

Soong Qingling

Madame Soong Qingling (1893–1981), wife of Dr Sun Yat Sen, was passionately committed to children and actively involved in China's revolution. Surviving her husband by many decades, she became torchbearer for his ideals, an ardent patriot, internationalist and peace advocate. Soong is remembered and revered in China (and abroad) as one of the true Great Idealists of China's Revolution, a sort of conscience of the Chinese Communist Party (CCP) throughout her life. Since her death she has become almost a patron saint of children.

Today one of China's premier schools is named after Madame Soong, a public-private hybrid called the Soong Qingling School. With both Chinese and International campuses in both Hongqiao and downtown, the school serves children pre-school through second grade, offering some of the best education in Shanghai. Expats have children in both campuses, depending on language skills. Waiting lists tend to be long, so put your name down early if you wish your child to attend.

Most international schools require uniforms, available for purchase through the school. Many expats find this convenient, considering the limited selection of 'cool' kids' clothes in Shanghai, especially for five- to ten-year-old boys, (see the section 'Shopping Till You Drop' in this chapter [pages 90–93] on the perils of finding plain jeans without Mickey Mouse AND Winnie the Pooh decals, waist to cuff!).

Most international schools enrol children from age three, through the American equivalent of either grade eight or grade 12. A plethora of 'play schools' are also available for toddlers, with programmes ranging from low-key 'mommy-and-me' play groups with names like Tiny Tots and Kinderworld, to highly structured day care at places like Little Eton, named after the prestigious British school!

STICKER SHOCK

Most international schools employ expatriate teachers, and the cost of home leaves and housing get passed on in tuition. Prices range from several thousand US dollars a year for a half-day of pre-school, to upwards of US$ 17,000 for a year of high school. Throw in bus fees, books and uniforms, and a year of school for a foreign student can cost nearly as much as a private international university. Most international school students in Shanghai have parents working for firms which include school tuition as part of benefit packages. Families without full expat packages more often home-school their kids, or send them to local Chinese schools.

Although these fees are in line with those of top college prep schools abroad, some expat families worry that quality may not always match prices. Local rules taxing foreign teacher salaries after two years of employment mean high teacher turnover. Also, few Shanghai international schools require the stringent testing that marks elite schools abroad; here, tuition money talks. In some cases, for instance, classes get slowed down to accommodate the language abilities of students whose parents paid high fees for them to 'learn English with the natives'. Native English-speaking students sometimes get frustrated by learning less content than they otherwise might, and/or get bored.

That said, many expats feel a price can't be put on the international exposure that kids gain from befriending diverse classmates. In fact, some parents (admittedly, a minority in the business community) take this further, and enrol their kids in local Chinese schools EVEN when an expat package would allow for international school tuition, creating the challenge of playing catch-up to learn content in Mandarin. Your child will, that way, almost certainly not be bored! As a bonus, in addition to fluent Mandarin, you may find after repatriation that your child has progressed well beyond home-country grade level in math and sciences, two topics particularly stressed in the Chinese curriculum.

EXTRA-CURRICULAR ACTIVITIES

School will take up much of your child's day, but there's still plenty of time after 3:00 pm or on weekends for bored rug rats to make trouble. Your best defence is getting involved with them in some of the many extra-curriculars available.

Classes, Sports and Clubs

Structured extra-curricular activities abound. Your child's lessons don't need to stop just because you relocate to Shanghai: tennis, swimming, ballet, piano and even horse riding lessons are readily available. Organised activity groups such as Roots and Shoots and Scouts offer more options. Ask friends or your child's school for recommendations. Mother-and-child play groups form and reform themselves rapidly, so the best way to find them is by word-of-mouth with other parents, though some teachers and schools take time to inform families of child-oriented activities available.

Active Kids Shanghai

Active Kids Shanghai, started in 2000 by a board of international moms and dads, runs activities for pre-school to high school kids in Shanghai. Day-to-day operations are handled by a small staff led by an energetic young Chinese-speaking Dutch national. Families buy memberships yearly every September; catalogues are distributed quarterly. Classes

Just Like Home

On a balmy spring morning, with the scents of cut grass and barbecued hotdogs wafting over, watching your kid hit a ground ball to third, you could be anywhere in the world. In reality, you just happen to be in Shanghai, on one of the four baseball diamonds donated to Active Kids by the US Consulate! Active Kids has helped bring 'normalcy' and a sense of home for many expat families.

range from ballet, tap and jazz to art and pottery. Team sports include soccer, baseball, basketball and others, organised by age, and played on fields and courts in Hongqiao. Moms and dads are encouraged to volunteer organising activities, passing out uniforms and coaching, just like at home.

FAMILY FUN TIME
Most families also enjoy spending unstructured time together. Many day trips and excursions discussed in the section 'Past City Limits' (*in* Chapter 7: Enjoying Life, *pages 213–220*) are terrific for kids. Local English-language publications like *That's Shanghai* often list theatre happenings, hotel or restaurant parties and other activities appropriate for kids, from holiday Easter egg hunts and Santa's Workshops to museum hands-on craft days. Many potential outings are listed below.

Outings
Opportunities for family outings in Shanghai are almost infinite. Following are some of one family's favourites. Start with these; you will quickly build your own 'top list'.

Parks
When asked in a class exercise what his favourite place in the world was, Susan Shulman's then five-year-old son answered: Zhong Shan Park. "We have travelled to more lovely destinations than I can count on my fingers and toes, so that says a lot for one of Shanghai's largest parks." Zhong Shan offers just about every play and activity area that any of the other city parks have, all in one place: an aviary, man-made lake with motorised leisure and bumper boats, a huge field filled with ball-kicking youngsters and kite-flying grandpas, and inflated moon-bounce 'palace' 10-m (33-ft) tall, complete with ropes to scale the sides and slides to come down the other end.

An amusement park completes the picture with other favourites: bumper cars, mini roller-coaster, tilt-a-whirl and the sky-bike, from which you can survey the whole scene while getting a thigh workout! Zhong Shan has the city's

A boy feeds the pigeons in Renmin Park.

largest Fun Dazzle—an indoor maze of ropes, tunnels and intertwined curvy slides.

To top it all off, the park offers Coney Island-style eats: popcorn, cotton candy, candy apples and so on. Swirled ice creams come in not just traditional chocolate and vanilla, but also lychee and green tea flavours, while the most novel treat there has to be candied sausages!

Other in-town parks with at least some of Zhong Shan's activities include centrally located Fu Xing Park, Renmin Park, Jing An Park and Pudong's Century Park (which boasts 21st century play areas, including a children's climbing wall). At all of these, adults can enter for just Rmb 2, and kids for just Rmb 1.

Another favourite is Shanghai Traffic Park, which offers almost everything you can experience from a Shanghai taxi window, without the honking! It's a magical world of miniature sites—Peace Hotel, Oriental Pearl TV Tower—all situated on quiet tree-lined pint-sized streets with tiny signs reading Huaihai Lu and Nanjing Lu. Hop in a little red corvette or Happy Birthday Rocket, and begin your sightseeing tour. Says Susan Shulman, "My three-year-old daughter's pre-school class comes on regular field trips, and in addition to enjoying seeing her joyriding with friends (a glimpse of the future, I fear!), I love watching the elderly Chinese who gather in this unique setting, knitting on tree-shaded benches, or practising *taiji* under the 'inner-ring road'."

Rides and treats in all Chinese parks are cheap by Western standards, but the fun your kids can have is world-class. Shanghai neophytes may only see rusty carts and slightly worn equipment, but children either don't notice or find it part of the charm. Bring handi-wipes and anti-bacterial soap for clean-ups when necessary, but otherwise just enjoy the day with your kids. If you choose to picnic, though, be prepared for a crowd; Shanghainese, although accustomed to seeing Westerners, are still interested in how they act with children, what they eat, etc.

Garden Picnic

A lovely picnic spot is the peaceful lawn of the Garden Hotel on Maoming Lu, offering shade trees, perennials, an elegant fountain, stone paths and usually a wedding or two on auspicious days. Enter, picnic basket in tow, and turn left. If security staff follow, smile sweetly and point to your plastic bag, as if to say, "I will clean up my litter!" If you speak Chinese this is probably not the time to let on; although occasional Chinese families also visit the Garden Hotel grounds, the latter is not a public park. Many expat familes assuage the guilt of taking advantage of their 'special status' as 'foreign guests' by reflecting that it is one of few places in the city where they can picnic without an audience!

Lions and Tigers and Bears, Oh My...

The Shanghai Zoo, built on a former golf course, is also a park, with animal exhibits spread over vast grounds that offer good spots for picnics and running around. Woefully under-funded, the Shanghai Zoo still houses animals in quarters not seen in major US zoos since the 1960s. Most expat families will want to avoid the 'Household Pets' section; Western kids are often disturbed seeing 'Lassie' and 'Garfield' in cages. Still, however they are housed, the elephants and giraffes and the rest are wonderful, and your kids will likely enjoy being able, for a few Rmb, to get a handful of giraffe nibbles to feed those gentle giants.

One Italian mother spoke, as only Italians can, of boarding a tour bus and being driven through exhibits of lethargic exotic animals, then stopping inside the tiger cage to watch ferocious cats stalk live chickens that had been placed in the cage for the viewing pleasure of bus passengers!

Another animal option is the Shanghai Wild Animal Park in Pudong. But again, saying that animal rights activists have not yet made it to Shanghai is an understatement. Another source of excitement was the opportunity to have a photo taken next to live—presumably drugged—panthers and lions. The Wild Animal Park is best left for older children, or those not overly sensitive.

Look Ma... No Hands

The famous Shanghai Circus performs almost nightly at Shanghai Circus World and the Shanghai Centre Theatre. Often, the skilled daredevils entertaining the crowd are no older than children in the audience! Girls bend their bodies into mind-boggling positions, boys tumble through hoops, clowns perform slapstick comedy, trapeze artists soar. At the larger, more remote Circus World, young men juggle flaming batons while balancing precariously on spinning wheels. Children, young and old, enjoy the acrobats. Remarks susan Shulman, "Our family has been going for years and no two shows have ever been identical!"

Winter Year Round

No, we are not describing Shanghai's weather! Even in the hot, sticky summer of this flat delta city, your kids can swish down a powdery slope at Shanghai Northstar Indoor Skiing! Those who have vacationed at Zermat or Aspen may not be impressed, but most kids are thrilled to don skis, boots, parkas and gloves, step on the carpeted escalator, and snow plow down a 380-m (1,246.7-ft) ski run. To one side, kids can build snowmen or be pulled in sleds. The facility also offers tennis, swimming, sauna and dining. Equipment (from skis and snowboards to gloves and hats) is available for rental and rumour has it that lessons will soon be offered after school and on weekends.

Rainy Day Fun

No, it is not always balmy and warm in Shanghai, but the cold and rain need not lock you in your apartment. The city offers museums and theatres galore to keep children entertained, and maybe they may even learn something at the same time!

Weekdays or holidays can be the best times to visit, for Shanghainese flock to these locales on weekends, and they can be unbearably crowded. Most new facilities are located on the Pudong waterfront, within easy walking distance of each other, if you choose to frequent several in one day. All of these facilities have nice gift shops—a good thing to keep in mind for birthday presents and party favours.

The Shanghai Aquarium in Pudong boasts underwater exhibits similar to any large international aquarium, complete with interactive displays that let curious youngsters learn about the East China Sea just over the Shanghai border. Another aquarium, older and less expensive, is centrally located in Chaofeng Park. Aquaria 21 features a shark tank, crabs and turtles you can touch, and even an open piranha tank into which you can throw live goldfish, if your child is so inclined! Aquaria 21 is Australian-managed, and throws great birthday parties that include a back-of-house tour and pizza lunch.

Also in Pudong, the Science Museum's Bug Museum features, well, bugs. Live exhibits show youngsters how these creatures exist and co-exist in their natural habitats. The Shanghai Children's Museum has partnered with the Baltimore's Children's Museum to feature many exhibits identical to Baltimore's world-class facilities. The museum also offers travelling exhibits—like a giant bubble machine that can be set up at your home for a birthday party; the museum provides English-speaking staff to man the equipment. The IMAX theatre features the same shows seen around the world, often in English. Some films are only in town for a short time, so book immediately when you find one your kids want to see.

A favourite indoor activity among Shanghai's two- to eight-year-old-crowd is Fun Dazzle, a private chain of indoor play-grounds throughout the city. The largest one is at Zhong Shan Park. Others are inside shopping malls like Kid World and Pudong's Babaiban. Of varying size, these outlets offer ball pits, slides, jungle gyms and trampoline-like enclosures. Costs vary by location, but range from Rmb 10 per hour to Rmb 25 per half day. Socks must be worn by adults and kids, so bring your own or be subject to purchasing Chinese nylons! Many Chinese children play at Fun Dazzle, so it is a good opportunity to let your kids practise Mandarin.

Summertime... and the Living is Easy!

Although many expat mothers and children still make a mass exodus from Shanghai when school adjourns, more and more use the summer to work on tans and spend quiet quality time together. Many South Americans, Australians and New Zealanders stay in Shanghai because at home it is winter, while many Americans and Europeans just don't like to have the family apart for 10–12 weeks. Enough members still take a long summer vacation that many women's groups still take the traditional hiatus from June to August (then hold a wild party in September!). But more and more, like the American Women's Club, have launched successful summer programmes for ladies braving the heat.

With more social clubs opening (including the Shanghai Racquet Club, complete with a man-made beach on its kidney-shaped outdoor pool), and with most five-star housing complexes offering pools and tennis courts, Shanghai is manageable in summer. The only change is that golf tee-times start at 5:30 am to avoid searing midday heat and humidity as well as the evening mosquitoes!

Summer Camps are springing up on the heels of the highly successful 'Camp Shanghai Centre' developed in 1996 by two American sorority sisters who bumped into each other at Shanghai Centre's Long Bar and needed summer jobs to extend their China visas. Shanghai Community

International School and Active Kids Shanghai also run half-day and full-day summer programmes in June, July and August.

TEENAGERS

Teenaged expats can easily find routine activities like shopping and frequenting arcades and Internet cafés. They can also easily find their way into bars, discos and karaoke lounges. None of these are illegal—for there is, in fact, no minimum drinking age in China (though by custom, Chinese families don't allow kids to drink till they're in college). But unsurpervised, teens tend to find such venues gateways to the illegal drugs that are, unfortunately, readily available in Shanghai.

Expat parents are very divided on teenage drinking and partying. Many believe in allowing teens to get 'wild oats' out of their systems in the relatively safe environment of Shanghai, where drivers can courier them home after an evening on the town, so the novelty will have worn off by the time they hit college. Other parents feel children should abide by whatever drinking age is enforced in their home countries and forbid their kids to join parties where alcohol is served. In Shanghai's cosmopolitan expat society, though, home drinking ages vary and this can cause schisms in friendships.

Sound Recommendations

The mother of an American teen living in Shanghai recommends parents question their child's potential school and talk with other parents, on after-school and weekend extra-curriculars, as well as if they have alcohol- or drug-related issues, and how these are handled. Some schools have more problems than others; schools with lots of activities seem to have fewer students with free time to get in trouble.

But as in any country, the best defence of all is strong parental involvement and a solid relationship with your kids that is grounded from the time they were toddlers.

MOMMY NEEDS A BREAK…
THE ALL IMPORTANT AYI

Whether mothers are in Shanghai to work, study or play, child care and home management is of utmost importance when mommy is away. As in any country, references are crucial, as are careful considerations of disciplinary and other standards. Some Western expats find cultural differences with Chinese *Ayis* difficult to overcome. Although Chinese tend to discipline their own kids fairly strictly, for instance, as *Ayis* in foreign households, they may let kids reign supreme and spoil them. Some families opt either to hire as nannies non-Chinese residing in Shanghai (such as Filipinos, who may be culturally closer to Westerners), or to 'co-op babysit' with other Western parents.

Most expat families do hire Chinese nannies, overwhelmingly by word-of-mouth. Few employment agencies offer domestic helpers and contracts are non-existent. Some families hire several *Ayis* with specific duties like child care, cleaning, shopping, etc. Others manage with just one, depending on how many kids are at home, how much the 'trailing spouse' works, and personal preference. Some expats hate to turn 'their jobs' over to a Chinese helper, while others are all too ready! Either way, the family must feel comfortable having the new hire in their home.

Many expats who hire Chinese as nannies, particularly for young children, pay for a physical exam—at a local hospital or private Western clinic—before they begin employment. Also, World Link Medical and Dental Centres offers a first-aid course in Chinese for domestic helpers, which is highly recommended. Many expat families quickly get used to having a live-in *Ayi*, which lets working mothers know their child is being cared for one-on-one, while routine evening babysitting gives married couples more 'date time' than they may have had in years!

Because Chinese who lived through the Cultural Revolution were reprimanded for thinking on their own, it is particularly important to set clear guidelines on duties and expectations for domestic helpers. Rarely will they do anything before being asked. This is frustrating to many foreigners, but needs to be understood in context. Also, many Chinese still lack modern household appliances in their homes. Clear demonstrations of how to use the washer/dryer—including lessons on separating darks from lights and what can and cannot go in the dryer, dishwasher, vacuum, iron and most cooking apparatus like blenders or mixers, are a must for harmonious relationships.

The Psyche of an Ayi

Ayi stories range from pure adoration to pure entertainment. The most notorious Shanghai *Ayis* in recent history were a group of women from an Anhui Province village, working for a group of foreigners in a Hongqiao apartment complex. Each new foreigner who moved in heard from a neighborhood *Ayi* who would 'recommend someone', then bring another woman from Anhui. They reached such critical mass that one night, someone returning early from a business trip found eight *Ayis* drinking beer and watching TV in his apartment. They waved him casually through, so he wouldn't block the TV.

Understanding that many of these women had never before used modern appliances, or dealt with formal business attire, we were not surprised to learn that one Anhui *Ayi* once gave a good lye-soap scrubbing to a silk tie, then hung it up to dry. The surprise was, she hung it on an open computer. By the time the owner returned, not only was the tie ruined (no matter how well-ironed), but so was the water-drenched laptop.

Humour aside, one of Shanghai's great joys is having a wonderfully competent country-woman help give your home some order and sanity, while sharing with you her sometimes surreal perspective on Shanghai. If you are careful with recommendations, and take time to make sure your *Ayi* knows how to use key appliances (and which to leave alone), you'll do fine and soon wonder how you ever made life happen without an *Ayi*.

Also give *Ayi* clear guidelines (with translation, if needed) on what children may and may not do, what they may and may not eat, and where they may and may not go. Most *Ayis* want their charges to be happy and would do anything to avoid tears. The American adage 'let them cry it out' at bedtime is unheard of; Chinese *Ayi* have been known to rock six-year-olds to sleep on a regular basis. Likewise, they may bring chocolates and candies for even the youngest children.

Many expat children learn their Chinese from their *Ayi*, who typically does not speak English. If having your child pick up Mandarin is important, make sure your *Ayi* knows not to use slang or dialect when speaking or reading to the children. Many local bookstores carry Chinese translations of Western nursery rhymes and Disney tales, as well as Chinese children's books about colours, body parts, etc. Says Susan Shulman, "Our *Ayi* has always read to our children and they both speak terrific Mandarin, thanks to her teaching." Chinese learn by rote, though, rather than experience or exploration, so don't expect your *Ayi* to substitute for a tutor.

With hourly wages hovering around Rmb 10 per hour, it is easy to see why most expat families have domestic help in Shanghai. Chinese helpers can simplify life in Shanghai, negotiating at the shops, running errands, taking care of household chores and caring for children. Many *Ayis* become part of the family, even travelling on vacation—a nice fringe benefit for them AND you!

ADULT EDUCATION

Lest grown-ups get forgotten in the world of the 'Little Emperors', adult education is available,. This is particularly important for trailing spouses looking for meaningful ways to enjoy Shanghai or for those not wishing to postpone higher education.

Ni Hui Jiang Zhongwen Ma?

The ability to speak basic Chinese is very important to one's sense of independence in Shanghai. Although many Chinese in the services industries—taxi drivers, shopkeepers, restaurateurs—speak at least some English, the ability to accomplish something on one's own—even if it is just getting to and from the grocery store in a cab or negotiating the cost of a handbag in the market—offers a feeling of belonging in a city where most expats stick out like a sore thumb.

Pick up any local expat publication, read any expat grocery store bulletin board and you will easily find advertisements for tutors or language exchange. Tutors typically come to your house or meet at a coffee shop. Tutors are not necessarily professional teachers and may or may not use a textbook.

Particularly if you have a private tutor, lessons will move at your pace. Tutors also offer flexibility in subject matter. Even if the tutor uses textbooks, if you never plan to borrow books from the Shanghai Library, simply skip the topic on 'Tushuguan', and move on to one better for your needs. But some prefer to share a tutor with two to three friends or colleagues, which can add a more social aspect to learning. Good tutors are found by word-of-mouth; expect to pay anywhere from Rmb 20–100 per hour. Tutors can offer insight into daily life, customs and traditions of the Shanghainese. But, do be cautious of locals just looking for 'foreign friends', if what you want is strictly a tutor.

Many non-degree language schools have sprung up in Shanghai as more expats want language instruction. Again, look for advertisements in local expat publications; though again, word-of-mouth is useful in finding a good programme. Instructors in these institutions, with corporate names such as 'Ease Mandarin', typically have some formal teacher-training. Confirm with programme coordinators prior to registration, if this is important to you.

Class structures vary, so most students can find programmes that suit their needs. Some institutes pack 30 hours of tuition into a month, while others follow more leisurely weekly programmes all year. Textbooks are followed, and in some cases exams must be passed to move on to the next level. Class sizes vary; some institutions even offer private tuition. Such formal programmes cost more than tutors, sometimes over US$ 500 per month, but realise you are in a structured programme delivered by a qualified instructor.

Continuing Education

Several Shanghai Universities offer certificate level Chinese language/culture programmes for foreigners. Fudan, Jiaotong and Huadong Shifan offer some of the best-known programmes. These programmes may be run in conjunction with standard study abroad programmes.

For those seeking higher degrees, several EMBA (Executive Masters in Business Administration) programmes in

Shanghai have recently appeared at the top of 'Best EMBA' lists. American programmes by Rutgers and Washington University's Olin School of Business (partnering with Fudan) both have offices in Shanghai with expat staff ready to answer questions or provide you with an application. The European CEIBS (China Europe International Business School) has a stand-alone school in Shanghai. And many global universities will arrange faculty mentors to guide independent research in Shanghai that can be applied toward a Master's or PhD.

Mistaken Identity

One Korean expat mom, with kids in school all day, has put herself in school too, attaining Mandarin fluency in just one year. She has enjoyed the camaraderie with young exchange students, not to mention the freedom and self-confidence when negotiating Shanghai. Although unsure how long her family will stay, she wanted to feel she was settling in, and be able to converse with the Chinese who mistake her for a Chinese!

The Fine Arts

For the creatively inclined, American potter Jeremy Clayton has opened the Hands In Clay Studio, situated in artsy Taikang Lu, offering a series of classes in sculpture and using one of five potter's wheels. Many expat women also seek out experts in Chinese painting and calligraphy, who are more than happy to serve as private tutors. From time to time, women form their own study groups or book clubs, focusing on anything from popular fiction to Chinese History reviews. See *Chapter 7: Enjoying Life* on pages 163–164 for more suggestions, and check with expat women's clubs for courses already in progress.

Although relocating to Shanghai can seem daunting to even the most seasoned expat families, with a little advance planning and a sense of adventure, Shanghai nearly always proves to be an exciting post, memorable for all members of the family; sadly departed and fondly remembered when the time comes to move on.

SHOPPING TILL YOU DROP

When Susan Schulman first relocated to Shanghai in the mid-1980s with her parents, her mom brought home a book called *Shanghai, Paris of the Orient*, dating from the Jazz-era heyday, which compared Nanjing Lu to New York's Fifth Avenue and the fashion districts of Paris, and the Number One Department store to London's Harrods. Susan and her sister were thrilled—until landing at dilapidated Hongqiao airport on a rainy, dismal Friday to find that streetlights went off at 8:00 pm to save power and grey Mao suits were haute couture.

Fast forward 15 years though, and Nanjing Lu DOES feel like Fifth Avenue again. Salvatore Ferragamo, Cartier, Hermes and other fashion icons have opened shop, with more top global logos on display daily. Chinese women who once seemed ready for *Glamour's* 'Fashion Don't' page are today dressed top-to-toe in brands: the latest Manolo Blahnik stiletto boots, Ralph Lauren jodhpurs tucked in, Prada jacket, Burberry cashmere scarf (with matching barrette) and Louis Vuitton mobile phone cover peeking from Chanel's latest tote.

In a way it's a shame: Chinese women seem to have lost some of their fearless fashion experimentation from years past, becoming slaves to the runways. But nobody can accuse them of being behind the trends.

HONG KONG PRICEY OR XIANG YANG DICEY: SPOTTING FAKES

Those logo-laden ladies are, however, sometimes pirates. Did that fashion-plate you passed spend thousands for her outfits in the Hong Kong-developed Plaza 66 Mall, where goods are indubitably genuine? Or was it all bargain-basement, just a few blocks over at Xiang Yang Market, where stall after stall hawks some of the best copies you ever saw? Perhaps not even her hairdresser knows for sure.

Many expat bargain-hunters end up shopping at Xiang Yang, for those times it just doesn't seem worth paying full price for Prada. If you're careful, you can indeed buy some copies so good that company reps may have trouble sorting them out. Indeed, rumour has it some Xiang Yang goods 'fall off the truck' from the same factories that make the real stuff.

Shopping at Xiang Yang is not for the faint of heart. Shifty-looking characters lead you from the market, up rickety stairs in dank and smelly houses, to bright rooms of expats and Chinese digging through boxes marked 'Montblanc' or 'Armani', where the latest fashions can be yours for prices lower than you imagine.

Many expats (and Shanghainese) go in circles about Xiang Yang. One day you think: "I want a matching 'Chanel' for every outfit, and why not? Why bother buying the real thing, when everyone will assume it's fake anyway!" Then a day goes by, you hear your spouse or other businesspeople complain about battling counterfeits, and you think: "That's it, from now on I will only buy from proper shops." Legality certainly and morality probably favours the latter stance. Your bank account will favour the former. Where you personally come down has to be a decision you make on your own.

Getting the Real Thing

It is perfectly feasible to buy everyday clothes in Shanghai for fairly reasonable prices, in stores where price tags don't require second mortgages, and which minimise pushy crowds and haggling. There are no legitimate department stores with the breadth of Western brands that a Nordstrom's, say, would carry in the United States. But the Japanese emporium Isetan carries the all-important nylons, underwear and some recognisable brands such as Ralph Lauren, Nine West and Calvin Klein.

Still, be prepared to pay premium prices relative to costs at home. Sizing is also an issue; sizes above 8–10 may be unavailable at legitimate stores, and many colours and styles come only in 2–4. Shopkeepers have been known to laugh as size 8 feet are removed from shoes. Remind yourself that fat is a sign of wealth in China, and thick skin is important.

CUSTOM TAILORING

Should off-the-rack fashions fail, try Maoming Lu just past Huaihai Lu, where shops make beautiful fashions with a Chinese flair to fit any size or shape. A personal favourite is Joy Luck Club, at 72 Maoming Lu. It is quite en vogue among savvy Shanghainese and expats to don Mao jackets

Stalls at the Xiang Yang cloth market.

with fur trim or sequined Chinese characters, traditional *qipao* of patchwork brocade with dirty denim, and so on. Not for penny pinchers, an outfit can cost hundreds of US dollars—well worth it to many. These are one of a kind and fun to wear.

Tailor-made Princess

For far less, most expats have tailors who make house calls, or are set up at fabric markets. Susan Shulman's daughter wore a gorgeous silk/velvet princess dress with matching bolero jacket, hat and purse to a London wedding. When complimented on her attire by a fellow guest, Stephanie replied, "Thank you, my tailor made it!" The whole outfit (fabric and tailoring), ran to about US$ 30.

One good place for tailors is the Fabric Market at Dongjiadu Lu (just off the Bund). Go with some idea of what you want; otherwise the rows of silks, brocades, taffetas, wools, cashmeres, linens and all blends between can boggle the mind—especially since almost every time you touch cloth, shopkeepers runs over with lighters to set bolts alight! This is meant to show fabric is genuine (since it burns instead of melting like plastic-fibre fakes). But it takes many trips to get used to vendors setting cloth aflame.

Even when cloth burns, buyers should beware. Not all genuine cashmeres or silks are equally well-woven. Pushy vendors may railroad you, slashing with fast scissors, then insisting you've bought cut pieces. Wave scissors firmly off until you've decided to buy AND finished bargaining on the price!

Then find a tailor. The Fabric Market has many, but what works for one doesn't work for all. Until you find someone who sews in ways that flatter you, buy cheap fabric you can toss if the outcome is not what you hoped. Most tailors do best copying existing garments, but some are amazing at working from photos, or even drawing verbalised gowns on scraps of paper, then turning them into creations fit for the runway!

There are also more established emporia like Silk King, whose several in-town locations offer fine selections of silk, cashmeres, wools and blends. Tailors at Silk King sew quickly, and have designed for the likes of Hillary and Chelsea Clinton. Although more costly, with no room for bargaining, Silk King—a state-owned retailer—guarantees fabrics and workmanship.

OSH KOSH... MY GOSH! SUITING YOUR LITTLE EMPEROR IN SHANGHAI

The infamous Xiang Yang market pirates well-known grade-school garment brands. Some mothers love bargain-hunting, daily scavenging trips, while others find it tedious to create wardrobes on the streets, where the latest Spiderman or Barbie logos are available, but quality control—especially for shoes—is problematic.

Several local department stores—like the Isetan in Meilongzhen Mall on Nanjing Lu; or the Hongqiao Friendship Store—have whole floors of kid's clothing and shoes. Kid World Mall (Nanjing Lu/Maoming Lu) features five stories of clothes, shoes, diapers and toys, with a Fun Dazzle indoor playground on the top floor! Local brands are priced below legitimate imports, but sales always roll around, especially at Chinese New Year. So if you are desperate for the latest Dolce and Gabanna smock for your four-year-old, visit Plaza 66's adorable new children's emporium in January!

TOYS

Danish block maker Lego has won the first successful piracy lawsuit in China against a local toymaker, so yes, even toys can be faked! Do be careful when buying local toys, though, as some Chinese toymakers ignore global safety standards. Many expats stock up for holidays and birthdays while on home leave, especially with computer software; pirated children's DVDs and Game Boy equipment are rife, but so are viruses.

For toddlers, try IKEA, which stocks kitchen sets, car and train tracks, basic musical instruments, art supplies and so on. Not surprisingly, most toy stores (and the French megamart Carrefour), stock many bicycles, tricycles and scooters at

Shoppers thronging the shopping district of Nanjing Lu.

prices so low you have to resist spoiling kids with one of each! Do buy padding and helmets at home, though, unless you are lucky and make it to Carrefour when they are in stock.

A BOOK IS LIKE A GARDEN CARRIED IN THE POCKET (CHINESE PROVERB)

The Foreign Languages Bookstore on Fuzhou Lu (a haven for art supplies to make Van Gogh jealous!) offers many coffee-table books on Shanghai/China, English-Chinese dictionaries and some great gift items. Upstairs is an entire floor of non-Chinese books, mostly English-language inexpensive classics, along with a few bestsellers, children's titles and business books. Many expats re-read titles unappreciated in high school, while others import books. When creating your library from overseas, it is best to hand-carry books in luggage; Amazon.com has successfully sent books to China, but many disappointed expats have had books confiscated at Customs and not returned to sender.

ANTIQUES AND 'ANTIQUES'— DONGTAI LU, HU & HU, ETC.

Many expats fall in love with traditional Chinese furniture and fittings. Stores and warehouses (often with English-speaking staff) have mushroomed throughout Shanghai selling antiques (rare) and reproductions (common) that range from shoddy to museum quality. Everyone has favourites. The larger ones advertise in expat magazines and take booths at seasonal shopping bazaars; smaller ones rely on word of mouth.

You can find great deals, if you approach these stores with common sense. Except in a few high-end emporia, assume the 'antiques' are reproductions; many factories specialise in 'rapid aging' with sandpaper and chemicals. Some are restored pieces 50–100 years old; many more are totally new, perhaps created from older wood. So ignore salesperson chatter on 'Ming-dynasty, ready for the auction block at Christie's'. If it WERE real and cheap, Christie's agents would probably already have bought it.

> **Telling It Like It Is**
>
> A good place to start is Hu & Hu Antiques in Hongqiao, which clearly distinguishes between beautifully restored originals and reproductions. A trip out to Hu & Hu for a coffee with the owner, Marybelle Hu, is a good place to begin learning about real Chinese antiques, and whether or not your budget can afford them.

Don't pay real-antique prices unless you're at a place like Hu & Hu that guarantees goods, or you are an expert able to discern real from fakes. Most expats simply go to reproduction shops, assume everything is new, decide what they like and what they're willing to pay, and bargain on that basis.

The nice thing about reproductions, of course, is that they can be adapted; most shops will custom-build in colours and dimensions of your choice—and can mix and match ('this moulding and that bronze hasp, with a lock like the one on the chest over there'). The not-so-nice thing is that many pieces have never been inside climate-controlled homes, and often crack: try to get recommendations on good workmanship.

At least two markets—an indoor mall on Fuyou Lu, and a pedestrian mall on Dongtai Lu—specialise in traditional knick-knacks, a mix of reproductions and fun older flea-market items. Writer SJ Perelman visited similar markets in the 1930s and was 'charmed at every turn by the indescribable wealth of imagination the Chinese lavish on their art… [He] bought three ivory back-scratchers you could not duplicate in San Francisco for less than a quarter.' Nothing much has changed!

Of course if, when decking your halls, you would rather pass on turning your home into a replica of the Forbidden City, Shanghai is home to IKEA, Bo Concepts, Thomasville and others stocking a range of Western home furnishings to suit a range of budgets.

STOCKING THE FRIDGE
Many expats are thrilled to have *Ayi* shop at local markets and make *ma po tofu* with garlic string beans every evening;

others require a daily dose of Kraft to keep them going. For the latter, City Shopping Groceries, with several branches of varying sizes carrying a huge range of 'foods from home', is probably the most popular. Watch carefully, though; key goods can still get depleted quickly after new shipments, with no replacements for months. Some expats react by hoarding.

Sticking to a home-country menu in China can be expensive as well as challenging. Imported food carries heavy tariffs: a medium box of cereal might easily cost the equivalent of US$ 8. Most expats find life is easier when they adapt to menus that are at least somewhat based on available foodstuffs.

Fortunately, availability is improving. Carrefour and German warehouse store Metro now have several branches each, carrying imported and local foods (as well as some home furnishings, etc.); so Costco addicts, fear not, you can buy bulk in Shanghai! Many hotels have delis stocking everything from meats and cheese to cakes and chocolates. The Sheraton Grande in Hongqiao is a favourite, while the nearby Australian-owned Glenmore Deli supplies lovely frozen foods, meats and fish, some fresh meats (including many sausages), wines, spices and gourmet magazines.

Gourmet Stores

As Shanghai becomes more cosmopolitan, locals and expats alike anticipate each new gourmet store opening. Cheese and Fizz in fashionable Xintiandi is a great addition, stocking amazing French cheeses along with bubbly accoutrements. The proprietor loves to help customers favourably pair his offerings; his café lets you try simple lunch and dinner specials. You can also secure moderate to excellent wines at quite competitive prices through the Montrose Food and Wine Company, which also organises a wine club complete with regular tastings and gourmet dinners.

So most adults—and kids—can live happily on foods available in Shanghai today, though for cost reasons you may want to ship any non-perishable staples you feel you can't live without on a regular basis. Baby products are also an issue. (*See the section* 'For Kids and Families' *in this chapter on pages 73–74*).

SUNDRIES AND NECESSARIES

Although local markets carry most personal hygiene products thanks to the likes of Johnson & Johnson and Unilever, if you have a favourite, ship it in. You may not find an exact match made in China-based joint ventures, and even if imported versions are available, high duties will make it pricier than at home. In addition, name-brand deodorants and feminine hygiene products seem to run out frequently, and you certainly don't want to be caught out in those departments!

In time, you may well find local or joint-venture products that become your new favourites. Most expats, though, continue to prefer bringing certain products from home, such as deodorant and hair colouring (blonde and other colours are hard to find in the world of the black bob!). Note that the carry-from-home rule is especially important for medications. (*See the section* 'Health care in Shanghai' *later in this chapter [pages 101–110] for details.*)

Finally, although many products in Western countries carry the 'Made in China' tag, don't assume you'll find it here. Most items made for export in China are truly exported. So do stock up on your favourite brands to load the luggage back to Shanghai, or be adventurous and pick a new preferred product available locally.

MONEY, BANKING AND CREDIT CARDS

China's local currency is Renminbi (literally 'the People's Money') or Rmb for short. The basic unit is the yuan, also called the kuai. One yuan = 100 fen = 10 jiao (the jiao is also called 'mao'). Coins come in 1, 2, and 5 fen, and 1 mao. Notes come in 2 mao, 5 mao, and in 1, 2, 5, 10, 20, 50 and 100 yuan denominations.

In terms of handling money, Shanghai is increasingly a global city, despite having a traditionally cash-based economy and a 'soft' currency (the Rmb can be traded for other currencies only under highly restricted circumstances). More and more shops, hotels and large restaurants now accept major global credit cards like Visa, Master Card, Diner's Club and American Express.

Credit card acceptance is hardly universal, however: you pretty much CAN leave home without them in Shanghai. Cheque writing is also tedious due to short expiry dates on Chinese checking accounts and other restrictions (not to mention the almost non-existent interest on savings or checking accounts in China), so cheques are generally used only in a business context, and only when necessary. Cash remains king.

Some expats open Rmb or foreign currency accounts at local Chinese banks, or at the handful of global banks now approved for individual foreign currency accounts. This can be handy if you will take a substantial portion of your salary in China (see below). But tedious procedures and low interest rates discourage many. Perhaps a majority of expats keep their funds largely overseas, and get cash as needed from ATMs—which spit out Rmb from local or foreign institutions. Most common is some combination, with expats getting salary wired to accounts overseas for paying credit card bills and similar, and taking hardship allowances and/or expense reimbursements in cash in Shanghai to use for day-to-day expenses.

In years past, such split-payment arrangements were sometimes used to skirt income taxes, claiming low income in China, while also claiming foreign-earned-income exclusions at home. Stronger enforcement, better record sharing, and computerisation have helped China's Tax Bureau (in full cooperation with the US Internal Revenue Service and its counterparts elsewhere) crack down on such practices nowadays. Tax evaders are getting caught, and heavily fined, and foreigners are top targets.

One final word: with the Rmb still a soft currency, a market remains for illegal street-trading of cash. But though street exchange rates are better than bank offerings, the margins are not what they were when the Rmb was fully banned from trading, and most expats find street trading no longer worth the risk. It is, after all, illegal, and unlikely worth losing your lucrative expat post and getting expelled over if some official decides to make an example of you. Then too, money-changers are known to 'launder' fake and/or stolen currency, and have found clever ways to short-change even experienced expats. And finally, they are a marginal part of society you may just not want to deal with. One American man stumbled into a deadly knife fight at the money-changer he had been frequenting for years! As they say: Buyer Beware.

But do enjoy Shanghai shopping. Every street offers something for purchase—from mom-and-pop shop laundry detergent, to a Ming Dynasty armoire in a dusty warehouse, to Waterford crystal in a fancy department store and everything in between! Most expats leave Shanghai with enough wares to open their own emporium at their next post.

HEALTH CARE IN SHANGHAI

Many new expats worry about health care options in Shanghai, probably more than they need to. The good news is that the Chinese health care system has improved dramatically in the past decade, and keeps getting better at lightning speed. Foreigners in Shanghai and Beijing especially have access to the best care in China: the most modern equipment and highly skilled doctors. Regulatory changes have opened the field for private medical and dental facilities in Shanghai (both local and foreign joint ventures) and local hospitals have imported more medical equipment.

Of course, new equipment and pleasant interiors aside, such 'invisible' factors as sanitation and sterilisation procedures and the training received by physicians remain critically important. There is wide variation in quality, so expats should visit several facilities, and choose their primary Shanghai health care provider BEFORE they get sick.

A Note About SARS

It's important to keep SARS in perspective and rely on official sources for information about the current level of risk. This disease, while more serious for elderly people and those with compromised immune systems, is far less serious for the average person than many other communicable diseases that are far more prevalent in China. Even at the height of the SARS crises, the World Health Organization (WHO) reassured people that 'the man in the street's chances in Hong Kong of getting this disease are very low'. The best preventive measures are awareness of the symptoms and current level of risk, avoiding sick people and washing your hands frequently. The wisest thing to do is keep updated by consulting the WHO website at:

http://www.who.int/en

or the Centres for Disease Control and Prevention (CDC) website at:

http://www.cdc.gov.

SHANGHAI'S HEALTH CARE SYSTEM: OPTIONS FOR FOREIGNERS

From an expatriate point of view, Shanghai's health care system can be divided into three broad categories:

- foreign-managed joint-venture facilities that have expatriate physicians
- foreigners' or VIP units in local hospitals (which usually offer English-speaking physicians)
- standard local health care system

Foreign-managed Joint-venture Facilities with Expatriate Physicians

These facilities adhere to global standards, offering medical care at the standards expats would expect in their home countries. Fees for foreign-managed medical facilities in Shanghai are similar to those in Beijing and other large Asian cities: a typical doctor's consultation will cost about US$ 50–100. These health care providers can often bill top global private health insurance companies directly: check with your health insurer for details. Some foreign-managed health care providers also offer discounts as part of a package of services to those who join as members of the facility.

Currently, there is only one Western-managed medical facility with expatriate physicians in Shanghai: World Link Medical and Dental Centres, which has a number of facilities (visit their website at http://www.worldlink-shanghai.com). Another facility, Shanghai United Family Hospital offers a range of services similar to what they offer in Beijing. International SOS has a call centre in Shanghai, staffed 24-hours a day with expatriate physicians who are trained in remote medicine; they offer members telephone consultation services and medical evacuation services in case of an emergency. There are also several facilities aimed at overseas Chinese and Japanese expatriates; but for most Western expats they have the disadvantage of not offering English-speaking doctors.

Local Hospitals with Foreigners'/VIP Units

Several local hospitals have foreigners' or VIP units that typically offer higher standards than average Chinese hospitals, and are usually staffed with English-speaking local physicians. Prices in these facilities for a standard medical consultation range from US$ 20–35. The most well-known of these are: Guangci, which also has a French-speaking physician; Huashan Hospital; International Peace Maternity Child Health Hospital, which has a partnership with Johns Hopkins University in the US for consultation and training; and the Shanghai Children's Medical Centre, a teaching hospital in co-operation with the international group Project HOPE.

There are other options as well; but the less famous VIP units may vary widely on how well they meet foreigners' expectations for sanitation and health care standards.

Payment policies vary too: keep in mind that if admission to a Chinese hospital is required, patients often have to pay an advance deposit of at least Rmb 10,000. Again, you should visit in advance, and choose the facility you plan to use BEFORE you get sick.

Beyond safety issues and payment differences, expats may run into cultural issues with Chinese-run health care providers. Chinese people traditionally are not active participants in health care, preferring to 'leave it to the experts', so many Chinese doctors are uncomfortable with talkative, questioning patients. You may need to be more proactive than you are used to in asking questions about diagnosis and treatment when seeing a Chinese physician, and you may need to finesse questions somewhat to get the answers you want. In addition, Chinese hospitals are often reluctant to release patient medical records, which foreign patients often want to give to physicians back home.

Finally, the style of medicine practised is also often different from what foreigners are used to, based on local cultural preference for fairly aggressive treatment. Chinese physicians may prescribe an IV drip for a complaint as mild as an elevated temperature, for example, and antibiotics are often given for colds. Local hospitals are also often eager to use their pricey new equipment, performing, for example, CAT-scans on patients where a foreign physician would not. Yet, in one area at least, Chinese physicians tend to treat less aggressively than foreigners are used to, perhaps following Nietzsche's maxim, 'That which does not kill us makes us stronger'. Chinese doctors tend to prescribe painkillers far more sparingly than many foreigners are used to.

Local Health Care System

Finally, there is the standard local health care system, where a visit to the doctor in a district hospital (the lowest level) will set you back about US$ 0.97. In the best hospitals, the cost of a general consultation skyrockets to US$ 1.33. There have been instances where foreigners have been refused treatment at purely local hospitals, referred instead to the hospital's foreigners' unit. But some foreigners do use local hospitals as their primary health care providers, finding the standard perfectly adequate for day-to-day care, and the low cost irresistible.

Local hospital personnel rarely speak English, so foreigners who use them must either speak fluent Mandarin or bring a friend to translate. In addition to the cultural differences noted above, local hospitals are also known for long lines, lack of freedom to choose physicians (patients often must see the first available doctor, even for follow-up visits), and pre-payment for all services (before the consultation, again before the X-ray, again before the lab test and again before the pharmacy). Finally, the US Consulate cautions that 'there is more than anecdotal evidence that that foreign residents regularly encounter medical care quality problems in China. Some are true medical care quality problems. Others are simply the consequence of being far from friends and relatives in a land where one doesn't speak the local language.' The good news is that the SARS scare probably increased the level of attention local hospitals pay to hygiene.

HEALTH INSURANCE

Most standard insurance policies do not cover medical care received abroad, but there are numerous insurance policies aimed at expatriates, which typically cover treatment abroad, plus a limited amount in your home country. Aetna Global Benefits and BUPA International are among the most common global providers; there are dozens of choices. Foreign-managed facilities usually have direct billing with several major insurers, which means you will not have to pay out of pocket for covered expenses, so many expatriates consider their facility's direct billing arrangements when choosing an insurer.

One critical component of health insurance for expatriates is medical evacuation coverage; International SOS is the best-known provider. In the event of a major medical emergency, this type of coverage will help arrange for immediate transport to your home country or to the nearest hospital with high international standards (usually in Hong Kong or Singapore), depending on the situation. Without this type of insurance, medical evacuation can cost anywhere from US$ 3,000–70,000, and consulates are typically not able to help with this cost for uninsured people.

OTHER HEALTH CONCERNS

Many foreigners take for granted that restaurants will serve meals prepared in sanitary conditions, that a simple

Evaluating Your Options

Consulates, relocation firms and chambers of commerce are all good resources for finding good health care providers, as are friends and colleagues. English-language magazines and expat-oriented websites have up-to-date listings of medical and dental facilities. Most providers willingly share information on their equipment and services. You should also probe into practice standards, addressing such issues as:

- How do the facilities look? Does an initial inspection reflect well on their apparent care for cleanliness and sanitation? Consider not just public areas and consultation rooms, but the bathrooms, laboratory and other areas.
- What are their standards for sanitation and sterilisation (for example, do they always use a new, sterile needle for each patient)?
- What is the style of medicine practised? Medical theory about the causes and proper treatment of diseases varies from country to country; you should be sure that you are comfortable with the style practised by the facility you choose.
- What is the level of education and experience of the physicians? Where have they practised and what languages are spoken? If the facility has both expatriate and local physicians, which physicians practise which specialties?

wash of fruits is sufficient, and that drinking water is safe. Unfortunately, that's not necessarily true in China, and expats need to pay close attention to health issues while they're here. Good personal hygiene (particularly proper hand washing) food and water hygiene ('Peel it, cook it, boil it, or forget it'), attention to where you eat out, safe sex (crucial, given the increasing prevalence of Hepatitis and China's burgeoning

- What style of management is used? Are you able to schedule a fixed time for your appointments? Is it possible to specify which doctor you would like to see?
- What are typical charges? What insurance is accepted, and can they bill the insurance firm directly? Will they accept credit cards? Are deposits required? Do they have membership plans that offer discounts or other benefits?
- What medications are available? Does the facility offer a proprietary dispensary stocked with Western, imported, and joint-venture medications? Keep in mind that there is some risk of counterfeit medications in Shanghai, which may be inactive or even harmful, and that risk may be higher in commercial pharmacies than in carefully monitored proprietary dispensaries.
- After selecting a health care provider, take the time to make a written record in English and Chinese of your preferred medical facility (including clinic name, address and phone number), a brief medical history of each family member (including any allergies, medical conditions and medications taken regularly), insurance provider and evacuation company, and people to contact in case of an emergency. A copy of this document should be readily available at home, in the office and at your children's school.

AIDS crisis), and appropriate vaccinations and immunisations are vital for staying healthy.

Keep in mind that most published information on vaccinations is focused on tourists; recommendations may be a bit different for people intending to live in China. A good source of to-the-minute information on vaccinations is the Centres for Disease Control (http://www.cdc.org) in the United States. Many cities in the US also have travel medicine centres with physicians knowledgeable about vaccination requirements, who can administer the first series of vaccinations. In general, Hepatitis A vaccinations are recommended for adults and children older than two years. Japanese Encephalitis vaccinations are usually only recommended for people who will be living in rural areas. Other recommended vaccinations may include typhoid, tetanus, polio, Hepatitis A and B, diphtheria, rabies and BCG (for protection against tuberculosis). Speak with your doctor, or the CDC.

TIPS FOR A HEALTHY STAY

Expatriates often tend to wait longer to see a doctor than they would in their home country, or to underestimate the seriousness of illnesses, given their busy schedules. Beware of this tendency, as earlier treatment generally leads to better outcomes. The US Consulate also recommends that all Americans take a first aid course including CPR; it's a simple process that could prove invaluable (note that Chinese ambulance staff are typically not trained in CPR).

Expatriates should prepare a modified first aid kit before leaving their home country. In addition to standard first aid items, the kit should contain a supply of preferred cold and flu medications and pain relievers, since masses of people with runny noses make colds all too common. All medications should be kept in their original containers, for Customs.

Remember, many brands are not available in China, and if purchased from foreign-managed facilities, will likely be pricier than at home. And while local Chinese pharmacies are amazingly well equipped with anything from Zythromax and birth control pills to Prozac and Viagra, all cheap and with no prescription necessary, these pharmacies carry the risk of

The Tong-ban-chun-tang pharmacy is well-known in Shanghai.

fakes that can range from useless to harmful. If you regularly take prescription medications, you might call or email in advance to the clinic or hospital you plan on using to ask about your preferred brand and dosage/format. Each facility is likely to stock only a few options of specific medications (e.g. asthma medications, birth control pills, etc.). Most physicians will write a six-month or one-year prescription for medications for people living overseas.

SUBWAYS TO BIKE LANES: SHANGHAI'S TRANSPORTATION

The sidewalk crowds of the 1980s have thinned to a degree since the advent of subways, and since more Shanghainese can afford indoor entertainment. Still, the crowding of Shanghai's sidewalks (and streets, subways and buses) is one of those sights, like the Great Wall, that really must be seen to be believed. While an efficient and growing subway system, rapidly rolled-out ring roads and high costs of private cars have kept Shanghai moving (to date) better than Bangkok or Jakarta, more and more Shanghainese can now afford cars, and traffic times of up to two hours to cross the city are increasingly common.

For the busy businessperson, rushing from office to meeting, lecture to networking dinner to evening show, transportation needs to be considered seriously. There are reasons why foreign heads of states, top Chinese leaders, and global CEOs, when they swirl through town packing in 16 meetings each day, hire police escorts.

But police escorts cost thousands, and aren't for everyday use for even the busiest resident. Nor are private helicopters; all private aircraft is banned in Chinese airspace, except jet landings/take-offs to/from foreign destinations, at select Chinese airports, following gruelling approval processes. Most Shanghai businesspeople use a combination of taxis, subways, company cars and feet (and, for the intrepid, bicycles), depending on destination, distance and time of day. Indeed, one key support that good local assistants give arriving executives is the gauging of how much time to leave between meetings in given parts of town at given times of the day—and when it's better to leave the car behind and take the subway.

TAXIS

Shanghai taxis are plentiful, mostly professionally driven, and cheap. Rush hour driving is aggressive; new arrivals often find this eye-popping and finish rides holding their breath. But it follows understood rules, and accidents are rarer than you'd think. Once in a while you'll find a cab piloted by an Anhui rustic whose previous driving seems to have been behind a tractor wheel, dreaming of the Grand Prix. But the government has tightened licensing requirements and such strange encounters are rare.

Most times, you can count on a reasonably clean, fairly well-driven cab, with a cabbie who knows the city and will take you anywhere in central Puxi, or central Pudong, for under Rmb 20 (somewhat more when crossing between the two). So for most businesspeople, most times, taxis are the transport tool of choice. Taxis can be found at hotels, department stores, office complexes and the like, or hailed on the street: the Chinese taxi hail is a cross between a high-five and what looks to Westerners like a farewell wave. Cabbies rarely speak English, but will often know key phrases

('Shanghai Centre'; 'the Bund'). Also, many expats use an excellent set of plasticised bilingual flashcards, available from AmCham, naming many popular destinations.

LONG-TERM CAR HIRE/CAR PURCHASE

Those who prefer the greater predictability and convenience of having the same car regularly available can arrange for long-term hire of a car and driver, either by their company or as an individual, either directly with a cabbie or through a car-hire firm. Long-term hires are typically far less expensive than outright car purchase, and as discussed below, are a very common choice for Shanghai businesspeople.

One note, however: hire arrangements are rarely available for high-end cars. Those who insist on riding in a Mercedes or BMW may have to purchase a car and hire a full-time driver. There are circles where you will hear this is the only way to go; indeed in some luxury trades, the 'lost face' of riding anything less than a Merc or Beemer might arguably affect business. But China's 250 per cent-plus tariffs on luxury cars, luxury usage taxes and maintenance costs, and the salaries/ benefits needed to keep skilled drivers full-time, mean a luxury car and full-time driver can cost upwards of US$ 100,000 a year, prorated over the five- to six-year useful life the car will have before it 'needs upgrading for face reasons'. Clearly, full-time use of a high-end car and driver exclusive to a particular executive is a luxury that goes along with US$ 15,000 a month garden villas: possible only for those with lavish expense accounts, and sensible only for those in trades where style is at least as important as substance.

More typical in most efficiently-managed businesses is one or more company cars, of the joint-venture Buick rather than the imported Beemer variety, leased or purchased for use by the company as a whole. Several managers might pool such a car for use when attending official meetings, leaving car and driver available between times for office errands, from picking up Public Security papers, to purchasing office supplies.

Most business people seeking exclusive use of car and driver for personal needs opt for long-term hire of a taxi. In such arrangements, car and driver are available for a given base of hours at a flat fee, with additional hours at a per-hour rate, and the driver is free to seek other fares between times. Cars available for hire range from thrifty Santanas, manufactured by Volkswagen's Shanghai joint venture, to mid-range Buicks from General Motor's joint venture, to occasional splashier cars. Prices vary based on car type, driver experience, direct vs. agency hire, and other details. Long-term hire of a Santana for, say, 15 hours a week might run Rmb 3,500–4,500 a month. Forty hours a week of a Buick might run Rmb 8,000–10,000 per month or more. Extra hours are typically around Rmb 20 per hour. Many businesspeople hire Santanas or similar for 10–15 hours per week to take working spouse to and from work, kids to and from school, and 'trailing spouse' to and from classes or volunteering, with some evening/weekend availability.

Car hire agencies can help locate good drivers, though that can be expensive and not always reliable. Often the best way is word of mouth. Find someone happy with their driver and ask for a recommendation; most good drivers know other good drivers.

Drivers rarely speak English (those that do come at a premium!). But the same flashcards that work with taxi drivers work with hire cars too. And over time, generally the driver will learn in English and/or the expat will learn in Chinese enough key phrases ('home', 'office', 'school', 'gym') to get by.

SUBWAY AND BUSES

Shanghai has an excellent subway system—the Metro—engineered by ADTranz, with the build-out starting in the late 1990s and slated to continue through 2008. Trains can be crowded at rush hour, but in Shanghai, as in many mega-cities, subways are the fastest way to travel, so almost everyone uses them sometimes. The cars are clean, air-conditioned and fast, with fares just a few yuan a ride.

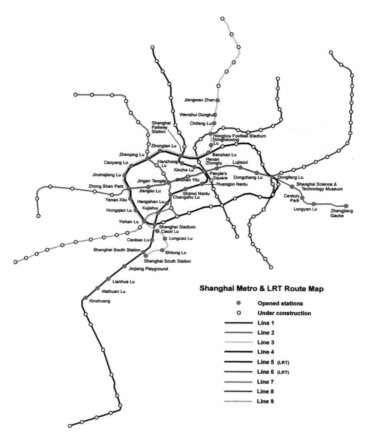

The Metro is the most efficient way of getting around Shanghai.

At the moment, the sy-stem is still limited. As the map above shows, more lines are 'under construction' than running; only three lines work now. Those cover some key districts, but there are still large areas where subways are useless (though that will change as the system expands). Still, if your regular commute happens to be near a current subway line, you may well find it's the fastest, cleanest, and most economical way to get around.

Shanghai's subway is something of a favourite among train buffs. For photos, fun facts and fan-fare, see:

- http://www.azagel.com/crail.html
- http://railwaysofchina.com/

The crowd at a subway station.

- http://www.metropla.net/as/shan/shanghai.htm
- http://www. subwayfuture.nease.net/ (a site set up by student Carl Yiu, who created the map for this book).

As planned extensions are phased in, subway convenience will only increase.

Buses are also increasingly clean and convenient, but are as crowded as the subway or more, without the speed advantage. A key transport choice for workers and students, buses are rarely used by business managers, expat or Chinese. For those who wish, a good English bus route map is available from the Xin Hua Foreign Languages Bookstore.

BICYCLES

A river delta, Shanghai is almost flat, and eminently bikeable. Most major thoroughfares have dedicated bike lanes. At rush hour, these can be crowded enough to require adroit balance and quick braking reflexes: the principle is that each rider watches only ahead and those behind take their chances with sudden swerves. With a little practice, though, Shanghai's bike lanes are easy to get used to, and can offer one of the best ways to see the city; after all, much it was built in the Jazz Era, when bicycles and rickshaws far outnumbered cars. Even today, the winding lanes of the French

Quarter, for instance, are easiest seen—or traversed—on bike or foot.

Inexpensive Chinese-made bikes are available in most department stores, and in bicycle speciality shops. A few speciality shops also sell Diamondback off-road bikes, made in the Guangzhou joint venture of the premium bike-maker, and sold for far less than in the West. Less practical for daily transport than the heavy Chinese Flying Pigeons and Forevers, the Diamondbacks are excellent for weekend mountain-biking in Hangzhou (*see the section* 'Past City Limits' *in Chapter 7: Enjoying Life, pages 213–220*), and make good buys for shipping home.

Most bikes in Shanghai come with small clip locks. These are adequate for inexpensive black clunkers; for anything better you should buy a good lock, as bike theft is endemic. In this city of bikers, bike parking can also be an issue. Most office towers, department stores and other destinations have bike lots with attendants, where you are required to park so as not to clog the sidewalk. Some office and apartment complexes require a bike parking permit, usually available from the attendant.

GETTING A SHANGHAI DRIVER'S LICENCE AND CAR

A small percent of Shanghai expats value wheeled freedom enough to brave the traffic jams, erratic driving and bureaucratic jungles associated with getting a PRC (People's Republic of China) driver's licence. China does not accept any international driver's licences; a PRC licence is required. Given how drawn-out the process of getting one is, this is NOT recommended for anyone staying less than a year. And those considering getting a licence should spend enough time in Shanghai first to get a sense of the city and to understand the idiosyncrasies of local drivers. Also, be aware that car rental agencies in China rarely rent to private individuals, so if you want to drive yourself, you must buy a local car.

If you're determined to buy a car and drive yourself, the basic process is:

- Register with the Public Security Bureau (PSB)
- Turn in your home country driver's licence
- Take a required local driver's education course administered by the PSB (this is regardless of how many years you have been driving internationally—although rumour has it that some 'instructors' will stamp forms verifying that you have 'completed' the course, without actually making you take it, for a 'modest fee')
- Take written test (in Chinese); wait for results
- Take practical exam; wait for results
- Pay registration fees, and get Chinese licencse

New Ministry of Public Security regulations are expected to streamline this process, but it will still likely take some time.

One final note: driving yourself in Shanghai should be considered mainly a leisure activity. It is unlikely to help you get from place to place during the workweek, for one simple reason: since almost everyone who rides cars in Shanghai hires them with drivers who wait with the cars, parking is rare in the central city. A few office towers have parking for commuters, but supply exceeds demand as fast as garages are built.

FEET

Last but not least, remember that walking is often a good option in this traffic-clogged town. The tours in the section 'Beyond The Bund' (in Chapter 7: Enjoying Life, on pages 176–209) should get you going—and a good map will keep you on track (there are several available in English from Xinhua Foreign Language Bookstore). Sometimes, walking will get you there as fast as or faster than a car.

LOGISTICS, FORMALITIES AND SAFETY

As with any relocation, an expatriate assignment to China can catch the unprepared in last minute issues and bureaucratic difficulties that make relocation feel like dislocation. Forewarned is forearmed. Take a little time to get educated on the nitty-gritty of China logistics beforehand and your transitions to and from Shanghai will be far smoother.

VISA MATTERS

A Lucky Break

Chinese visa formalities are not to be taken lightly. An expat was once stopped at exit when trying to catch the first morning flight to Hong Kong for an important business meeting. His China visa had expired three months earlier, and he was given to understand in no uncertain terms that he wouldn't be flying anywhere any time soon! He was fined Rmb 5,000 (a little over US$ 600) on the spot, and had to travel across town to get a one-day visa in order to leave the country. Luckily, he spoke good enough Chinese to be able to make the next day's afternoon flight.

The fact is, laws and regulations in China are complicated, and... they change often. Fortunately, more changes than not are for the best. The governing body for all China visa matters is the Entry & Exit Administration under the Public Security Bureau (PSB). All relevant regulations are now accessible online at:

http://www.shanghai.gov.cn/shanghai/node8059/index.html

The Shanghai office of the Entry & Exit Administration also takes inquiries over the phone at tel: (021) 6357-7925, and your nearest People's Republic of China (PRC) consulate should also have a listed number for visa inquiries. Given how frequently rules change, the following should be taken only as a general guideline; touch base with a consulate or the PSB for updates.

Shanghai Visa Types

China, like most countries, offers many visa types, from simple tourist visas to business visas to work visas to residence permits or 'Green Cards'. The easiest way to come to China is on a tourist visa, which can be later converted to a work visa, the 'Z' visa. Switching to a 'Z' visa is a complicated process that usually takes up to a month. Having a capable administrative assistant who knows how to navigate the system definitely helps. In the past, at least officially, applicants had to apply for the 'Z' visa abroad, or at least from Hong Kong, but since 2002, the PSB has plans to allow this process to take place entirely in the mainland.

Shanghai Visa Procedures

Once you obtain a work visa, you must immediately obtain a temporary residence permit. This involves undergoing a full physical examination (including testing for HIV/AIDS) at a designated site to receive the requisite health certificate; a certificate from your home-country doctor will almost never be accepted. The work visa and health certificate will then allow you to apply for a residence permit—the 'Green Card'.

If you do not yet have an official employer in China, and want to come over and test the waters, the easiest way is to come on a tourist visa, which can later be converted to a resident (work) visa once employment is found. You can apply very easily for a tourist visa to the country in the PRC consulate nearest you. It is even easier to simply fly to Hong Kong (for which US, UK and many other nationals do not need a visa at all), and get a PRC tourist visa through one of the many visa service providers in tourist hotels there.

HOUSEHOLD GOODS RELOCATION
...to China

Relocation of goods can be a major headache if it is not done right. Customs regulations are Byzantine, and a missing 't' or an undotted 'i' can provide an excuse for Customs to collect a fine, an opportunity they will rarely miss.

The key to getting household goods relocation right is planning. As a general rule, you should plan at least three months from when you decide to move to China to when you receive the last shipment of goods at your door in Shanghai. Most people use a combination of air freight for day-to-day necessities (which will arrive in 7–14 days, but is expensive), express shipment of crucial items (2–5 days, but exorbitant) and ocean freight for the bulk of the goods.

A professional relocation agency will make this whole process hassle free for you.

One expat who relocated quickly just shipped off his goods without ANY of the required paperwork, and hoped for the best. The hapless shipper had all his worldly possessions impounded for more than six months as a result, in the end paying fines worth some 30 per cent of the total cost of the goods to get them released. Don't let it happen to you.

There are many service providers in this area, each having their own strengths. Some have offices around the world; those without worldwide offices typically have a strong team on the ground in China, and affiliate networks outside of China.

Choosing an Agency

When choosing an agency, it's important to look at two indexes. One is whether or not they are fully licensed (for example, are they capable of clearing Customs on their own or do they need to engage a subcontractor). The other factor is staff— not just sales staff, but down to the levels of moving supervisors, packing and transportation workers. Some international agencies do not directly employ these people, and instead work with local affiliates, whose quality may vary. Some of the biggest-name agencies include Sino Santa Fe and Crown Relocations. It is worth getting on their websites and getting educated, even if you then shop around for cheaper agencies.

Most foreigners moving into China work with an agency active in China and leave it to them to work shipments out with overseas affiliates providing 'door-to-door' service; this is especially true when China employers are paying for the relocation costs. Other people do it the other way around, feeling more comfortable with the help and consultation they can receive from familiar freight forwarders in their home country, which then must line up China affiliates. Either arrangement can work, so long as all agencies and affiliates involved are reputable.

A quality, professional relocation agency will evaluate your belongings and provide you with customised advice as to what to pack and what to leave behind. There are some general rules though, and these are especially important to pay attention to if you're working on a shoe-string and trying to ship goods without paying for a full-service freight-forwarder or relocation agency:

- DO be extremely punctilious about paperwork. There are literally dozens of forms to fill out, and the requirements change often. If you are not familiar with the freight forwarding process, you're probably better off paying someone to do it for you.

- DO be selective about the wine/liquor, cigarettes and electronic appliances you bring in. Many of these items incur a very high import duty, but are easily available in China. The import duty on furniture is much lower, and zero on personal effects if you have your work permit and residence permit.

- DON'T try to bring in very large numbers of video tapes or VCD/DVDs. Customs may decide you are part of a pirating chain and confiscate and/or fine you on their value. At best, Customs officials will go through them one by one and decide whether or not they are pornographic. You will then have a chance of your tapes being returned to you in two to four weeks… maybe!

- DON'T bother trying to ship in pornography or banned materials. It's just not worth it. One copy of the Dalai Lama's autobiography is unlikely to cause problems, but still it is best to carry it in your suitcase rather than ship it. A thousand 'Free Tibet' pamphlets in your household goods shipment may mean a VERY short stay for you as a China expatriate.

…Home

Leaving China? Remember that exporting household goods takes a process that can be almost as complicated as the relocation into China. It also requires presenting to Customs, again, all the records that prove you brought the stuff into China legally in the first place and thus do not owe duty. Be sure to keep track of all those forms!

Some other items to watch out for include antiques over 150 years old (illegal to export) and knock-off VCD/DVDs (ditto, and likely to be confiscated). Pets are always a hassle to bring in and out, but as long as you plan sufficient time for the quarantine process, it should be fine. Some people simply give away pets acquired in China before they leave the country, rather than put pets through the lengthy quarantine process.

TELECOMMUNICATIONS

Shanghai, as one of the fastest growing cities in the world, is getting more connected and wired by the day. Telecommunications options are abundant, from traditional landline phones, to mobile phones running GSM and CDMA; even broadband Internet connections are easily obtained.

Telephone Codes

China's country code is '86', and Shanghai's city code is '21' (add a '0' when dialing within China). All local Shanghai phone numbers now have eight digits, a reflection both of the desire of the government to appear 'modern', and of the sheer mass of Shanghainese needing phone numbers.

While China Telecom still has over 80 per cent of the market, its monopoly has been broken, and service is improving every month. Mobile phones are available everywhere and prices are getting more and more competitive. The two main operators, China Mobile (formerly a division of China Telecom) and Unicom, have also both started adopting the US sales approach of giving away free phones as long as consumers commit to certain monthly usage fees (usually US$ 25) for a 12- to 18-month period.

Buying a mobile phone is not a problem for foreigners. The easiest thing to do then is to get a pre-paid phone card. An alternative is to register with the operator and get charged a fixed fee of Rmb 50 (US$ 6) per month. This will save you the hassle of having to repeatedly deposit money into the card. Foreigners are not yet allowed to register into the network without a local Shanghai resident's ID card (*shenfenzheng*). This can be easily accomplished, however, with the help of a Chinese friend or colleague or even your *Ayi*! As competition between China Mobile and Unicom intensifies, there are ever more promotions to benefit consumers. Having a local friend or colleague check out current offers will help you get the best deal.

Connecting to the Internet via dial-up connection is easy and inexpensive. Shanghai now boats a multitude of ISPs.

A good example is 8888. You just need to create a new dial-up connection for your modem, using '8888' as username, password and phone number, and you are ready to surf at speeds anywhere from 28k to 56k. A token per-minute fee will be charged to the phone you are calling from, but unless you leave the computer logged on 24 hours a day, it's unlikely to add up to much.

Attaining broadband Internet connection is a bit more complicated, although you only need your passport and you are on your way to surfing the net at warp speeds. Broadband is a phone call away, but as of this writing, that call still needs to be made to the semi-monopoly Shanghai Telecommunications Bureau. The telephone number to reach this bureau is '1000'. Again, probably a good idea to ask your *Ayi* for some help! You will be connected and surfing at ISDN or ADSL speeds within days. Installation and usage rates are also quite reasonable.

SAFETY & SECURITY

Overall, Shanghai is very safe, far safer than probably most other cities of comparable size worldwide. Even within China (which is on the whole quite safe by world standards), Shanghai is recognised for good social order. In most neighbourhoods, you can walk around at two in the morning without having to worry about security. Aside from an effective and well-functioning municipal government, the strong safety record of the city may have much to do with the stereotypes of Shanghainese men and Shanghainese as a whole—always minding their own business and choosing verbal altercations over fisticuffs when encountering any type of confrontation.

That said, it doesn't hurt to remember a few tips just to be on the safe side. As developed as Shanghai is compared with other Chinese cities, bear in mind the widening gap between rich and poor. Be vigilant when exposing money in public places, especially in crowded subways or buses, or in markets like the (in)famous Xiang Yang market. Some good personal protective measures include wearing purse or backpack on the front of your body, keeping valuables in a

safety pouch when browsing crowded markets, and keeping mobile phones tucked safely inside bags or purses rather than hanging outside (although in China that is a fashionable thing to do!).

When choosing your place of residence, do a little homework about the neighbourhood. To say that Shanghai is on the whole safe doesn't mean that every neighbourhood is hassle-free. Without prejudice against the millions of migrant workers who have made such tremendous contributions to the city's development, as a general rule, try to stay away from neighbourhoods with large numbers of *nong min gong* ('peasant workers'). These neighbourhoods tend to be overcrowded, volatile due to ever-changing residents and less well-managed than the government wants them to be. For these reasons, they are sometimes hiding places for fugitives and criminals. In other words, much though you may sympathise with the down-and-out of Shanghai, you are less likely to enjoy having large numbers of them as immediate neighbours.

It is difficult to pinpoint such troubled districts, as they shift with the 'floating population' of migrants. But as a sweeping generalisation, old, rundown districts such as you may find in corners of Yangpu or Hongkou, should raise a red flag. More developed areas such as Xuhui, Jing'an and Lu Wan are generally safer, and certainly quieter and cleaner.

Security in the Home

When talking about 'household security', one China-specific phenomenon is that nearly everyone with money has an *Ayi*. This includes virtually all foreigners and a very significant percentage of Shanghainese as well. Most *Ayis* are honest, hard-working people, and many expats end up seeing their *Ayis* as friends, if not as part of the family. Still, it is important to realize that when you take on an *Ayi*, you will be giving the keys to your home to a person who most often comes from a background so much less wealthy than yours that the most minor embezzlement from your worldly goods might contribute substantially to her family's well-being. It's not worth getting paranoid about, but it is worth exercising some common sense.

First and foremost, be careful who you take on as an *Ayi*. Some expats will only accept *Ayis* from official agencies, whose employees are bonded. We don't believe it is necessary to go that far, but it is crucial to get references, and to interview people carefully. It is probably best to hire based on a personal recommendation by a Chinese person you trust. In China, a personal recommendation carries substantial weight, since if anything goes wrong with the new hire, the recommender loses enormous face. Thus, having the recommendation creates pressure between recommender and recommendee, which gives a serious disincentive for the new hire to misbehave.

Secondly, if you pay and treat your *Ayi* fairly, and provide little perks like vacation pay and Chinese New Year gifts, she will likely feel less of an incentive to try to get more for her time by padding the grocery bills. And finally, even with the best *Ayi*, it may still make sense to have a lockbox for the top valuables. An old saying in the Jewish tradition calls it unfair to put stumbling blocks before blind men, or to expose people to temptations so large they will find them hugely difficult to resist. An *Ayi* who may, for instance, have sick relatives at home whom she's trying to support on the US$ 150–200 per month that she gets between two or three part-time *ayi* positions may find it a very large stumbling block indeed to dust every other day around a diamond necklace she knows she can hawk for US$ 5,000. Again, common sense will help ensure a happy stay.

Security in the Office

One final note: the largest security issue most expats will deal with in Shanghai is security of intellectual property on the job. Chapter 9: Business Unusual (*pages 245–274*) offers a few tips in this area, but it is a major subject in its own right, beyond the scope of this book. It is a subject well-worth spending substantial time exploring, since many companies operating in China identify violations of intellectual property rights (IPR) as the single largest threat to their future in China (*see the section* 'Shopping Till You Drop' *in this chapter, pages 89–101, for some of the reasons why*).

A short note on IPR resources: several agencies specialise in corporate and/or IPR security in China; among the best-regarded are Pinkerton's and Rouse & Co, Ltd. There are intellectual property-focused business organizations, like the Quality Brands Protection Committee (*see* Chapter 9: Business Unusual *[page 256] for contact information*), and almost every chamber of commerce and other business organisation has an intellectual property sub-group. There are also specialised publications in this area: the global law firm Baker & McKenzie, for instance, has a regular IPR Watch newsletter. For an excellent overview, see *Kluwer Law International's Chinese Intellectual Property Law and Practice* (to which—truth in advertising alert—one of the co-authors of this book is a contributor).

EATING YOUR WAY AROUND SHANGHAI

CHAPTER 6

'Job's-tears seed, almond, and lotus-seed congee!'
'Rose chip and white-sugar rice cakes!'
'Shrimp won-tons with noodles!'
'Tea-eggs here!'
—Lu Xun, *Business in the Shanghai Longtangs*

Eating in Shanghai is serious business. The old saying '*Min yishi weitian*' (meaning 'hunger breeds discontentment') seems to have inspired an explosion of creativity in this food mecca of 30,000-plus restaurants, and easily ten times that many snack vendors. Nobody, in this century, should ever go hungry in Shanghai. With a little creativity and sense of adventure, you could easily spend years exploring the city's many cuisines, and never have the same meal twice.

Cooking and eating well is an important part of life across China; gatherings around a loaded table are signs and symbols of wealth, happiness and prosperity, a peaceful family, a successful company and a good business deal. You will no doubt spend plenty of time at banquet tables in Shanghai—as well as at family dinners, picnics, buffets, cafés and maybe even a tea-egg vendor or two. It's worth exploring enough to get familiar with your options.

EATING IN

Shanghai is very much a city of restaurants, and of small apartments. As a result, many expats find they eat out more often than at home, especially for business entertaining. Much of this chapter is devoted to restaurant eating.

That said, meals at home, with friends or family or even business associates can be a wonderful way to relax and share food and ideas in a comfortable environment. It's a good idea to be prepared.

PREPARING FOR GUESTS

The stores listed in the previous chapter (*see the section entitled 'Stocking the Fridge' pages 96–98*) will also help you lay in a stock of supplies for guests. It is a good idea to keep non-perishable treats around for last-minute visitors: sodas, bottled juice, some wine and beer and perhaps a few other drinks, and some nuts and other simple snacks.

Holding dinner parties is a regular part of social life for many expats, a wonderful way to share good food and conversation. Business entertaining at home can also be a fine way to network and strengthen relationships.

Given local labour costs and the ubiquitous availability of good *ayis*, holding a dinner party in Shanghai may well be much easier than in your home country. If you are blessed with an *ayi* who can cook well in several cuisines, you are set. There are also excellent caterers, servers, bar-tenders, in-home chefs and other support available to be hired on a case-by-case basis for more formal entertainment; ask among friends and colleagues for recommendations.

This labour help frees you up to concentrate on your guests, starting with the all-important issue of what to serve. Chinese guests will almost always be happiest with Asian foods, but may well enjoy trying something new. Just be sure to consider local tastes, including the lactose intolerance common among Chinese; a cheese board followed by cheesy lasagna will not impress Shanghainese visitors.

Consider the evening as a whole. Do you want a large party where guests can mix and mingle over trays of hors d'oeuvres? Or are you aiming at an intimate table and in-depth conversation? Are your guests drinkers? Smokers? Will they appreciate quiet background music, or after-dinner entertainment? How will your apartment best accommodate and welcome your guests, and help create the atmosphere you want?

You should also consider carefully the specific mix of guests you are inviting, particularly in cross-cultural groups. Many Shanghainese are as sophisticated in international exchange as any of their global counterparts, and will mix easily with non-Chinese guests and be relaxed about protocol, focusing more on the quality of the food and conversation. Other Shanghainese, often including senior government officials or executives from state-owned enterprises, may be very traditionally Chinese in their outlook, and be very concerned with protocol. Make sure you know who you are dealing with and plan accordingly.

PROTOCOL FOR ENTERTAINING TRADITIONAL CHINESE GUESTS

Whether entertaining at home or in a restaurant, if your guests include senior Chinese with a traditional outlook, there are several important points of protocol to remember. Your overall goal as host is to provide everything possible for the comfort of these guests, from non-stop filling of wine or liquor glasses, to a groaning table loaded with dishes, to a ready ashtray and extra cigarettes for smokers. For all these reasons, many expats find it easier to entertain senior Chinese guests in restaurants, although with help and plenty of planning, in-home entertaining can be especially face-giving.

Be available, if possible, to greet your senior guests individually, immediately on arrival, ideally at the door to your building, so you can escort them to your apartment or to the private room you have booked at a restaurant. Ensure that something (at least tea and snacks) is served immediately. Seat your senior-most guest as far as possible inside, facing the door, with the main host on his/her right, and make sure the guest is comfortable. Throughout the meal, seek to personally serve your senior guests special delicacies, and refill their drinks. It is also very appropriate to hold toasts, both generally to the group and individually with each guest. At the end of the evening (generally signalled by the last course, unless specific after-dinner entertainment is planned), escort your guests out of the building and to their cars.

Two final points. First, while traditional Chinese are highly attuned to protocol, traditional Chinese table manners are generally quite relaxed. Show no surprise if your senior Chinese guests blow noses loudly or reach across the table to help themselves or you or each other to delicacies, or even spit on the floor.

Second, business entertaining occasions with traditionally-minded Shanghainese and other Chinese should focus on general relationship-building, not directly on business. Traditional Chinese detest negotiating over meals; but the rapport developed over a pleasant meal can bring dividends when you return to negotiations in business hours.

And now to the many restaurant options in Shanghai.

EATING YOUR WAY ROUND THE WORLD

Of course, many options most popular with expatriates are restaurants offering foods familiar from home. Cosmopolitan Shanghai offers a wide range of international flavours, from American sports-bar food to French haute cuisine, Italian pizzerias to Indian curry shops. From Middle Eastern to Mexican, tapas to Thai, in four- or five-star hotels and privately-owned restaurants, Shanghai today can satisfy virtually any food craving, at virtually any level of formality. You can grab a burger and fries 24 hours of any day at one sports bar or another. You can sip the best imported wines over chateaubriand or charcuterie with a view of the Bund or a trendy renovated district like Xintiandi. You can savour the flavours of India in a setting decorated to suit a sultan. And you can find just about anything in between.

Our list of favourite restaurants that follows later includes a short sampling of the city's best opportunities for culinary globetrotting. You can read about more of these in any of the expat-oriented magazines listed in Chapter 7: Enjoying Life (*pages 173–174*), and/or hear about them from other expats, for the variety and quality of international foods in Shanghai is a common topic among Shanghai expats.

At the same time, Shanghai is also a mecca for top chefs in all the cuisines of China, offering a range of splendid eating sometimes less well-appreciated by the average expat. And so, with apologies to those who might wish it otherwise, our list of favourite restaurants focuses primarily on prime local eateries that the average expat may be less likely to hear about on the expat grapeline. Our goal is not to snub the many fine non-Chinese restaurants listed in any copy of *That's Shanghai*, but rather to encourage expats to look (and taste) beyond that list.

But first, just a few notes on what to expect with Chinese food as you will experience it in Shanghai.

CHINESE COOKING IN CHINA

If your past experience with Chinese food has been limited to 'one from Column A, two from Column B' take-out joints, you're in for a treat. Forget the overcooked, candy-coloured sweet-and-sour pork. Think crisp vegetables in light, subtle sauces; meats slow-cooked with star-anise and rice wine; seafood so fresh it was alive just before you ate it. Think, in other words, of rich, distinctive flavours that you will likely savour and be surprised by.

There are also sides of authentic Chinese cooking that are less attractive to many expats. Traditional Chinese cooks are frugal, making use of organ meats and virtually every other part of the animal, as well as incorporating exotica from sea slugs to swallow-spit (in bird's-nest soup). Shanghainese are not as given to eating exotica as their

Cantonese cousins, who are famous, in the words of one commentator, for 'eating everything that moves, and some things that are still moving'. But you are likely to encounter a few surprises in your Shanghai stay that you'll be happier pushing around your plate than shoving down your throat.

Take it all as an adventure and try as much as you feel able. You'd be surprised at how many once-squeamish expats who have developed a taste for the velvety richness of Shanghai river-eel, for instance. And there's plenty of Shanghainese cooking, and other Chinese cooking in Shanghai—from sautéed greens, to beer-cooked duck, to steamed chicken in spicy peanut sauce—that you will likely enjoy right off, and about which you'll find yourself saying, "I never knew that Chinese cooking was so varied."

THE MANY CUISINES OF CHINA —IN SHANGHAI

Chinese people divide Chinese cooking into 16 major regional styles, each with their own universe of sub-cuisines. Some of the most famous Chinese cuisines include:

- Jing Style (from Beijing: hearty northern cooking)
- Chuan Style (spicy food from Sichuan)
- Yue Style (fine food in light sauces, originally from Guangdong province)
- Yang Style (rooted in Jiangsu province)
- Lu Style (fresh, garlicky seafoods and vegetables from Shandong)
- Min Style (from Fujian province)
- Xiang Style (hot, garlic-spicy food from Hunan)

Shanghainese call their native style *Benbang cai*, literally 'local-type cuisine', reflecting the style's roots in farming and fishing family cooking. Shanghainese use river fish, seafood, chicken, duck and vegetables as raw materials, cooked into tastes they categorise as salty, salty-sweet, sweet-sour, sweet-spicy and/or pickled. Many famous *Benbang cai* dishes are braised in soy sauce, such as *Hongshao Rou* (pork braised in brown sauce), which paints the dishes a rich brown that can be unbearably oily in bad versions, but in good versions is meltingly luscious. Many others are smoked or steeped in tea and soy sauce, a combination called *lü*. Lü-style eggs, tofu and other treats are common snack foods and appetisers.

Shanghainese are such devotees of *Benbang cai* that when foods from out-of-town got introduced, they traditionally needed to get 'Shanghai-ised'. After the major wartime immigration wave of the 1930s, for instance, many out-town cooks landed in Shanghai and opened shops along the old Xizang, Nanjing, Jiujiang and Fuzhou Lu, serving foods that were different from local Shanghai food in cooking style and taste. Those that were too different quickly went out of business. The successful out-town cooks modified styles and flavours to satisfy local Shanghai tastes: a little sweeter than before perhaps, a little less spicy, maybe a bit more oil.

Nanjing Lu's famous Meilongzhen restaurant is a good example. Originally a fiery-flavoured restaurant serving homesick wartime refugees from Sichuan, Meilongzhen found itself too spicy to attract many Shanghainese. After the war, to expand its clientele, Meilongzhen ordered its chefs to tone down the spice and add a bit more sugar. Today, almost any Shanghainese will tell you they love the 'unique'

The famous Sichuan restaurant, Meilongzhen.

and 'original' take on *Benbang* cuisine that is represented by Meilongzhen, but relatively few will name the restaurant's Sichuan-style origins.

Another classic example is borscht, the famous Russian beet soup, widely introduced in Shanghai in the 1920s by White Russian émigré cooks. Today, in many *Benbang cai* restaurants, you can get a red beet-based soup, usually served a little sweeter than you would find it in Eastern Europe or the United States, but quite tasty, called variously *tiancai tang* ('beet soup') or *ba-she tang* (a transliteration of borscht). Most Shanghainese, who grew up more familiar with the soup than with Russian émigrés, will tell you it is a traditional speciality of Shanghai.

Shanghai Fusion Cuisine

The 'Decade of Chaos' known as the Cultural Revolution (1966–1976) effectively shut down Shanghai's restaurant sector, along with much else. Most well-known restaurants were closed. The few 'acceptable' restaurants allowed to stay open had to serve a limited menu of basic dishes that had been pronounced politically correct. Any attempt at individual style could be suspect, so everyone from chefs to servers steered clear of special flavours or flourishes. The result was a half-generation of badly-trained restaurant personnel, and visitors to the city in the early to mid-1980s still suffered the after-effects.

Late Chinese leader Deng Xiaoping's policy of reform and opening brought a rebirth to the city's food markets, however, and Shanghainese re-took to the restaurant world with gusto. Old-brand restaurants re-opened with new decor. International hotel chains established branches, bringing global food and service standards. The post-reform immigration wave brought more out-town dishes to Shanghai and this time, in keeping with post-reform openness, Shanghainese pressured less for 'Shanghai-isation', and more for 'authentic' new cuisines. Many excellent new wave restaurants from across China, including many listed below, are authentic enough that new arrivals from their areas of origin patronise them whenever homesick.

Facing competition from these new restaurants, many of which offer lighter, less oily fare than traditional *Benbang cai*, many local restaurants and dishes have undergone a 'reform' of their own. Still using carefully selected raw materials for colour/display, *Benbang cai* is becoming a little lighter and less oily than in the past. Many restaurants have also borrowed presentation techniques from the West: a greater attention to serving dishes, utensils, tablecloths, atmosphere, and décor. This new 'fusion *Benbang cai*' is called by the Shanghainese *Haipai Shanghai Cai* (Shanghainese cuisine with overseas characteristics).

A SHORT LIST OF LONG-TIME FAVOURITES

Any attempt to briefly summarise the 30,000-plus restaurants of Shanghai is doomed to failure, as someone's favourites will inevitably get left out. This list is by no means exhaustive, but rather an entirely idiosyncratic list of a few of the authors' favourites; perhaps it will get you out beyond the well-trodden pathways between Malones American bar and the Starbucks in Shanghai Centre.

We have tried to include a range of nice eating spots, from places with an interesting history, to high-end venues good for formal business entertaining, to places suited for casual dining with friends and family, to good cheap eats for lunches and quick dinners out, to street foods. For each location, we have rated facilities and décor, service as well as average cost per head for a typical meal.

Please note as one final requirement, given how quickly restaurants open and close in Shanghai: we have only listed restaurants that had been open for at least 18 months as of this writing. If this requirement leaves out some of the hottest new venues, we apologise; we figure if they're that hot, you'll hear of them anyway and better err on the side of caution than have every other restaurant we direct you to turn out to have been a six-month wonder that is now closed.

> **Key**
> - Facilities and décor (F&D)
>   † (minimally acceptable) to † † † † † (fantastic)
> - Service (S)
>   ‡ (they won't poke you in the eye) to ‡ ‡ ‡ ‡ ‡ (you will wish you could live there)
> - Average per head cost (APHC)
>   Every $ = Rmb 50 (US$ 6)
>   For instance, a restaurant with 5 $'s will cost on average Rmb 250 (US$ 30) per person for a full meal with a little beer or wine.

A note on tipping: traditionally one never tips in Shanghai restaurants, and many people still never do. In local hole-in-the-wall restaurants, it is still rarely done, but in many of the nicer restaurants, it is increasingly becoming expected, with 10 per cent of the bill an average tip. In some of the fancier places, especially if you come in a large group, a tip will be added right into the bill.

Benbang cai (Shanghainese) Favourites
Shanghai Lao-Fandian (Shanghai Old Restaurant)
上海老饭店
242 Fuyou Lu
Tel: (021) 6355-2275
F&D   † † † †
S   ‡ ‡ ‡
APHC $ $ $ $
Established in 1867, serving fine traditional Shanghainese food, especially known for chicken, duck and fish dishes.

Lao-zheng-xing Restaurant 老正兴菜馆
556 Fuzhou Lu
Tel: (021) 6351-5496
F&D   † † †
S   ‡ ‡
APHC $ $ $

Lu Bo Lang Restaurant 绿波廊酒楼

131 Yuyuan Lu

Tel: (021) 6328-0602

F&D   † † † †

S   ‡ ‡ ‡ ‡

APHC $ $ $ $

A national special class restaurant and one of the appointed restaurants for overseas tourists in Shanghai, located in the famous Yu Garden in the old Shanghai downtown area. Known for its authentic Shanghai cuisine, Shanghai *dim- sim*, crab dishes, shark's fin, etc. Lu Bo Lang has hosted more than 40 state leaders and VIPs, from former US President Clinton and Britain's Queen Elizabeth II, to Fidel Castro.

Wang Bao He Dajiudian (Central Hotel) 王宝和大酒店

555 Jiujiang Lu (Fujian Zhong Lu cross)

Tel: (021) 5396-5000

F&D   † † † † †

S   ‡ ‡ ‡ ‡

APHC $ $ $ $ $

Wang Bao He is famed for its crab dishes and southern China rice wine (Huangjiu, literally meaning 'yellow rice wine' describing the colour of the liquor). The restaurant claims to be the King of crab and God of wine.

Big Fan Restaurant 大风车小馆

1440 Hongqiao Lu

Tel: (021) 6219-7514

F&D   † † † † †

S   ‡ ‡ ‡ ‡

ACPH $ $ to $ $ $ depending on dishes selected

This 30s-retro restaurant is set in a Spanish-style compound in Hongqiao that dates from the 1920s. General Claire Chennault's 'Flying Tigers' were housed in the compound during the war. Today, in addition to the Big Fan, the compound also houses a health spa. It is next door to some good antique reproductions shops, and to the old Sassoon Villa, one of the more splendid Jazz-era private residences.

Lulu Restaurant 鹭鹭酒家
No 1, Lane 336, Shuicheng Nanlu
Tel: (021) 6270-6679
2-3/F, 66 Lujiazui Lu
Tel: (021) 5882-6679
F&D   † † † †
S   ‡ ‡ ‡ ‡
APHC $ $ $

Herry's Restaurant 亨利餐厅
8 Xinle Lu
Tel: (021) 6473-3448
F&D   † † † †
S   ‡ ‡ ‡ ‡
APHC $ $ $

The Gap 锦亭
8 Hengshan Lu
Tel: (021) 6473-4828
F&D   † † † †
S   ‡ ‡ ‡
APHC $ $ $ $

Xi Jia Hua Yuan (Xi's Garden) 席家花园
1 Dongping Lu
Tel: (021) 6474-7052
F&D   † † † †
S   ‡ ‡ ‡ ‡
APHC $ $ $ $

Shanghai Lao Zhan (Shanghai Old Station) 上海老站
201 Caoxia Bei Lu
Tel: (021) 6427-2233
F&D   † † † † †
S   ‡ ‡ ‡ ‡ ‡
APHC $ $ $ $

Lao Man Ke (Always Full House) 老满客饭店
1599 Yan'an Xi Lu

Tel: (021) 6213-7988
F&D   † † † †
S   ‡ ‡ ‡ ‡
APHC $ $ $

Mei Lin Ge (Merrylin) 美林阁

- 77 Songshan Lu (at Huaihai Zhong Lu cross)
  Tel: (021) 6355-5116
- 816 Zhangyang Lu (at Laoshan Lu cross)
  Tel: (021) 5835-3666
- 1885 Hongqiao Lu (inside the Xianxia Tennis Centre)
  Tel: (021) 6262-9966
- 85 Wuning Nan Lu (at Wuding Xi Lu cross)
  Tel: (021) 6246-3788

F&D   † † † †
S   ‡ ‡ ‡ ‡
APHC $ $ $

A chain restaurant, but a good one.

Xian Qiang Fang Chuan Cai 鲜墙房传菜

(Xian Qiang Fang Traditional Dishes)

- 57 Nanchang Lu
  Tel: (021) 5383-9893

F&D   † † †
S   ‡ ‡ ‡ ‡
APHC $ $ $

- 1468 Hongqiao Lu
  Tel: (021) 6295-1717

F&D   † † † †
S   ‡ ‡ ‡ ‡
APHC $ $ $ $

Yuan Yuan Restaurant 圆苑

- 550 Wanping Nan Lu (at Lingling Lu cross)
  Tel: (021) 6438-1015

F&D   † † †
S   ‡ ‡ ‡ ‡
APHC $

- 201 Xingguao Lu
  Tel: (021) 6433-9123

F&D   † † † †
S   ‡ ‡ ‡ ‡
APHC $ $

Jia Chang Fan (Family Dishes) 家常饭
217 Tianyaoqiao Lu
Tel: (021) 6438-9036

F&D   † † †
S   ‡ ‡ ‡ ‡
APHC $

Jie Shi Restaurant 吉士酒家
41 Tianping Lu
Tel: (021) 6282-9260

F&D   † †
S   ‡ ‡ ‡
APHC $

Grape Restaurant 上海格瑞普酒家
55 Xinle Lu (at Xiangyang Lu cross)
Tel: (021) 6472-0486

F&D   † †
S   ‡ ‡ ‡
APHC $

Helong Restaurant 合隆酒楼
267 Huashan Lu (opposite Hilton Shanghai)
Tel: (021) 6248-1588

F&D   † †
S   ‡ ‡ ‡
APHC $

Chuan-cai (Sichuan Style)
Meilongzhen Jiujia 梅龙镇酒家
22, Lane 1081, Nanjing Xi Lu
Tel: (021) 6253-5353

F&D   † † † †

S   ╪ ╪ ╪ ╪
APHC $ $ $ $

Established in 1938, the famed Sichuan-style restaurant in Shanghai is located in an old building along the busy shopping area of Nanjing Lu. The Meilongzhen board above the entrance was written by Mr Liu Haisu, one of the most famous artists and arts educators in modern Chinese history.

Da Ling Gang (Darling Harbour New Concept Chuan-cai)
达伶港新概念川菜厅
1782 Nanjing Xi Lu
Tel: (021) 6248-1818
F&D   ╪ ╪ ╪ ╪
S   ╪ ╪ ╪ ╪
APHC $ $

Chuan Guo Yan Yi Hotpot 川国演义火锅
2/F, Guangdong Development Bank Building
555 Xujiahui Lu
Tel: (021) 6390-1436
F&D   ╪ ╪ ╪ ╪
S   ╪ ╪ ╪ ╪
APHC $ $ $

Hangzhou-cai (Zhejing)

Hangzhou is a beautiful city in the Zhejiang Province, about two hours driving distance from Shanghai. The city's ten historical scenic spots surrounding the West Lake (Xi Hu) attract thousands of overseas and local guests. Delicious food at reasonable prices is another attraction of the city; local wags claim prices are so low that no Hangzhounese ever cook at home. About three years ago, Hangzhou cuisine entered the Shanghai market and took a remarkable share of Shanghai's food sector.

Zhi Wei Guan 知味观
345 Fuzhou Zhong Lu
Tel: (021) 6322-5266
F&D   ╪ ╪ ╪

S   ⴕ ⴕ ⴕ

APHC $ $

Opened in 1930, Zhi Wei Guan was one of the first 'modern wave' restaurants in Shanghai serving Hangzhou dishes. The name of the store Zhi Wei Guan (know-taste-observe) means 'if you'd like to know my taste, you would know it from observing my selection of raw materials'.

Zhang Sheng Ji 张生记

2-3/F, 446 Zhaojiabang Lu

Tel: (021) 6445-5777

F&D   ⴕ ⴕ ⴕ

S   ⴕ ⴕ ⴕ

APHC $ $

Xin Kai Yuan 新开元

560 Xujiahui Lu

Tel: (021) 6466-8866

F&D   ⴕ ⴕ ⴕ

S   ⴕ ⴕ

APHC $ $

Hong Ni Dajiudian (Red Earth Restaurant) 红泥大酒店

121 Yanping Lu

Tel: (021) 6246-2777

2000 Pudong Dadao

Tel: (021) 5851-9777

F&D   ⴕ ⴕ ⴕ

S   ⴕ ⴕ ⴕ

APHC $ $

Wan Jia Deng Huo 万家灯火

1 Dapu Lu

Tel: (021) 5396-1077

F&D   ⴕ ⴕ ⴕ

S   ⴕ ⴕ ⴕ ⴕ

APHC $ $

Huai-yang-cai (Jiangsu)
Yangzhou Fandian 扬洲饭店
2-4/F, 72 Nanjing Dong Lu
Tel: (021) 6358-3788
F&D　† † †
S　　† † †
APHC　$ $ $
Opened in 1950 as 'Mo Youcai Kitchen' (owned by Mo Youcai, then a chef with Bank of China Yangzhou branch), the restaurant moved and changed to its current name in 1970. It still serves great Yangzhou food.

Su Zhe Hui 苏浙汇
1-2/F, 388 Zhaojiabang Lu
Tel: (021) 6415-9918
F&D　† † † †
S　　† † † †
APHC　$ $ $

Lao Ban Zhai Jiulou 老半斋酒楼
600 Fuzhou Lu
Tel: (021) 6322-3668
F&D　† † †
S　　† † †
APHC　$ $

Jing-cai (Beijing)
Jing-cai in its more than 1,000-year history has combined the best of Beijing local, Shandong provincial, royal and vegetarian dishes, and is known for mutton and duck.

Quan Ju De Peking Roast Duck 全聚德烤鸭店
4/F, 786 Huaihai Zhong Lu
Tel: (021) 6433-7286
F&D　† † †
S　　† † †
APHC　$ $ $

Yan Yun Lou 燕云楼

755 Nanjing Dong Lu
Tel: (021) 6322-0496

F&D	† † †
S	⧾ ⧾ ⧾
APHC	$ $ $

Named Nanhua Jiujia originally, before 1948. The current name Yan Yun Lou means 'northern swallow heading south'. The calligraphy is by Guo Moruo, a respected author and historian with an important role in China's revolutionary history.

Ya Wang (Duck King) 鸭王

2/F, 20 Tianyaoqiao Lu (at Zhaojiabang Lu cross)
Tel: (021) 6464-9169

F&D	† † † †
S	⧾ ⧾ ⧾ ⧾
APHC	$ $ $

Another roast duck brand from Beijing.

Dong Lai Shun Mutton Hotpot 东来顺

9 Sinan Lu
Tel: (021) 5306-4407

F&D	† † †
S	⧾ ⧾ ⧾
APHC	$ $

Da Qing Hua 大清花

466 Changde Lu
Tel: (021) 6289-6666

F&D	† † † †
S	⧾ ⧾ ⧾ ⧾
APHC	$ $

Muslim

Shanghainese people first encountered the cuisine of China's Muslim peoples via the *Yangruochuan* (mutton cubes roasted on a skewer). Since the most concentrated area of Muslims in China live in the Xinjiang autonomy district in the north-west, Shanghainese tend to call all Muslim food 'Xinjiang dishes', even though some Chinese Muslim cuisine is, strictly speaking, that of the Hui (Muslim traders and merchants who settled throughout China), and not from Xinjiang. In today's Shanghai, Xinjiang food is very popular.

Hong Chang Xing Mutton Restaurant 洪长兴羊肉馆
10/F, Baodaxiang Building, 685 Nanjing Dong Lu
Tel: (021) 6352-9700

F&D   † † †
S   ⸸ ⸸ ⸸
APHC $ $

Established in 1913, it is said to be the best place for mutton in Shanghai.

Hui Feng Lou 回风楼
89 Henan Nan Lu
Tel: (021) 6328-1795

F&D   † † †
S   ⸸ ⸸ ⸸
APHC $ $

Ba Yi Mei Shi (Ba Yi Taste) 巴依美食
Room B, 79 Songshan Lu (at Huaihai Lu cross)
Tel: (021) 5306-3386

F&D   † † †
S   ⸸ ⸸ ⸸
APHC $ $

Qian-cai (Guizhou)
Qian Xiang Ge 黔香阁
171 Pucheng Lu (at Shangcheng Lu Cross)
Tel: (021) 5887-1717

F&D   † † † †
S   ⸸ ⸸ ⸸ ⸸
APHC $ $

Qian Guo Ju 千锅居
2/F, 1716 Nanjing Xi Lu
Tel: (021) 3214-0392
F&D   † † † †
S   ‡ ‡ ‡ ‡
APHC $ $

Xiang-cai (Hunan)

Hunan is the hometown of the late Chinese leader Mao Zedong. Rumour has it that the Hunan classic version of *hongshao rou* (pork in brown sauce, spicier than the Shanghai version) and chillis were Chairman Mao's favourites. You can find plenty of pork and plenty of chillis in every *Xiang-cai* restaurant in the city.

Dong Ting Chun Xiang-cai Guan 洞庭春湘菜馆
58 Yuanyang Lu
Tel: (021) 6466-9501
F&D   † † †
S   ‡ ‡ ‡
APHC $ $

Xiang Yuan 湘圆
2/F, Qianjin Building, 151 No 1 Ruijing Lu
Tel: (021) 5306-7216
F&D   † † †
S   ‡ ‡ ‡
APHC $ $

Gu Yi Xiang Wei Nong (Guyi Hunan Restaurant)
古意湘味浓
1/F, Jufu Building, 89 Fumin Lu
Tel: (021) 6249-5628
F&D   † † † †
S   ‡ ‡ ‡ ‡
APHC $ $ $

Yue-cai (Guangdong/Cantonese food)

Cantonese are famed both for good cooking and for brave cooking, eating (in the traditional phrase) 'everything with legs but tables, everything that flies but kites, and everything that swims but boats'. *Yue-cai* is, in fact, known for seafood, and is considered one of China's best cuisines. Today, it is a fine and face-giving gesture for a host (especially a foreign host) to treat Chinese people to a good meal in a fine *Yue-cai* restaurant.

Xin Hua Lou 杏花楼

343 Fuzhou Lu
Tel: (021) 6328-0504
F&D † † † †
S ‡ ‡ ‡ ‡
APHC $ $ $ $

Established in 1857, today Xin Hua Lou can serve 800 people at the same time with more than 100 dishes, from seafood to snake, chicken to *dim-sim*. Local people queue up at Xin Hua Lou prior to Zhongjiu Jie (Md-Autumn Festival on the 15th day of the eighth month in the Chinese lunar calendar or around mid- to late September on Western calendars) every year for its renowned Cantonese mooncakes, a must-have at Zhongjiu Jie when people gather together to appreciate the family ties.

Xin Ya Yue-cai Guan 新雅粤菜馆

719 Nanjing Dong Lu
Tel: (021) 6320-7788
F&D † † † †
S ‡ ‡ ‡ ‡
APHC $ $ $ $

Opened in 1926, to date, the restaurant has served several hundred thousands customers from over 100 countries and regions in the world, including former US President Nixon.

Shanghai Mei Yue Hua Restaurant 上海美粤华大酒店
222 Zhaojiabang Lu
Tel: (021) 6437-7979
F&D   † † † †
S   ‡ ‡ ‡ ‡
APHC $ $

Zen 采蝶轩
Xintiandi
Tel: (021) 6385-6385
F&D   † † † †
S   ‡ ‡ ‡ ‡
APHC $ $ $ $

Tang.com (soup online) 汤.com
267 Maoming Bei Lu
Tel: (021) 6267-1861
F&D   † † †
S   ‡ ‡ ‡ ‡
APHC $ $

Vegetarian

Buddhism was once China's state religion, and vegetarian cooking was a natural outgrowth of the religion, using bean curd and vegetables to cook tasty food, symbolising non-violence and peace.

Shanghainese, in their enterprising way, went the traditional Buddhist position one better, developing a local sub-cuisine called 'Fat Buddha Cooking' (*pang-fo cai*) of complex vegetarian dishes made to imitate various meats. Thus, the sophisticated Shanghai Buddhist could have fake duck, fake ham, fake goose, even (remarkably convincing) mock shrimp made of tofu, tree-ear mushrooms and similar ingredients.

Besides the restaurants listed below, you will find vegetarian restaurants at each Buddhist temple in Shanghai, with some of the best-known at the Jade Buddha Temple, the Jing'an Temple and the Longhua Temple. In vegetarian restaurants, there is no meat or fish, and often no smoking, alcohol, or even eggs (Chinese cooking, of course, almost never uses dairy). Still, the food is delicious and you will rarely leave a meal feeling healthier.

Gong De Lin Vegetarian 功德林素菜馆
445 Nanjing Xi Lu
Tel: (021) 6327-0218
F&D   † † †
S   ‡ ‡ ‡
APHC $ $

Chun Feng Song Yue Lou 春风松月楼
17 Ninghui Lu, Yu Garden
Tel: (021) 6355-3024
F&D   † † †
S   ‡ ‡ ‡
APHC $ $

Zao Zi Shu (Jujube Tree) 枣子树
600 Fuzhou Lu
Tel: (021) 6322-3668
F&D   † † †
S   ‡ ‡ ‡
APHC $ $

Owned by Ms Zeng Fangying from Taiwan, the restaurant opened in January 2001, and quickly became a famed place for vegetarian food. How did the Jujube tree come to represent a vegetarian restaurant? The Chinese pronunciation for 'Jujube Tree' (Zao Zi Shu) is a near-homophone for Zao Chi Su (meaning 'eating vegetarian early'). The following lines from Zao Zi Shu may bring you into the spirit of Vegetarianism: *To him / there is no bad thing in the world / everything is good / both Chinese cabbage and radish are good / even salty and bitter vegetables are good / everything has its own taste / everything is great.*

Tea Food

At tea food restaurants, every dish is made with tea. It makes for a really unique theme meal, and the food and presentation are terrific. You can also order a tea ceremony with your supper.

Tian Tian Wang Tea Restaurant 天天旺茶宴馆
258 Fengxian Lu
Tel: (021) 6212-5758
F&D † † † †
S † † † †
APHC $ $ $

SHANGHAI DIM-SIM AND SNACKS

Shanghai has its own typical *dim-sim*. To name a few:

liangmian-huang 两面黄	double-side fried noodle with seafood dressing
xiaolong mantou 小龙馒头	bun with meat stuffing steamed in bamboo utensil
shengjian mantou 生煎馒头	fried stuffed bun
youtiao 油条	deep-fried twisted dough sticks
doujiang 豆浆	Soya-bean milk
yangchunmian 阳春面	noodle in plain soup with no dressing
zong-zi 棕子	pyramid shape dumpling made of glutinous rice wrapped in bamboo or reed leaves
yuanxiao 元宵	sweet dumplings made of glutinous rice flour
xianrou shaomai 鲜肉烧麦	steamed meat stuffing dumpling with the dough gathered at the top
jiuniang yuanzi 酒酿圆子	ball of glutinous rice flour in fermented glutinous rice soup

zaotianluo 糟田螺	river snail in distiller's grains
cairou hundun 菜肉馄饨	meat and vegetable stuffed dumpling soup
youdou fuxi fentang 油豆腐细粉汤	fried bean curd in vermicelli (made from bean starch) soup
paigu niangao 排骨年糕	pork ribs fried with New Year cake (made of glutinous rice flour)
ji zhou 鸡粥	congee with chicken soup and sliced chicken meat
guihua tangou 桂花糖藕	steamed rice-filled lotus roots in sweet-scented osmanthus dressing
youzha choudoufu 油炸臭豆腐	deep-fried stinky toufu (preserved bean curd)
sanhuangji 三黄鸡	chicken served with soy-sauce
yuantou miantiao 浇头面条	soup noodles with all kinds of dressing

You can have Shanghainese *dim-sim* from street vendors, but be careful, as few of these have modern hygiene facilities. You might do better at one of the following restaurants, which specialise in making meals out of traditional snacks:

Wang Jia Sha 王家沙
805 Nanjing Xi Lu
Tel: (021) 6253-5202

Qiao Jia Shan 乔家栅
1460 Zhonghua Lu
Tel: (021) 6377-1661

Shen Da Cheng 沈大成
636 Nanjing Lu
Tel: (021) 6322-5615

Xian De Lai 鲜得来
98 Yun'nan Nan Lu
Tel: (021) 6311-0777

Wu Fang Zhai 五芳斋
136 Sichuan Bei Lu
Tel: (021) 6321-6647

Xiao Shao Xing 小绍兴
118 Yun'nan Nan Lu
Tel: (021) 6373-2890

Cang Lang Ting 沧浪亭
691 Huaihai Zhong Lu
Tel: (021) 6327-5738

Nan Xiang Xiao Long Man Tou Dian 翔小龙馒头店
Yu Garden shopping area

Xia Mian Guan (Xia's Noodle Restaurant) 夏面馆
798 Zhaojiabang Lu
Tel: (021) 6472-8504

INTERNATIONAL CUISINE

And finally, as we promised, we have listed below a few international favourites. These have not been rated for décor or service: most will be adequate for the average expat—indeed a number are familiar chains, managed in ways very similar to their branches in your home country. A few that really stand out as special for décor or service are noted below.

American
Hard Rock Café
1376 Nanjing Xi Lu
Tel: (021) 6279-8133

Rain Forest
4/F CITIC Plaza, 1168 Nanjing Xi Lu
Tel: (021) 5298-4998

Friday's
4 Hengshan Lu
Tel: (021) 6473-4602

KABB (Kathleen's American Bistro Bar) 凯博西餐厅
House 5, North Block, Xintiandi
Lane 81, Taicang Lu
Tel: (021) 3307-0798

Malone's American Cafe
257 Tongren Lu
Tel: (021) 6247-2400

French
M on the Bund
7/F No 5 The Bund (at Guangdong Lu)
Tel: (021) 6350-9988; fax (021) 6322-0099
Email: info@m-onthebund.com
This award-winning French-inspired restaurant was the first
opened in Shanghai by famed chef Michelle Garnaut. Today,
it is one of Shanghai's great pleasures to eat in, look at or just
hang out in (nightly sessions in the 'Glamour Bar', overlooking
the Bund, are a 'must-do' at least once).

La Maison
Unit 1, House 23, North Block, Xintiandi
Lane 181, Taicang Lu
Tel: (021) 3307-1010

German
The Paulaner Bräuhaus 上海宝莱纳餐厅
150 Fenyang Lu
Tel: (021) 6474-5700

Indian
Tandoor
59 Maoming Nanlu (within the old Jinjiang Hotel)
Tel: (021) 6472-5494

Italian
Pasta Fresca Da Salvatore 沙华多利意式
4 Hengshan Lu
Tel: (021) 6473-0789

50 Hankou Road Bar & Restaurant 五十号菜馆
50 Hankou Lu
Tel: (021) 6323-8383
One of the first really interesting, upmarket foreign restaurants in town, 50 Hankou serves fusion Italian in a soaring space near the Bund decorated with wood carvings inspired by South-east Asia.

Japanese
Yi-Teng-jia 伊藤家
24 No. 2 Ruijin Lu
Tel: (021) 6473-0758

Weiqian Noodle 味千拉面
518 Huaihai Zhong Lu
Tel: (021) 6372-5547
165A, Grand Gateway, 1 Hongqiao Lu
Tel: (021) 6407-5130

South-east Asian
Irene's Thai
263 Tongren Lu
Tel: (021) 6247-3579

Others
Park 97
Gaolan Lu 2, inside the west gate of Fuxing Park in the old French Concession
Tel: (021) 5383-2328 (for Baci, Tokio Joe and California Club)

Direct from Hong Kong, Park 97 consists of four outlets: Baci's Italian Cuisine (serving wonderful Italian food including a delightful weekend brunch), Tokio Joe (serving sushi and rolls), California Club (disco) and Upstairs at 97 (lounge).

FUSION FOOD

International 'fusion food' is popular in today's Shanghai. It's a style in some ways created by expats who came to China in late 1970s to early 1980s, probably the first group of foreigners working and living in this re-opened country. After returning to their home countries, they missed the delicious food they had in China, and some came again to Shanghai to open East-meets-West style restaurants. They inspired many local chefs to follow suit, creating food combining the best of Chinese and Western cooking and serving styles.

The Door Restaurant & Bar 乾门西餐音乐酒吧
3/F, 1468 Hongqiao Lu (at Yan'an Lu cross)
Tel: (021) 6295-3737
F&D   † † † † †
S   † † † †
APHC $ $ $ $

The Door is owned by Mr Wang Xingzheng, a former textile merchant and fashion designer who also runs the famous *Benbang cai* style Xian-qiang-fang Restaurant. At The Door, Wang has combined his love for Chinese history with his taste in textiles and in antiques from across China and Southast Asian countries. The result is visually stunning, a feast of colours and textures for the eyes that mixes the ancient and modern. In fact, everything at The Door is fusion, from the food to the entertainment. On a huge barco screen, loop-taped Charlie Chaplin films play from early evening till 10:00 pm, when a live band plays. Dressed in traditional Chinese costumes, the band includes such traditional Chinese instruments as the *er-hu* fiddle, bamboo flute and *suona* horn, combined with a keyboard, to play Asian and Middle Eastern pieces set to modern Western rhythms. The results are reminiscent of the Ang Lee movie *Crouching Tiger, Hidden Dragon*. It's an odd place, but fun.

Colours Restaurant & Bar

Building No 11, 118 Ruijin Lu, No 2, Ruijin Guesthouse
Tel: (021) 5466-5577

F&D ✝ ✝ ✝ ✝ ✝
S ✠ ✠ ✠ ✠
APHC $ $ $ $

Hong Fang Zi Xi Cai Guan 红房子西菜馆

(Red House Western Food Restaurant)
37 Shanxi Nan Lu
Tel: (021) 6437-4902

F&D ✝ ✝ ✝
S ✠ ✠ ✠
APHC $ $ $

Started in 1945 by an Italian businessman, The Red House is an East-meets-West shop that's been serving fusion French-Shanghai food since before the word 'fusion' was ever applied to food. It is named for the red walls that distinguish it inside the Donghu Guesthouse compound.

One final note on fusion eating habits. Traditionally, as noted in Chapter 4: Shanghai Lifecycles, Chunjie (Spring Festival, the Chinese Lunar New Year) is a family celebration, featuring a dinner cooked at home. In the last few years, however, eating out for Chunjie has become a hip trend, and tables at the most popular restaurants are being booked solid for Chunjie six months ahead!

Clearly, more changes and innovations in Shanghai food are on the way.

ENJOYING LIFE

CHAPTER 7

'He was borne on to the conclusion that they must
make a night of it after all they had been through.'
—Vicki Baum, *Shanghai '37*

ASKING ANYONE WHAT WAS THE MOST FUN they have ever had in Shanghai causes a long pause as they mentally search for not a moment, but THE moment.

Was it the holiday evening where they bluffed their way past the elevator security guard to get to the executive floor of the Portman Ritz-Carlton, and from there snuck up the cement staircase to the helicopter pad for their first Moon Festival in Shanghai, then having a picnic of delicious cakes while gazing at the full moon over the city, feeling like they were staring at the ocean from the top of a cliff? Maybe it was the open mike Sunday night at the Cotton Club when Chinese 'Godfather of Rock & Roll' Cui Jian showed up, and the entire room made music together. A theatre event perhaps? Les Miserables? Or maybe dancing all night with everyone at the old Judy's, and being shocked that the sun was up upon emerging—as a few curious 60-year-olds walked by backwards, slapping themselves for early morning exercise.

An alley wander where they were invited to sit down and play mahjong with a group of cutthroat chain-smoking grandfathers. The first dinner at a private Shanghai flat. A moonlit spring evening wine tasting on the balcony of swishy M on the Bund, transported back to the 1920s while waiting for the lights to go out. This chapter offers some ideas to get you started. You will find the options are as extensive as your energy level, and as varied as the city itself.

SPORTS AND OUTDOOR ACTIVITIES

Whatever your exercise passion, you can find comrades in Shanghai. One of the oldest expat exercise groups is the Hash House Harriers: the 'Hash', 'the drinking club with a running problem'. The main Hash meets Sunday afternoons for a run or walk through different Shanghai neighbourhoods, following preset chalk marks down streets and through alleys, until their dinner and drink conclusion. The Taiping Hash, for hard-core distance runners, meets Saturdays for runs outside of the city.

While the Hash may be one of the oldest groups, the Expat Football League (for soccer) is one of the most emotionally involved. With diehard loyalty to their sport, long-standing teams like the Lions and Vikings play league games every Saturday. Most teams are sponsored by local restaurants or bars; if a group of men in heated debate about football sit near you late on a Saturday afternoon, chances are you have happened into the home of one of Shanghai's teams. Each year, they passionately battle for the League trophy, and occasionally travel to other Asian cities for tournaments.

Jinqiao Rubgy Pitch in Pudong houses Shanghai's Rugby League, Ultimate Frisbee Team, Cricket Team, and Gaelic Football Team. Each weekend, athletes, families, dogs and other enthusiasts arrive at the field for kids' games, adult games and amateur games. The field also hosts the notorious Shanghai Hairy Crab Rugby Team, which holds an annual game that draws 'alumni' back to Shanghai from around the world to demonstrate that physical and beer drinking endurance do not diminish with age; or at least that reserves remain available for short bursts of prowess and glory.

As of winter 2002, you can no longer use the expression, 'I'll believe that when I can ski in Shanghai' because a large indoor ski facility has opened in Hongqiao. The facility boasts a graduated slope for beginners and early intermediates, with jumps for snowboarders to catch air—along with hot tubs, saunas and a restaurant. For non-beginners, the fun is going to the ski facility to see the wonder of Shanghainese experiencing snow in quantity for the first time.

Shanghai also boasts a community of ultra-sport enthusiasts, whom you can meet through the Shanghai Bike Club (bohdi@ bohdi.com.cn), or at Luo Ben outdoor store on Fuxing Lu, owned by adventure traveller Christopher Peres (http://www.luoben. com), who biked across China in 2001 to raise money for heart transplants for Chinese kids. They hold 5:30 am weekday group runs in the old French Concession (p.zwahlen@swisscenters.com). On weekends, most run/bike at Sheshan or in Hangzhou, where they have mapped more than 60 km (37.3 miles) of trails through tea plantation-dotted mountains. Adventure races in and around Shanghai include people cross-training with the Masterhand Rock Climbing Club. Shanghai is also the organising home base for the Mongolia Sunrise to Sunset race (http://www. ultramongolia.com). Many Shanghai ultra-athletes run this amazing non-profit marathon/ultra-marathon, whose proceeds support Hovsgol National Park.

Hotel Ratings

When Shanghai's corps of ultra-athletes started training years ago, their first undertaking was Hong Kong's 100-km (62-mile) Trailwalker ultra-marathon. Because Shanghai gyms were then limited and they needed hill work for leg strength, each evening they would run mountain substitutes in Shanghai—the stairwells of five-star hotels. They became connoisseurs of which hotels had the best internal maintenance, and the best food available outside the back door—at that time the Hilton won top marks.

Air quality, traffic, and overcrowding can make exercising outdoors a challenge. Many gyms are available for membership, either independently or through international hotels, and offer activities from Tai Bo boxing to aerobics, *taiji*, strength training, indoor triathlons, and weekend treks. The yoga craze has also hit Shanghai. In addition to yoga classes in gyms, a couple of independent studios specialise in different forms of yoga. A favourite is the Bikram Yoga class (http://www.bikramshanghai. com).

Serious golf became a craze in Shanghai in the late 1990s, resulting in at least 18 courses being built within an hour's drive of each other, some designed by world-renowned golf legends like Jack Nicklaus. Within city limits, several driving ranges are open late into the evening for aspiring Tiger Woodses to practise swings. Most golf courses are for members only, but will allow non-members to play for fees ranging from Rmb 250–830 on weekdays, or Rmb 625–1,250 on weekends. For die-hard golf enthusiasts, several courses in Shanghai have homes built around them (*see the section* 'Golf Course Living' *in* Chapter 5: Settling In, *on pages 67–68*).

Tennis is reputedly a passion for senior government officials in Shanghai. Hosting tennis' Masters Cup in late 2002 caused a swell of interest citywide. Most large living complexes have tennis courts, as do many member gyms at hotels. For the serious player, the Shanghai Racquet Club (in Minhang, past Hongqiao Airport) boasts two international tennis coaches and 13 courts, with housing on-site for hard-core enthusiasts! Downtown, the Regal International Hotel on Hengshan Lu has several indoor and outdoor courts. The city offers many other mostly outdoor courts.

Many forms of martial arts are available for those interested in exploring these ancient Chinese methods for creating mental and physical harmony. In several *wushu* centres, novices can learn with experienced masters. In addition, various forms of Japanese martial arts have taken root in Shanghai, and one can find a master to study under if a particular form is a passion.

Even horses have returned to Shanghai with the opening of the Bridle Club in Hongqiao. From riding to racquets, rock-climbing to orienteering, Shanghai's sheer size assures you of finding people who share your interests. Local entertainment magazines like *That's Shanghai* have contact details for many sports interest groups; or you can always take an ad in the personals section and start your own group.

INTELLECTUAL CLUBS

The more cerebral can also find many groups to get involved with. There several book clubs, which range from simple volume exchanges of hard-to-come-by English-language titles, to more organised discussion groups. As most of these are informally structured within larger groups, check with members of the Expat Professional Women's Society or the Shanghai Expatriate Association for recently formed book clubs. Also, Rick Foristel, head of Webster University's MBA programme in China, informally leads a popular ongoing contemporary China history workshop.

Many of the world's university alumni groups have associations in Shanghai, with an increasing number holding global reunions within the city. There are also as many geographically-focused groups to belong to as one can slice or dice on the map. A person can join the Cascade Club (for people from or fond of the US Pacific North-west). There is the Cercle Francophone de Shanghai, Club Italia, Canuck Connection, German-Speaking Club, and a multitude of others depending on either where your home, or your heart, is.

One of Shanghai's most popular and long-standing groups is the Shanghai Historic House Association, which in its early days had a street scout to sniff out signs that beautiful old houses might be torn down, then either immediately begin negotiating for old doors and fireplaces, or begin petitions to stop the city from destroying an architectural art piece. Eventually, the city government was converted, coming to understand the appeal (and financial/tourist value), of these buildings to foreigners and returnees; many are now voluntarily preserved. The Historic House Association holds tours of the city's beautiful old landmarks. A favourite lecturer is Tess Johnston, respected author of several books on China's foreign concession architecture/history, and longtime Shanghai resident.

From Toastmasters to Chess Club to Palm Pilot Club, there are groups for any interest you may have. The great thing about Shanghai is if you can't find a group you want to be a part of, you can just go out and create your own, and soon enough have a strong membership. Again, check the pages of expat magazines for contact details, or to take out an ad to start a new group.

TAKING TO THE STREET

A delight unearthed by many Shanghai newbies soon after their arrival, as jetlag pops their eyes wide open at 5:00 am, is an early morning wander to take in Shanghainese morning exercises in parks and along stretches of sidewalk. From *taiji* to sword exercises to ballroom dance, the Bund and most of the parks are full of middle-aged to elderly Chinese dedicated to their early morning exercise and social gatherings. In addition to organised groups, you will find backslapping old men walking in reverse as they take in the morning, lines of little old ladies with their legs propped up on fences stretching and catching up on neighbourhood gossip, and intent-faced men shouting at trees in the middle of the parks. You will be a welcome addition to any good-spirited group if you step into a back row and begin and follow along.

MASSAGE

One of the pure indulgent luxuries of Shanghai is affordable massage. What often starts as a single experience ends up a weekly addiction, for foreigners and locals alike. There are four basic types to opt for: head and shoulder massage, traditional Chinese full-body massage, Western full-body massage, and foot massage.

Every city block offers small hairdressing salons, where you can drop in without appointment for a hair wash with head-and-shoulder massage. Throughout the city, you'll find traditional Chinese massage parlours, many employing Shanghai's blind population. These recreational massage parlours range from the refined Green Massage, which employs and trains sighted people near Xintiandi, to generically labelled 'Blind People Massage Parlours', run by individual owners all over the city. A one-hour massage typically costs Rmb 60–120.

Conversely, many medical universities and hospitals have medicinal massage specialists who focus on pressure points to adjust *qi* that is out of alignment. *Qi* is the Chinese concept of energy that flows within the body; in traditional Chinese medicine, misaligned *qi* causes illness. Specialists have a feel for *qi* alignment, and adjust other people's *qi* with their own energy force.

With the opening of the Banyan Tree Spa at the Westin, pampering has taken on new meaning. This exclusive line of Asian spas provides any Western or Asian full-body massage you may desire. Most five-star hotels offer full-body oil massage, with the Spa at the Hilton having some of the best massage therapists. Many locally-run day spas throughout the city offer hybrid East-West treatments. One of our favourites—for women only—is the Rizz Plaza, located in the Aijian Building on Lingling Lu, near Tianyaqiao Lu.

One of China's most ancient massage forms is foot massage. Chinese medicine connects pressure points on the foot to different internal organs and systems; foot massage stimulates these pressure points for better health. Most 'blind people' massage parlours offer foot massages, as do excellent specialist chains like Henan Foot Massage, with 12 locations citywide.

'HIGH CULTURE'

Shanghai is becoming an ever-more interesting global culture centre with the Art Museum and Shanghai Grand Theatre hosting world class exhibitions and performances. Some older theatres, like the Shanghai Concert Hall, also have beautiful traditional architecture that lends something special to performances. The Shanghai Acrobats, now in a redesigned performance space, are also worth seeing. The pure physical challenge of Chinese acrobatics is unmatched in most other sports.

Shanghai now offers at least 80 commercial art galleries, and burgeoning artists' studios; check lifestyle magazines for listings. One of the best for emerging artists is ShangArt (at the Gaolan entrance to Fuxing Park). Famous for capturing stills of China's changing face is the Gang of One photo gallery at Tianshan Lu, home gallery for photojournalist and art photographer Wang Gangfeng.

The Tai Kang Lu Warehouse District is interesting to wander through and gallery-graze, as is the area around the Old China Hand Reading Room on Shaoxing Lu, near Shanxi Nan Lu,

Art galleries in the Duolun Lu cultural and historical area.

where you can browse the Reading Room while drinking tea in a manner reminiscent of 1920s Shanghai.

From the Hua Xia Sex Museum (1133 Wuding Lu) to the Museum of Public Security (518 Ruijin Nan Lu), a walk through Shanghai's more out-of-the way museums can be a unique experience, both for what Chinese view as museum-worthy, and for exhibit contents. In a Shanghai suburb, we stumbled on a museum housing real mummies, a wax museum, temple, fishing pond and model historical village, all for an entrance fee of Rmb 15; easily the best museum value for money we ever had.

A noteworthy new museum is the Shanghai Science Museum near Century Park in Pudong, which houses China's first IMAX theatre. An oldie-but-goodie is the Museum of the First National Congress of the Chinese Communist Party, where the fresh-faced idealists made it all come to life.

Shanghai also has some of China's best antiquing. For details, see the section *'Antiques and 'Antiques'—DongTai Lu, Hu & Hu, etc.'* in *Chapter 5: Settling In* on pages 95–96

LATE NIGHT PROWLING

In the mid 1990s, outside of hotel lounges, Shanghai had about ten bars and four discos. In the bad old days, everyone knew the weekend migratory pattern between bars and saw each other repeatedly at about the same time each Saturday night. At one of Shanghai's first discos, which had a dress code, a person in casual attire could lease of a pair of waiter's pants from an entrepreneurial employee for a couple dances, return them, change back into shorts, and be off to the next place to keep frolicking.

Today, you have to arrange in advance if you want to meet friends, for the discos and nightclubs have multiplied, with host DJs from around the world dictating the tempo of the night. You would not dare, at most of these chic hot spots, to cadge spare pants from a waiter; more likely you will peruse your wardrobe before heading out to see if you still have anything cool enough to wear. There are so many choices that bars can be grouped by interest: university bars, gay bars, dance clubs, jazz bars, pubs and comedy clubs.

For a newcomer, the best way to approach Shanghai nightlife is geographically, one neighbourhood at a time. Areas to focus on include Xintiandi, the Tongren Lu/Nanjing Lu area, the section of Julu Lu near Huashan Lu, Maoming Lu

A souvenir stall in Xintiandi.

bordering the Ruijin Guesthouse, a broad area of Hengshan Lu, the clubs encircling Fuxing Park, and a few good dance spots on both sides of the Bund.

For people-watching enthusiasts, Xintiandi is an unlimited treasure chest. A hot new landmark, Xintiandi offers some of Shanghai's best restaurants, speciality shops and bars. From Chinese tourists to foreign dignitaries, Xintiandi is now a must-see for Shanghai visitors. When staid APEC (Asia Pacific Economic Co-operation) met in Shanghai, president's and prime minister's wives were sneaking out for 'bathroom break' shopping sprees at Anthony Xavier's designer clothing store. Xavier admits to keeping his shop open till 2:00 am during APEC, to facilitate secret splurges by well-dressed ladies of the world.

If you missed all that, not to worry: Xintiandi still has plenty to see. Live bands play nightly at the Ark, Luna and Paulaner Brauhaus. To see and be seen as one of Shanghai's beautiful people, try Kabb, Che and the Va Va Room at the top of VaBene.

Moving to Tongren Lu, people you forgot you ever knew re-emerge at the Long Bar, one of Shanghai's oldest, and an institutional hangout from the bad old days. The Long Bar is Shanghai's version of the Boston bar from the American TV show *Cheers*, one of few bars in Shanghai with a lively after-work crowd. For those with abundant testosterone or a love of the extreme, Tuesdays and Thursdays after 9:30 pm are 'model night', where the women's bathroom is draped with feathers, sequins and padded pushups, and the 'models' count steps in sync down the bar, avoiding eye contact with cat-callers, and ignoring occasional drunks who, kicking and strutting, join their line.

Another Shanghai institution is Malone's, an American-themed sports bar with a dance floor at ground level and pool table above. Club Le Belle is an increasingly popular wine-bar/night-spot, reputed to stay open long enough on Saturday nights that people can finish dancing in time for Sunday breakfast at Malone's. Further down Nanjing Lu in Jing'an Park is beautiful Bali Lagoona, whose bottom floor is submerged below water level. At the rim of the large circle leading to Jing'An subway station is the Rmb 10 per drink university hangout Windows, where dancers sway to the steamy rhythms of Africa.

If a street could be notorious, it is Julu Lu. The bar names—Goodfellas, Badlands, Latina—remind one of Humphrey Bogart movies. The experience, which hits full swing after 2:00 am, gives the same feel. A real Julu Lu experience means wandering bar to bar as it suits your fancy, meeting other late night prowlers, being harassed by old cigarette sellers or sized up as business prospect/potential threat by prostitutes, and generally having good fun in whichever bar suits your liveliest whims.

Many night-prowlers end up at Julu Lu after spending the early evening on Hengshan Lu. There, for laid-back visiting and Irish music, people move between O'Malley's (another Shanghai institution, with a great outdoor garden for nice weather), and a newer favourite: the Blarney Stone.

Lost and Found
One of Shanghai's best-ever parties was O'Malley's Christmas-season opening in the late 1990's. After a night of mind-blasting fun, two chalkboards appeared at the bar entrance, reading: 'Things Lost' and 'Things Found'. Written under 'Things Lost' were the names of several people who did not emerge for days.

One of Shanghai's best places for live music is the Cotton Club, opposite the American Consulate on Huashan Lu. Guitar- player Greg blew in for "a few weeks" after a gig in Russia, and has yet to leave. The Cotton Club is one of those bars where every once in a while pure music magic happens, and you get to be a part of the kind of night that makes jazz and blues legends.

To see emerging local talent, visit the M-Box, where Hengshan Lu meets Huaihai Lu. Each band plays an hour-plus set, and many an emerging China Spice Girl has been spotted on stage. Across the street is dance club Maya, which has private karaoke rooms with not-so-innocent hostesses. It is sister club to hot dance spot Pegasus, further down Huaihai Lu.

For a Shanghainese nightlife experience, visit Real Love on Hengshan Lu, across from the New Orleans theme bar Bourbon Street. A hot dance spot for Shanghai's university co-eds, Real Love teems on weekend nights with China's real new-generation leaders. Bourbon Street itself is an on-again, off-again hot spot, depending on police 'good' or 'bad' lists. It has fine décor and a cigar bar on top, and when in full swing, it is a great place to dance.

The street of our most consistent fond weekend memories is Maoming Lu. There Judy's Two, elegant sister to the closed firetrap Judy's (where all in Shanghai in the 1980s cut their nightlife 'baby teeth'), starts the weekend with Thursday 1980s nights where you can tear up the dance floor, jump-starting a long weekend with plenty more to go.

As in most places, in Shanghai, bar owners tend to be people of character and stamina. Some are also people of passion, like owner of House of Blues & Jazz, Lin Dongfu. Lin loves jazz that goes beyond the sometimes moribund Big Band of the official Peace Hotel Band. For many years, through many iterations of House of Blues & Jazz, Lin has filled a real music need in Shanghai—and not just as a bar owner. Lin is also the Chinese voice of some of the world's steamiest male stars: he spent his earlier career as a voice-over artist and popular TV actor. A genuine spirit of the soul of Shanghai, past and present, Lin is well worth getting to know.

Anyone who knows Shanghai well knows that when you say you finished the night at the Manhatten Bar, you were in for a long evening and a tender head the next day. The ladies of the Manhatten Bar know regular male customers by name, and know how to treat them well. Across the street from the Manhatten Bar, and a standard that you can bring the new day in with, is Buddha Bar, with its elevated dance floor.

A little more civilised but equally fun, two favourites for enjoying the flow of a Shanghai evening are the Blue Frog and Face. Both are owned/managed by some of Shanghai's finest, creating a unique atmosphere and welcoming feel that will have you lazing the night away laughing, people-watching, and/or kicking up heels.

Two hot dance places at Fuxing Park are favourites with Hong Kong and Taiwanese visitors: Park 97's California, and Guandii. Both play house and trance music, for those who like the throbbing tempo of techno. California was first on the scene, and is still one of Shanghai's top clubs; it is constantly packed. Guandii, opened by a group of Hong Kong celebrities including David Woo, is also attracting vogue crowds. A lower-key old standby is Shanghai Sally's, one of the first independent bars. Sally's hosts visiting comedians, and is still a popular dance spot.

For emerging hot spots, keep an eye on Tai Kang Lu's warehouse district. Home to many art galleries and designer shops, and to the beautifully designed bar Mei, Tai Kang is a fine new addition to Shanghai's emerging arts culture.

A few other spots do not fall easily into neighbourhood divisions, but should not be forgotten. First is Tropicana, a Bund-area salsa heaven with two floor shows choreographed by talented leggy Russian dancers who tailor acts to include Latin band members. With Latin dance teachers and regulars on-site nightly to teach a novice the moves, Tropicana throbs with energy, and is especially fun with a group.

Another spot with outstanding bands is BATs, in the basement of the Pudong Shangri-la. But nothing has more magic than the Glamour Room, at M on the Bund. On weekend evenings, the Glamour Room showcases talented jazz singers, many from overseas. A beautiful venue that does justice to its name, it is one of Shanghai's iconic night spots. Sitting on the balcony at M watching lights go out on the Bund late on a steamy evening with a fat full moon over Shanghai, you will feel the city's magic as nowhere else.

COMPETITIVE KARAOKE

Wherever you travel in China, you'll find a karaoke lounge full of smoke and crooners. Shanghai is no exception. Karaoke was invented for all of us that ever had two-minute fantasies of rock-n-roll stardom, or touching an unrealised love through a song. Karaoke can be sung after plates are cleared at most neighbourhood restaurants; those good at multi-tasking can sing right through dinner—belting out 'Like a Virgin' between bites of spicy tofu. One popular chain of karoake clubs is PartyWorld, with branches in Fuxing Park and on Urumqi Lu near Yan'an Lu. People typically go in groups, piling into private rooms served by dedicated wait-staff, and spend the night punching in song codes, each singer trying to outdo the last. It makes for a great staff outing for teams with a sense of humour, and is fun for anyone at least once.

Ad-lib

One of us had her personal best karoake singing a duet with a man more illiterate than her at reading Chinese prompts. At least she knew the characters for 'man' and 'woman'; he kept singing the woman's part. The team made up words to their 'love song' based on screen images of a dreamy woman by a duck pond at sunset, tossing her hair at intervals. At performance's end, the duet partner's wife asked in wonder: "How did you know the words? Were they in English on that small screen?"

RECREATIONAL GUIDES

The most popular English language lifestyle monthly is *That's Shanghai*, which keeps its proverbial finger on the pulse, and has recently begun publishing a sister monthly in Beijing. Another solid bilingual resource is *City Weekend*. One of the oldest guides is *Shanghai Talk*, best thumbed through for society-column style with lowbrow photos.

Website on Shanghai

Many websites about Shanghai, some affiliated with the magazines above, and others independent, are great resources. One of our favourites is:

http://www.shanghaisoup.com.

Finally, a high-end Chinese-language society magazine has emerged, called *Shanghai Tattler*, loosely affiliated with 'visionary artist' Chen Yifei's growing media/lifestyle brand in China. The best thing about the magazine is its editors' utter disregard for getting people's names right under society photos. Anyone who knows the who's who of Shanghai can get endless entertainment from the ten 'filler names' that keep appearing each edition, regardless of gender, for people not properly identified at the time each photo was taken.

FESTIVALS

This list below is not exhaustive, and includes only the major festivals. For a more complete list, see *Mooncakes and Hungry Ghosts: Festivals of China* (Carol Stepanchuk and Charles Wong; China Books and Periodicals, 1991).

Those marked ** are officially recognised by China's government, and firms must give at least one day off from work with pay (for Spring Festival, employees will expect up to a week). Others are traditional Chinese holidays, but do not require work holidays. China tends to recognize official UN holidays, but does not necessarily grant days off for them.

Traditional Chinese holidays are marked on the lunar calendar, which varies slightly year to year relative to the Gregorian calendar, and are thus it is difficult to provide exact dates.

Major Festivals

1 January

New Year's Day**

Late January–Early March

Spring Festival/Chinese New Year**

Two weeks later

Lantern Festival (15th day of first lunar month)

8 March

International Women's Day

Late March–Mid-April (23rd day of third lunar month)

Birthday of Mazu (religious festival important in South China)

1 May

International Labour Day**

May–June (fifth day of fifth lunar month)

Dragon Boat Festival

September (15th day of eighth lunar month)

Mid-Autumn Festival

1 October

National Day**

December–February (23rd day of 12th lunar month)

Kitchen God reports to Jade Emperor (an important family holiday in Southern and Western China)

In the next section, we will discuss Chinese New Year and some recommendations on how to spend it in Shanghai. Many people prefer to make Chinese New Year in Shanghai a one-time experience and use the vacation time other years to travel. Be forewarned, though, Chinese New Year is a VERY difficult time to travel inside China, as seemingly the entire population of China is travelling then as well. All transport is jammed and reservations must be made many months in advance. Many expats find Chinese New Year a good time to take home leave or vacation outside China.

Chinese New Year

The closest thing to a street party for 15 million that you will ever experience is the Lunar New Year in Shanghai. Anyone old enough to light a match is shooting off fireworks from streets and balconies that would require special permits in other parts of the world. The firework display is a sensory experience as mind numbing as it is dazzling.

It is best to watch 360 degrees of Shanghai illuminated by cascading fireworks from a tall building mid-town. Some brave souls hit the streets and enter the frenzy, but be forewarned: every year sees serious injuries.

A Harrowing Experience

In her first (and last) Chinese New Year at street level, one of us got trapped in the entrance of a large compound as revellers set off bottle rockets that bounced randomly off walls and passing taxis. After ten minutes, when smoke cleared enough to see a way through, she bolted out the entrance, across the street. Traffic was clogged for blocks in both directions, while boxes of factory-made fireworks were being ignited with a cigarette in the street by a pot-bellied 50-year-old who sprinted surprisingly well. Some brave taxi drivers crept by the fireworks, seemingly impervious to the danger of exploding car and passengers.

Forget going to bed before 3:00 am. All Chinese New Year's Eve and through the early morning, chains of firecrackers are lit to chase bad spirits away and encourage wealth, happiness and all of the other good things that make life in Shanghai special.

BEYOND THE BUND: SHANGHAI'S MANY NEIGHBOURHOODS

For many new arrivals, the most immediately striking fact of Shanghai is its architecture, a living object lesson in how cultures shape and are shaped by a sense of space. As historian Tess Johnston has written, in older neighbourhoods 'low Chinese buildings jostle with the Shanghai built by foreigners for foreigners, in the styles of the countries from which they came... The ensuing melange of styles is what makes Shanghai unique'. Meantime, throughout the city, ever-taller newly built towers shape the modern horizon. Materials and styles overlap in levels and layers that form an urban pentimento of all Shanghai's prickly history and a uniquely cosmopolitan setting for the city's contemporary life.

Exploring these paradoxes on foot is an excellent way to start getting to know the city. In the next section, we offer a street-level guide to Shanghai's eclectic neighbourhoods. As local architectural critic Luo Xiaowei has written, 'architecture is the mirror of social life'. For anyone with an aesthetic sense of humor, Shanghai is never dull. Nor is it ever fixed, changeless as a moth on a pin. Shanghai's neighbourhoods are alive, varied, vibrant, works in progress as the city continues to grow.

Of course, this change makes describing Shanghai's neighbourhoods a challenge. One week's favourite walking tour might be flattened the next by a new shopping centre, or razed for a new ring road. That said, city planners are becoming more selective about preserving islands of 'traditional character' (in all the varieties that phrase evokes in Shanghai). Though the metropolis sprawls for kilometres, many of the neighbourhoods still have distinct flavours best savoured at walking pace. We have made every effort to ensure the walking tours suggested below are accurate as of this writing, but with the speed Shanghai changes, some details may well alter by the time the book reaches print. Still, these descriptions should be a useful guide.

One note: we have not attempted to reproduce the many excellent tourist guides to Shanghai, nor yet to provide a street by street treasure-map to lost history. For the former, see *Further Reading* (pages 322–326); for the latter, Pan Ling's *In Search of Old Shanghai* is unmatched. Rather, this section aims to provide new arrivals with a sense of today's Shanghai as Shanghainese see it, while encouraging expats to look beyond the limited neighbourhoods where foreigners most often congregate, and enjoy the city as a whole.

OLD CITY

Before Shanghai was Shanghai, there was a walled village nestled into the bottom of the S-curve of the Huangpu. The arced walls are gone now, replaced by the inner ring roads Zhonghua Lu and Renmin Lu, whose major intersections are still named for former city gates (*men*): Xiaodongmen, Laobeimen, Laoximen. Inside, while many old twisting lanes have been cleared for air-conditioned shopping malls, enough remains for a flavour of traditional Shanghainese life.

Old City is still one of the best areas to see *shikumen*, or 'stone-framed gate' style houses, a uniquely Shanghainese architectural form. These two to three storey stone-and-concrete buildings were mostly arranged in gated lanes (called *longtang*) that housed several families. In this crowded and fire-prone city of vagabonds and thieves, *shikumen* and *longtang* replaced the low wood-frame *siheyuan* courtyard houses and open *hutong* alleys popular in northern China. Many wealthy-but-cautious Shanghaiese families lived in 'great houses', at the end of a *longtang* of lesser homes filled with servants and poor relations, who both disguised and guarded their patron's wealth by their presence. After 1840, many *shikumen* incorporated Western architectural elements, and the remaining *longtang* offer great examples of Shanghai's cultural mixing.

Elite Shanghainese tend to enjoy Old City for its heritage, while middle class residents often find it faintly uncomfortable—a too-vivid reminder of all they have,

An example of *shikumen* (stone-framed gate) residential buildings.

perhaps, only recently escaped. But most visit at least occasionally, if only to buy the famous dumplings at Lao Shanghai Fandian, which has operated for some 300 years. Today's Old City residents are mixed—some elite intellectuals in pricey renovated *shikumen*, next to largely poor workers staying in unrenovated *shikumen* without heat or running water, because they can't afford anywhere else. These poorer residents most often seem happy when their turn comes to relocate to Pudong, as yet another section of the Old City is either razed in favour of tourist shops or renovated for yuppies. Every now and then, though, old-timers resist gentrification and street protests in sections marked with the *chai* ('demolish') character are not unheard-of.

Old City Walking Tour
5–7 km (3–4 miles) depending on exact route

Start at Laoximen, the 'Old West Gate' at the corner of today's Zhonghua Lu and Fuxing Donglu. Proceed north-east on Wenmiao Road (just south of Fuxing) to the Confucius Temple, one of few really ancient buildings remaining, today a thriving open-air book market.

Meander through alleys north and east, crossing Henan Nanlu, watching for vestiges of tradition: old men playing elephant-chess while listening to caged songbirds, girls playing *biandong* with stretched rubber bands (half jump-rope, half cat's-cradle), boys waking their grandmas with firecrackers. You may hear an *erhu* fiddle or someone running through an aria from traditional Kunju opera. In smaller lanes, you may have to duck under laundry, press against the wall as a bridal party passes (accompanied by thundering firecrackers), or hold your nose past a *chou doufu* ('stinky tofu') stand. Enjoy it all. This is the Real Thing—these back-alleys aren't set up for tourists. But watch out for pickpockets—another traditional Shanghai lifeway that years of modernisation have failed to wholly stamp out.

Just south of the Yuyuan complex, make a stop at the Buddhist nunnery Chenxiangge, at 29 Chenxiangge Lu. Built in the Ming Dynasty, it is named after its chief treasure, a statue of the Guanyin Bodhisattva inlaid with agalloch eaglewood (*chenxiangmu* in Mandarin). On rainy days, you can still catch a whiff of its fragrance. Nunnery living areas are closed to casual visitors, but the main courtyards and prayer halls are open to the public in return for a modest donation, and offer an oasis of calm in the bustling Old City.

Eventually, make your way to Lishui Lu, gateway to the complex of shops and restaurants around Yuyuan, the garden retreat of a 15th-century mandarin (today a museum) which has most of the rest of Old City's authentically ancient buildings. The surrounding complexes are recent mock-ups, but well done, and the shops are fun.

Be sure and stop for tea at Huzhongting Teahouse. In business since the 16th century, the probable model for 'Willow Pattern' blue-and-white dishes popular in 19th-century Chinese export porcelains, Huzhongting serves tea in traditional ceremonies, accompanied by upmarket snacks. Afterwards, slip into Yuyuan and just relax. Enjoy the way nooks and crannies throughout that maze of ancient gardens allow the illusion of privacy, even in a space that today is crowded with sightseers.

Leaving the Yuyuan complex you might stop at Lu Bo Lang Restaurant, kitty-corner from Huzhongting. Serious shoppers will want to continue north to narrow little Fuyou Lu. Though most of the stands selling 30s-retro collectibles, real and fake, have been moved indoors, a few street-sellers can still be found, and the indoor flea-market is well worth the price of admission.

Finish meandering your way north through the alleys to Renmin Lu and grab a cab home with your flea-market treasures, secure in the knowledge that at least that part of traditional Shanghai that is marketable for tourists, will never die.

THE BUND

Famous from photographs, stories and song, the consummate image of Shanghailander's Shanghai, the Bund needs little introduction. We won't reproduce here the building-by-building descriptions available in Pan Ling's *In Search of Old Shanghai* or Tess Johnston and Deke Erh's *A Last Look*. That bold swath of Western-style bank buildings and insurance firms, hotels and clubs, some today once again housing their original owners, was built to make that section of Shanghai look like London or New York—and it succeeded. While average Shanghainese today view those symbols of past glory with mixed pleasure, still they come to stroll Huangpu Park and enjoy fresh river breezes. A Bund visit is practically required for expatriates.

Bund Walk
About 2 km (1.2 miles), north to south

In fact, the Bund is worth returning to, to enjoy its many moods. Try strolling Huangpu Park (now open to all races) on a spring afternoon, when breezes off the river whip flags, sending band music scattering over the crowd. Or come on a summer evening to watch the light show on the old buildings, followed by a nightcap at M on the Bund, or dinner on the 20th-floor balcony at Shanghai Mansions, with its sweeping view up the Bund. On a warm day, climb the tower of the old astronomical observatory at the south end of Granite Row, today the Bund Museum. On a cold, rainy evening, walk swiftly beneath those glowering stone façades and pretend you're Marlene Dietrich, or will soon meet her. Go ahead, it's a minor sin to imagine yourself a dramatic role in the city's naughty-glamorous past, and it's free.

FUZHOU LU AND RENMIN SQUARE

The entertainment heart of the former International Concession is today the cultural and political heart of the city. The streets leading from Bund to Renmin Square are studded with arts, crafts and antiquities shops, bookstores and fine restaurants, while the square itself features City Hall and the spectacular new Opera House and Museum.

To appreciate the area's status today requires remembering what it once was. Back in the 1930s, a busy Bund banker might set out after work for the Racecourse, a convenient rickshaw ride away, watch a few races, have drinks at the Jockey Club, then eat at one of the area's upmarket supper clubs. All well and good—but that wasn't the only entertainment the area offered. If he went out afterwards to the naughty Dashijie ('Great World') entertainment centre, or the naughtier Huileli ('Meeting with Happiness Alley', which until 1949 held 150 + bordellos), he probably involved no colleagues, for Shanghailanders were supposed to be above such things.

What Great World Was Like

Hollywood producer Josef von Sternberg, happily for us, was not above such things when he visited Shanghai, and his *Fun in a Chinese Laundry* vividly describes Great World then. He found 'gambling tables, singsong girls, magicians, pickpockets, slot machines… girls whose dresses were slit to their armpits, a stuffed whale, storytellers, peep shows, balloon masks, a mirror maze, two love-letter booths with scribes who guaranteed results, 'rubber goods', and a temple filled with ferocious gods'. On the roof, von Sternberg said, was an open space 'where hundreds of Chinese, so I was told, after spending their last coppers, had speeded the return to the street below by jumping from the roof'.

Tess Johnston interviewed many 'old Shanghailanders', but none would 'admit to ever having been' to Great World in the old days, 'except perhaps once—as a child 'taken there by my Amah'.' This, Johnston says kindly, 'may even have been true'.

Today, Huileli is a residential street, while Great World (which still displays its old name) houses a shopping mall and offices. Government offices help fuel restaurants and shops, which in turn help support movie theatres, a concert hall and several other performance spaces. Apartment towers in the area house mostly well-to-do Shanghainese who enjoy living in the cultural centre; for many locals, it is a natural area to visit for an upmarket evening out. But most expatriates visit, if they do at all, only for the museum or for Western operas. That's a shame, for some of the city's best eating and browsing is nearby for those who can read a Chinese menu or aren't afraid to point.

Walking Tour:
Bund to People's Square via Fuzhou Road
1.5–2 km (0.9–3 miles)

Start on the Bund at the corner of Fuzhou Road, named (in the old spelling) Foochow in the old International Concession, after the ever-prosperous southern Chinese province. Given the utilitarian name *Si-ma-lu* ('Road Number Four') after the establishment of the People's Republic, the road today is once again (in the new spelling) Fuzhou.

On the north side of the street you'll see a five-storey, 32,000-sq-m (344,445-sq-ft) wedding-cake of neo-Greco stone, the original Shanghai headquarters of the Hong Kong and Shanghai Banking Corporation (HSBC). Built in 1923 to the direction of then HSBC director Sir Ronald Macleavy, KCMG, the building is worth a peek at the gorgeous art-deco lobby, with its domed ceiling and 'century mural'. Featuring air-conditioning imported at a cost of ten million taels of silver, and gold coins from around the world buried in the opening ceremony for luck, HSBC's home was known in its day as 'the most elegant building between the Suez Canal and the Bering Straits'. The main door features copper lions, the moulds for which were destroyed to ensure there would be only two pairs; an identical pair guards the entrance to the British museum in London.

When HSBC returned to Shanghai in the 1980s, they reportedly negotiated for the building, but found the price tag asked by local authorities for its return and renovation too exorbitant. Today, it is the headquarters of the Shanghai Pudong Development Bank.

Across Fuzhou road is 9 Zhongshan Road East, former headquarters of the formidable China Merchants Bank, founded by Qing Dynasty Prime Minister Li Hongzhang. Li was a moderniser who sought to import Western industrial innovations to strengthen the dying dynasty. Having witnessed the power of Western warships in the Opium Wars, Li was determined to obtain a modern navy and merchant-marine for China and founded China Merchants as a maritime financier. This headquarters (still today a branch office of China Merchants) was built in 1916 in

One of the copper lions guarding the former HSBC building, now the headquarters of the Shanghai Pudong Development Bank.

Renaissance style. China Merchants, meanwhile, has become arguably China's most successful investment bank, with interests from telecoms to aerospace and beyond.

If you need nourishment, pop into the Bonomi Café, attached to the old HSBC building—founded in 1886 and now in renewed operation. Then head west on Fuzhou Road.

Your first major intersection will be with Jiangxi Zhonglu. Note there the Fuzhou Tower, and its first-floor 'Magic Restaurant', which features nightly performances that are worth taking in at least once. Across the street is the fading but still elegant Metropole Hotel (Xincheng Fandian). Opened 8 September 1934, it was one of Shanghai's chicest spots in the few years before Japan's bombs fell. The semi-circular baroque tower somehow perfectly symbolises Shanghailander excess: it was a birthday gift from Sir Victor Sassoon to his daughter. Today, the Metropole has fully re-opened, including the basement bar (today a disco).

Continuing west on Fuzhou, start looking around, after you cross Henan Beilu, for bookstores, antique and curio shops, music/art stores and shops selling the tools of Chinese calligraphy—inkstones, brushes, rice paper, silk matting—all lovingly displayed, for calligraphy has returned to Shanghai as a refined art for the intellectual elite. This section is called 'Fuzhou Culture Street', and offers some of the best book, music, computer software and other browsing in the city. Since the stores are state-run, you can be reasonably sure most of what they sell is genuine. Meantime, itinerant peddlers selling imitations have blanket stalls right outside. Fuzhou Culture Street has to be one of few places in the world where you can buy real and fake Mont Blanc pens within steps of each other.

Stores of special interest include the China Science and Technology Book Corporation, Foreign Languages Bookstore, Shanghai Ancient Books Store, Scholar Bookstore (a privately-owned chain with a Starbuck's in each branch) and, biggest of all, Shanghai Book City, at 465 Fuzhou Road. This seven-storey palace of books represents some 136 Chinese publishers and features nearly a quarter-million books ranging from literature, history and the arts to geography and the natural sciences. The store also sells audio and video recordings.

Fuzhou Culture Street also houses several media groups and cultural agencies, from Shanghai headquarters of *Guangzhou Daily*, to China headquarters of China's first book club, launched by German media giant Bertlesman. In GIVEMCO Tower (318 Fuzhou Lu, at Shandong Zhonglu) are the Cultural and Educational sections of the German and British Consulates-General.

Should you be hungry, Fuzhou Lu offers abundant choices. From east to west, our top picks are:

- Xinhua Lou (343 Fuzhou), one of Shanghai's best Cantonese restaurants, dating from 1857.
- Wugong Dajiudian (431 Fuzhou) is famed for noodle and fried rice dishes from East China cuisines like Wuxi and Suzhou.
- Laobanzhai (600 Fuzhou) has been offering top Yangzhou-style cooking since 1905.
- Wangbao He (555 Jiujiang) is one of Shanghai's best places for the famous local 'hairy crab' when it's in season, best served with plenty of *huangjiu*, the smooth local rice wine.

Continuing west, across Yunnan Lu, you'll see the Yifu Theatre and Tian Chan Chinese Opera complex, a mecca for fans of everything from Peking opera to Shanghai's Kunju opera to local specialities like Ping Tan, Yu and Hu opera.

Finally, across Xizang Lu, you will reach the massive Renmin Square ('People's Square') which is 137,000 sq m (1,474,655.7 sq ft) large. On your right is City Hall (the large grey marble and granite building) and associated government offices, including the Shanghai Urban Planning Exhibition Centre. Just past them is the Shanghai Grand Theatre, the gleaming new opera, designed by a Sino-French architectural team, and featuring innovative sound baffles from the same sound engineers who created Sydney's Opera House. Directly across the square is an old granite tower with a big clock—a little out of place among the new buildings, but dignified still. It was the former Racecourse clubhouse and the grandstands have since been torn down. Today, it houses part of the Shanghai Library.

To orient yourself spatially, remember that less than 100 m (328 ft) north is the main shopping drag of Nanjing Road. Time orientation requires more adjustment. You might check out basement displays at the Urban Planning Exhibition Centre, with its mock-up of a typical Shanghai street scene circa 1930. As you emerge, looking south on Xizang Lu, you'll see Shaowansheng, a hundred-odd-year-old emporium of pickles and other preserved foodstuffs that was part of that 1930s display, and remains remarkably unchanged. But looking north on Xizang Lu, where there once were low houses, you'll see the towers of Raffles City, an ultra-modern skyscraper complex. In this part of town, the clash of eras can be jarring.

For a longer-term view, finish your walk at the magnificent Shanghai Museum, built in 1996 with some US$ 60 million in donations from corporations and wealthy individuals seeking favour with the government. Private collectors donated much of the museum's 120,000 treasures (some of which were also confiscated from local families after 1949). Today, the unified collection offers a magnificence that is truly timeless.

Designed to look from the outside like a *ding*, or traditional bronze ritual vessel, the Shanghai Museum is state-of-the art, from impeccable bilingual displays (acousti-guide tours available) to preservation techniques that include sensors so many objects are gently lit only when visitors near them. In addition to perhaps the world's top collection of Chinese bronzes, the museum features displays of paintings, ceramics, sculptures, calligraphy, furniture, textiles and ancient seals, which the Chinese used instead of signatures. The museum is a must for anyone with any interest in Chinese culture—which should include every Shanghai expat for at least one visit. Besides, there's a nice teahouse on the second floor where you can rest tired feet.

JING'ANSI AND NANJING ROAD

Further south-west, around the well-to-do area of the old International Concession—once known as Bubbling Well

Road—today rises the gaggle of hotels and offices and high-end shopping centres known as Jing'an District. Historically, and today, Jing'an is from the perspective of average Shanghainese expensive, exclusive and not always welcoming—a source, at times, of tension.

Most expatriates spend a lot of time in Jing'an District, at work and play and perhaps at rest; indeed, some seem to hardly ever leave it. In Chapter 5: Settling, we discussed Jing'an's residential options (*s 58–60*); here, we'll highlight just a few attractions sometimes overlooked by expats, however much time they spend in Jing'an.

First and foremost, the district takes its name from the small but lovely Jing'an Temple on Nanjing Lu near Huashan Lu. Less famous than Jade Buddha Temple and smaller than Longhua, Jing'an is still a gem. Its thick yellow walls shut the world out, offering a refuge of calm amid one of the city's busiest areas. Two other nearby oases are Jing'an Park, and the small but lovely gardens behind the Jing'an Guesthouse.

The heart of expatriate Shanghai is still arguably Shanghai Centre on Nanjing Lu, with its hotel and restaurants, luxury apartment towers and bars, wine shop, cheese shop, Starbucks, City Shopping Groceries, entertainment complex, boutiques and art galleries. You will no doubt spend at least some time in Shanghai Centre, that triumph of expatriate engineering and preferences. When you're tired of noisy Shanghai exuberance and just want to pick up a bagel and mug of Joe and sit in the air-conditioning and pretend you're home, there are few better places. Still, take some time, at least once, to really pay attention to that other extraordinary complex across the street: the old Shanghai Exhibition Centre.

Originally the private residence of Sir Silas Hardoon, the Exhibition Centre was redecorated/rededicated during Sino-Soviet co-operation as the China-Soviet Friendship Hall, and the re-done façades still incorporate red stars and other motifs (most hammers and sickles were removed after the Sino-Soviet split). The oddly church-like exteriors give way inside to muscular paeans to agriculture and industry, with vaulting ceilings and arched doors carved with friezes of heroic farmers and workers with massive plough-horses and tractors.

Today, with little flavour left of either its Sephardic Jewish origins or its detour into Russian motifs, the complex is used for industrial, tourist and other exhibitions. It is worth a wander through. It may still be something of an outdated tribute to an outmoded political philosophy, an anachronism that seems almost blindingly ironic next to that other complex across the street. But it remains one of the first complexes in Shanghai that Shanghainese transformed fully to their own uses after the foreigners left. Most Shanghainese are rather fond of it still, even as its crumbling look ever more out of place in a district more distinguished today by soaring glass and steel.

As Nanjing Road continues to modernise, such vestiges are disappearing or are being moved. The classic traditional Chinese medicine emporium Lei Yun Shang was shifted from Shanghai Centre's neighbourhood to near Jing'an Temple. With advice from McKinsey, Shanghai's government is exploring a Rmb 18 billion plan to refurbish Nanjing Road as a 'world-class commercial street'. It is to be hoped that the renovation plan will leave at least a little local tradition in place.

For now, a few older buildings still adorn Nanjing Road, peeping between the modern façades. Like the wonderful traditional photo shop at the corner of Xikang Lu, full of rental costumes for brides and grooms to deck out as everything from Emperor and Empress to Rhett and Scarlett from *Gone With the Wind*. And in an alley just past Jiangning Lu is an 18th-century opera house turned eatery; the Meilongzhen Restaurant remains a must-try for local fare.

Finally, on Yan'an Lu (history's Avenue Foch—Avenue Edward VII nearer the Bund—the International District's border with the French Quarter), at the corner of Ulumuqi Lu, stands one of th greatest private Shanghailander residences, Marble Hall, home of the Kadoories (see later in this chapter, the section on Jewish History [page 203–209] for details).

THE GUESTHOUSE DISTRICT

South of Jing'an is a graceful area home to many of the wealthiest former French Quarter residents. The sycamores they planted still line streets in this part of town, as do many of their graceful mansions and guesthouses.

Some of these today are restaurants or clubs, others are sub-divided as apartments, and a few still leased whole (see Chapter 5: Settling In [pages 58–70] in for details). A few of the largest have become government-operated guesthouses, offering gracious respites of green space amid the mega-metropolis that are part of why, despite similar populations, Shanghai feels less frenetic than New York. As a result, while relatively few Chinese can afford to live in the guesthouse district (most of those in small *longtang* that once housed servants), it is still an area much enjoyed by most Shanghainese. It's a district of winding roads and small lanes, by far best seen on foot or by bicycle. The following provide only initial suggestions; the entire area is worthy of a stroll.

Guesthouse District Walking Tour:
3.5–4.5 km (2.2–2.8 miles)

Start at the corner of Huashan Lu and Ulumuqi Lu, a block south on Ulumuqi from the Equatorial Hotel. To your north and west is Huadong Hospital, formerly the County Hospital, built by donation 'for the benefit of the foreign residents of Shanghai without distinction as to nationality or religious belief'. Even today, one section is set aside for near-exclusive treatment of foreign residents. The main building was designed by renowned Shanghailander architect Ladislaus Hudec (who also designed Xujiahui and Sheshan Cathedrals); the grounds are also lovely.

Now proceed east on Huashan till it makes a 90-degree turn where Changshu Lu begins heading south. Skip across this intersection onto little Julu Lu and keep heading east, enjoying the old mansions along the way, and the street markets that have sprung up in front of them (noting also the bars and nightclubs you may want to return to some evening!). Turn right (south) on Fumin Lu and follow this to the five-way intersection with Yanqing Lu and Donghu Lu. Follow Donghu Lu and you'll find the Donghu (East Lake) Guesthouse on your right, which now houses a gated complex of luxury garden villas that rent for upwards of US$ 15,000 per month, nearly 100 per cent to business executives whose firms are not exactly firm about housing budgets. The complex also features Club 7, an upmarket eatery and cigar bar.

The Donghu's lawns and gardens are pleasant to stroll, and most foreigners will not be disturbed. Technically, however, they are a private pleasure reserved for villa residents and outsiders (particularly, alas, Chinese outsiders) wandering too far from the open area around Club 7 may be evicted upon any complaint from a resident. The irony of selective eviction of Chinese, even today, from these lovely gardens in the heart of a Chinese city, is not lost on most Shanghainese; there is an excruciating depiction of such an eviction in Zhou Weicui's *Shanghai Baby*.

At the next corner is Huaihai Zhonglu—history's Avenue Joffre, the great shopping street of the French Concession, and still a major commercial strip. Browse shops and boutiques as you head east on Huaihai, then turn north on Maoming Lu.

On your left will be the Garden Hotel Shanghai, whose delightful gardens are, thankfully, open to all. After a stroll in them to clear away street dust, pop into the hotel. You might try one of the coffee shops in the old two-storey art-deco masterpiece that was the former Cercle Sportif Francais (the old French club), one of few private drinking and sporting clubs from Shanghailander days that admitted women. Should you want something upmarket, let elevators whisk you to the top of the modern 34-storey tower added to the Garden by Japan's Okura chain. There you'll find one of the best Japanese restaurants where you will ever have the pleasure of dining.

Across the street from the Garden Hotel is the Jinjiang, a complex of hotel, apartments and offices that includes the magnificently restored Grosvenor House, where several US presidents, UK premiers and other global leaders have held banquets for government hosts in Shanghai. There is rumoured to be a secret underground passage between the Garden and the Jinjiang that Mao Zedong used to reach the swimming pool.

Once you've explored the Garden and Jinjiang, head east on Changle Lu, one block north, to Ruijin Lu. Turn right onto Ruijin and walk about 2 km (1.2 miles) south, enjoying the mix of architecture and boutiques along the way. Half a block south of Fuxing Zhong Lu, on your right, you'll find the Ruijin Guesthouse, whose graceful buildings include wide verandas with porch swings, one of the best places for cool drinks on a hot Shanghai day. The Ruijin's #1 Building had the dubious distinction of housing Jiang Qing in luxury reserved for her use on visits to Shanghai after becoming Madame Mao. Today, her rooms are rented out as a hotel suite. You, too, can lie in the bed of the Greatest Harpy of All Time, for just US$ 240 a night.

Just across from the Maoming Lu entrance to Ruijin guesthouse, and up an alley, is the Bird and Flower Market, a colourful mass of plant and animal life that must be seen to be appreciated, and an excellent place to accessorise your apartment. The market grew on the site of the former Canidrome, a dog-racing track which, with its clubhouse ballroom, was once one of Shanghai's premier hot spots. At the far end of the Bird and Flower Market is a delightful bookstore/café called the Old China Hand Reading Room, a good place to browse, relax and finish your Guesthouse District tour.

THE FRENCH CONNECTION: LU WAN DISTRICT

From the larger perspective of modern Chinese history, the French Concession's great contribution was not lovely guesthouses, but the shelter that tolerant French magistrates of the 1920s and 1930s gave zealous Chinese men and women with revolutionary ideas. Political meetings were illegal but the Gendarmes pursued organisers with little zeal. Most early founders of the Chinese Communist Party (CCP) sheltered at some point in the French Concession from Nationalist Party (Kuomintang or KMT) witch hunts. Many key intellectual/political leaders (from Mao to Sun Yat Sen, Kang Youwei to Zhou Enlai to Lu Xun) lived there for years, and as discussed above, it is no accident that the CCP was founded there.

A surprisingly concentrated district, traditionally called Lu Wan, held the cafés and apartments and underground printshops where revolutionaries congregated, often behind shops on fashionable Huaihai Lu (then called Avenue Joffre). Several revolutionary haunts have been lovingly preserved as shrines to the birth of modern China. Others have been converted into upmarket shopping/ dining venues, especially in

Whatever one feels about the CCP today, or the several disastrous meanders in its history, it is hard not to admire those intense young dreamers who founded it and saw it through the revolution. Armed (at first) only with ideas, with a vision of a world redeemed from opium barons and starving coolies, and with the courage to keep writing and speaking despite KMT death threats, these revolutionaries were perhaps the ultimate proof that pen can be mightier than sword. That many of their ideas have failed the test of time, that later leaders perverted their vision or simply fell into corruption, does not make them wholly wrong or unworthy of respect the newly renovated slice of historic Lu Wan known as Xintiandi.

Proudly aware of how their city is helping drive the engines of China's markets, most Shanghainese give lip service at best to revolutionary teachings today—but most still take some pride in their city's role in the revolution. It is worth the time of expats today to make the pilgrimage to the former haunts of the visionaries, to remember and reflect.

It is also worth enjoying the stores and shops of the now once-again fashionable Huaihai Lu, and of Xintiandi. The irony of Lu Wan's mix of Chinese tradition, colonial legacy, Marxist-Leninist-Maoist icons, and modern materialism would not have been lost on Lu Xun or his contemporaries. It's all just part of what makes Shanghai unique.

French Connection/ Lu Wan Walking Tour
5–6 km (3–3.7 miles)

Start at Fuxing Park, one of Shanghai's finest, planned by the French Concession Council in 1909 with two major scenic areas. The park's north end features flowers and green areas in European-style gardens with fountains and pools (look for the pool with the marble statue of Marx and Engels, added after China's Revolution). The park's south end is a Chinese traditional garden, with rockeries, corridors and waterside pavilions. Today, Fuxing features several hot entertainment spots as well (see pages 166–173 earlier in this chapter for details).

As you wander Fuxing Park today, bright with flowers and Mylar balloons, take some time to picture the scenes of the 1920s. Perhaps there, in the shelter of those large old sycamores, Lu Xun read essays to eager students. Over there, by the fountain: perhaps the stolid peasant-teacher Mao Zedong (who never left China) sat in the café beside it, drinking green tea and debating historical necessity with a young Zhou Enlai, just returned from his studies in Paris. Back yonder, in that small granite house with the arched doors at No. 7 Xiangshan Road (the south-west corner of the park), revolutionaries certainly gathered for wisdom and blessings from Dr Sun Yat Sen. His residence, a two-storey building

For those familiar with US history, Sun is China's Ben Franklin—the elder statesman counselling caution to young hotheads in his circle—with the tragic difference that Sun's circle was divided. Sun strove to bridge the gap between KMT and CCP. It was on the lawn of this house, where he lived from 1918–1924, that Sun arranged the first meeting between Communist and Nationalist party representatives, in September 1922. That meeting helped bring together the short-lived 'United Front' against Japanese aggression. Tragically, as mentioned earlier, the United Front ended in a blood bath in 1927 when Chiang Kai Shek responded to concerns in the foreign community about 'Reds', and turned the KMT army against the largely unarmed backers of the CCP.

bought for and presented to him by Chinese Canadians in 1918, is today a museum and well worth a visit.

That Dr Sun never permanently healed the inter-Party breach seems to have been one of several great life disappointments. After years of fomenting revolution against the corrupt last emperors of the Qing Dynasty, Sun was in exile in Denver when the Qing finally fell in 1911. Returning to China, he saw the principles of 'his' revolution ravaged in the bitter warlord years. He failed in several alliances with seemingly 'enlightened' warlords, before allying with the Soviet Union and the CCP. Perhaps the most fortunate event of Sun's eventful life was his timely death in 1925, before the United Front fell apart, early enough for him to be remembered yet today in both the mainland and Taiwan as the 'Father of Modern China'.

Enjoy the Sun Yat Sen museum, and take time to visit the ShangArt gallery next door. Then exit Fuxing Park, turning west on Fuxing Zhonglu. At No. 517 Fuxing Zhonglu, you'll find the former residence of Liu Yazi, one of the gentler war-era revolutionaries, an example of how even small acts of defiance reverberated during the Japanese occupation. Liu is best remembered for locking himself into his house, refusing to exchange courtesies with the new overlords. In a gesture poignant with all the stifled feelings of the occupied Chinese, he re-dedicated his house with the name for which it is remembered still: the Temple for Being Buried Alive.

Continue on Fuxing to the intersection with Sinan Lu and turn left (south). At No. 73 Sinan Lu, you'll find the former residence of Zhou Enlai. Modern China's most beloved premier is best remembered in the West as the urbane statesman who negotiated with world leaders from India's Nehru to US President Nixon. Within China, Zhou is remembered as the gentle mediator who strove to mitigate Mao's worst excesses. His pre-war Shanghai home is as graceful as his memory deserves. He stares out of youthful photographs, disturbingly direct, with a challenge that borders on arrogance. His later photos seem softer, ever more cautious and veiled as the years went by. His death in 1976 released a wave of national mourning that in some ways has never stopped.

Continue to No. 87 Sinan Lu and turn for a moment from revolutionary to artistic history. This four-storey Spanish-style garden house was the Shanghai residence of famed Peking opera star Mei Lanfang. Here he kept his wife, mother-in-law and several sons and daughters all through the war. Like Liu Yazi, Mei locked himself in during Japan's occupation and refused to perform onstage for eight years until China was again free—an act for which, more even than his legendary singing, Mei is revered.

Returning to Fuxing Zhonglu, turn right (east), noting the mix of relatively well-preserved old French villas with modern construction, where buildings were knocked down for the Chongqing Nanlu flyover. Among the few historic buildings well-preserved is No. 185 Chongqing Nanlu, the wartime home and office of American journalist Agnes Smedley, a CCP sympathiser and colleague of Edgar Snow. Many key leftist intellectuals and artists met here while Smedley was in residence, from 1929–1931.

Continuing to Huangpi Nanlu, turn north and proceed to No. 338, the 30,000-sq-m (322,917-sq-ft) historic, cultural and commercial development known as Xintiandi. Designed by an international consortium experienced with historic reconstruction and managed by Hong Kong's Shui On Development Group, Xintiandi is fast becoming a Shanghai cultural and entertainment mecca.

The north block of Xintiandi has filled meticulously restored *shikumen* residences with some 30 fashion and antique stores, and with fine restaurants, pubs and

'Xintiandi' literally means 'new paradise', or 'new horizon'. It represents, for many, a new stage in Sino-foreign co-operation towards returning Shanghai to its once-and-future greatness. Already, many are saying it will be a model for the planned renovation of the rest of this graceful district.

cafés featuring international cuisines. The south block was completely rebuilt, and features retail, dining, recreation, KTV and cinemas in contemporary architecture. Between south and north blocks, high-end residential towers are under construction around a man-made lake. As of this writing, despite unfinished construction and a price tag of US$ 2,000 per sq m, all flats have sold out.

Before leaving Lu Wan, visit one last 'sacred site' from the revolutionary era, at No. 374 Huangpi Nanlu/No. 76 Xingye Lu (the building straddles the corner). This small museum commemorates the First National Congress of the CCP, held here in the home of then-delegate Comrade Li Hanjun on 23 July 1921. Thirteen representatives of then 53 total Party members attended, developing the first Party constitution and electing leaders who helped organise the CCP's official establishment. French Gendarmes raided the meeting and turned the young comrades out, but then showed their relative tolerance; instead of being arrested, the revolutionaries were

The First National Congress of the Chinese Communist Part was held in this building.

released with a warning. They finished their meeting on a boat in Nan Hu Lake in Zhejiang Province on 30 July.

Two other famous revolutionaries lived outside the French Concession. Lu Xun's residence is in the northern suburb of Dabazi, and Sun Yat Sen's beloved widow Soong Qingling lived for years after his death in a modest house on Tianping Lu. Both of these are now museums worthy of a visit, on another day.

Simon Leys has noted that of the 13 comrades at that original meeting, five were later executed by the KMT, four more defected to the KMT and were killed in the war or executed as spies, and two were beaten to death by Red Guards in the 1960s. Only two original delegates—Dong Biwu and Mao Zedong—died of old age, a ratio that's perhaps an apt symbol of the Party's tortuous history.

For now, retrace your steps and rest tired feet while sipping a cappuccino in Xintiandi, with the site of the CCP's First National Congress in view, while reflecting on the oddments and ironies of history in Shanghai.

XUJIAHUI AND LONGHUA: MARTYRS CHRISTIAN AND COMMUNIST

The Xujiahui (formerly 'Siccawei') area was the far southwest corner of the French Concession, and site, then, of a great French-Jesuit college offering studies from chemistry to meteorology (part of their astronomical observatory still remains). They also engaged Czech-born Shanghailander architect Ladislaus Hudec to design what is arguably China's loveliest Western-style religious site, St Ignatius, a soaring building that can stand with the best European cathedrals.

Much of the Jesuit college has been transformed into campus for today's Jiaotong University. St Ignatius, now renamed 'Xujiahui Cathedral', also remains active, offering regular services, drawing hundreds if not thousands of Chinese Christians, and welcoming Western visitors as well.

Most Shanghainese today know Xujiahui better, though, for worship of a more commercial sort. A cluster of high-end shopping malls offer top brands in a slick, glass-and-neon space geared to the high-tech tastes of China's Generation X. It is worth a wander through the interconnected malls centred in the traffic circle where Caoxi Lu meets Huashan Lu and Zhaojiabang Lu, to get in touch with the latest in Chinese pop culture. If you like, you can then retreat into Xujiahui Cathedral at 158 Puxi Lu for some reflection; up-to-the-minute-ism meets timelessness.

Further to the south is the Longhua area, named for Longhua Temple, Shanghai's largest Buddhist complex. Longhua is a livably interesting residential area where expat and Chinese residents mix far more readily than in, say, Jing'an. Today's Longhua boasts apartment towers, a subway stop and the massive Shanghai Stadium (with attached gymnasium complex), where soccer cheers help quiet ghosts of the district's difficult past (see below). The district also includes small Longhua Airfield, commandeered by the Japanese in World War II and used as a prison camp for expatriate prisoners of war, as in the film *Empire of the Sun*.

Longhua Walking Tour:
Total distance 4–5 km (2.5–3 miles), depending on park route

Start on Longhua Lu, at the main gate of Longhua Martyrs Park (Longhua Lieshi Gongyuan), also called the Cemetery of the Martyrs. This stately park of marble and granite walkways and monuments commemorates several groups of CCP martyrs killed in Shanghai between 1924–1949. Wander north through the park, past sculptures both overwrought and haunting, and you'll come to a small cemetery where cremated remains were interred. Many cemetery markers bear porcelain copies of photos; take some time to look at those terribly young faces on the graves and reflect on why their deaths are still mourned in this city.

The park also offers lighter entertainment, as children play while their parents practise Tai Ji Quan or ballroom dancing, for open space is too rare in Shanghai to reserve for solemnity alone. But on Martyr's Park's eastern edge stands a row of whitewashed buildings with barred windows that demand solemnity. This now-refurbished museum was first built as a prison. It served as a warlord lock-up for 1916 rebels, a KMT hold for suspected Reds, and a pen for Japanese war prisoners (including some foreigners). But Shanghainese remember it best for the night of 7 February 1934, when KMT guards, under order to eliminate Reds, opened fire into locked cells, killing 24 early CCP leaders, the '24 Martyrs of Longhua'. You can wander into the small cells with their high, tiny windows, and imagine just what that was like.

Exiting the prison buildings, go out the east gate of Martyr's Park and turn right on Wanping Lu, past Longhua Hotel, to the juncture with Longhua Lu. Follow Longhua around a curve to your right to Longhua Temple, where noisy temple gongs and incense pouring from barrel-sized burners should help clear away prison ghosts. The buildings are mostly open and, if you're of a mind, the temple also features a fine vegetarian restaurant, jointly managed with Longhua Hotel.

From the temple gate, turn left again on Longhua Lu, then follow as it curves through the 'Hy.Mall' shopping complex (built in 1999 to imitate circa 1799 architecture), becoming Longhua East Road, and past a Kentucky Fried Chicken (for those unready for temple fare). Continue to the first light, which in this confusing part of town proves to be the intersection of Longhua East Road with Longhua West Road. Turn left (south) onto Longhua West Road and continue past several apartment buildings and over Longhua Creek. Perhaps 200 m (656.2 ft) ahead, you'll see some cracked tarmac and the crumbling remains of a control tower. This is all that remains of Longhua Airport.

It was a fashionable place in its day, where Shanghai ladies in gorgeous *cheongsam* might gather for aperitifs while waiting (or pretending to wait) for foreign boyfriends to return from Hong Kong. Then, in the dog days of World War II, as Japan's control over Shanghai crumbled, foreigners by the thousands got herded into a tent city on that tarmac. Unless it has been developed into a disco by the time you read this, you can walk right into the old waiting room and listen to echoes. Out back, you'll see more tarmac, though less each year as an apartment complex eats steadily closer to the new buildings on the left: appropriately enough, the vocational school of China's Civil Aviation Administration, the CAAC.

The Chanel Mystery

Retrace steps back out of the hangar and turn right onto Fenguo Lu, passing the CAAC complex on your left. At the back of the compound, you'll see three planes—probably in some disrepair, since they're regularly disassembled by students learning aviation fundamentals. There's an old B-3406 twin-prop from the early days of China Eastern Airlines, an older A-64 from the now-defunct revolutionary Chinese People's Airline, and a war-era biplane incongruously branded 'Chanel'. If anyone reading this can solve the wee mystery of how a Coco Chanel-branded biplane ended up abandoned at Longhua Airfield, the authors would appreciate hearing from you.

On your right, about level with the biplane (unless it has been built on by the time you read this), you'll see the main airfield runway, where many *Empire of the Sun* prison tents were set up. Take a moment to listen to wind off the runway whistle through the biplane's creaking prop, say a quick *sic transit gloria mundi* for all that history gone by, and be on your way.

HONGQIAO: MISTRESSVILLE AND THE SUBURBS OF THE WEST

In Shanghailander days, Hongqiao was 'Pudong': the up-and-coming commercial district. Hongqiao Airport, built in the 1970s, made Hongqiao the fashionable suburb of Western Shanghai. Apartment towers went up and older guesthouses were refurbished. But before Hongqiao really took off, plans for Pudong emerged and Hongqiao became the 'also-ran' of Shanghai's future. Today, it remains an odd mix of commercial, residential and warehouse areas, convenient to the ageing Hongqiao Airport (still used for domestic flights) but rather far from the Bund and Pudong. Residents are a mix of Shanghainese and expats who enjoy open space fairly near city centre, at prices less astronomical than the Guesthouse District.

Hongqiao is too spread out for walking tours, but key points of interest include:
- The Shanghai Zoo, with its fine collection of pandas and other fauna

- The Xijiao Guesthouse, with decent restaurants and lovely grounds that are a delight to walk around. The garden apartments and villas in the Xijiao, while expensive, are more affordable than counterparts downtown (*see* Chapter 5: Settling In, *pages 55–70*).

- The Big Fan Restaurant, serving wonderful traditional Shanghainese food in a '30s-retro setting, part of a complex of Spanish-style villas that, in the 1930s, housed General Claire Chennault's Flying Tigers. Just west is the Sassoon Villa, built in British Tudor style by the Iraqi Jew Sir Victor Sassoon, today owned by a Japanese business. Just east are several fine faux-antique furniture shops, where 1930s chests and armoires are refinished to look like Ming.

- A little further west on Hongqiao Lu is *tai-tai cheng*, or 'Mistressville'. This complex of faux-Greek and Italianate temples and palazzos houses many families and married couples, expat and Chinese. But enough apartments act as love nests for Shanghainese mistresses of mostly Asian businessmen to give the area its name. And the ratio of pricey restaurants to vegetable markets in the neighbourhood gives credence to the thought that many residents are not cooking on a budget.

JEWISH HISTORY AND THE HONGKOU 'GHETTO'

Vestiges of Jewish history remain throughout Shanghai. Key highlights are as follows.

Ohel Rachel Synagogue and the Shanghai Jewish School

500 Shaanxi North Road is the most important Jewish community building remaining. From 1920–1952 (except for two years during World War II), it was the primary synagogue for Shanghai's Sephardic community, founded by Sir Jacob Sassoon in memory of his wife and consecrated by Rabbi W Hirsch. The buildings are now occupied by the Shanghai Education Bureau; appointments are required to visit (and can be arranged by today's Shanghai Jewish community).

The Shanghai Jewish School was founded in 1900 by DEJ Abraham, on the grounds of the former Shearith Israel synagogue, and transferred to this location in 1932 by Horace Kadoorie. All other buildings are post-1952. There used to be a Mikveh beside the school (where there is now a six-storey building), and a separate entrance on Xinzha Lu (still visible).

Pacific Gardens and the Toeg House

With the synagogue nearby, Shaanxi North Road had many Iraqi Jewish residences. Pacific Gardens (near Beijing Xilu) was popular with upper middle-class families like the Abrahams, who carried British passports, and spent the war in Longhua Prison. The Toegs were in the second tier of rich Iraqi Jews; their house was split for ten families after they left in 1951. The Toegs were very involved in the community and synagogue; during the Japanese occupation, the synagogue furniture and Torah scrolls were hidden in their house.

Old Market Area, Uptown Theatre, Jewish Shops

Further down Shaanxi North Road, turn west on Nanjing Road. This area had many small Jewish retail shops because of the high concentration of customers. Today, Shaanxi North Road has a church on the right just past Beijing Road. Just across from it, on the back lot of what is today a skyscraper, there once was a thriving multi-storey market (with a kosher butcher) where Jews of all nationalities shopped and many languages could be heard. The Uptown Theatre was a landmark, where local residents attended new films; it still stands at the south-west corner of Nanjing Road and Shaanxi North Road. Heading west towards the Portman, you will pass the Mandarin Hotel on your left, where a Jewish bakery once stood.

Exhibition Hall, Originally Hardoon Gardens

Sir Silas Hardoon was among the most flamboyant Shanghailanders—and known as one of the richest. A Sassoon employee, he branched out on his own into real estate. Rumour claimed he was forced to pay for paving

Nanjing East Road when city leaders learned he owned 40 per cent of the buildings on the street. Although he built Beth Aharon synagogue (after, he said, having a dream about it), he was not overly close to the Jewish community and married a Eurasian prostitute. They adopted over 20 Chinese orphans and built Japanese and Chinese gardens on their huge estate, today the Shanghai Exhibition Centre. Old Shanghainese still know it as Hardoon Gardens. The street immediately to its west was originally Hardoon Road.

Marble Hall

Sir Horace Kadoorie was one of the three richest members of Shanghai's Jewish community (together with Hardoon and Sassoon). His magnificent residence, Marble Hall, includes an 85-foot ballroom, and originally had 43 servants and 18-foot chandeliers in every bedroom. It still stands today, across from the Equatorial Hotel. You can sneak a peak without an appointment as it is, today, the municipal Children's Palace.

Abraham, Hayim, Moses and Ezra Houses

No longer easily accessible because of walls or ownership, these residences are some of the loveliest remaining. Ezra House on Huaihai Lu is quite impressive, but is currently an army compound and only visible from the street. The Ezras were among Shanghai's first Zionists and started the city's first Jewish newspaper, *Israel's Messenger*, in 1904. DEJ Abraham was president of the Sephardic community for many years, and his huge mansion was the place of Shabbat football (soccer) matches during the 1930s. It is now also occupied by the army and hard to see. Hayim house was behind it. Moses house on Huashan Road was very close to the British School and is now part of the East China Hospital.

Jewish Club/Music Conservatory

On Fenyang Lu, south of Huaihai Road, was a Russian Jewish Club that eventually became a club for the whole community. News of the establishment of the State of Israel, including

Prime Minister David Ben-Gurion's speech, was read here in 1948; most fitting, as Russians were the greatest Zionists in Shanghai. The club is, today, the Shanghai Conservatory of Music and is open to the public. This is also a fitting tribute; Jews from central Europe and Russia trained many of city's leading musicians for decades.

Jewish Hospital/Eye-Nose Hospital

The Shanghai Jewish Hospital at 83 Fenyang Lu was originally the B'nai Brith Polyclinic. Founded in 1934, it adopted its new name in 1942, when headed by Dr Max Steiman. Today, the site is the Shanghai Otolaryngological Hospital. While not as great as in music, Jewish influence on medicine was also significant. Jewish German doctors played a large role after their arrival in the late 1930s.

Jewish Recreation Club

On Maoming Beilu, around the corner from the Abraham house (probably today's No. 39), this building was the centre of Jewish sports. Originally run by Russians, it also later opened to the whole Jewish community. Jews led Shanghai in boxing and had strong football and other teams. Leo Meyer, a German refugee, had been a star in Dusseldorf and led the refugee team to a close second in the 1939 Shanghai league championships, and to victory in the same year's mini-soccer championship. The Jewish Recreation Club also hosted Mir Yeshiva students teaching local Jews about Judaism. Although most *yeshiva* students studied elsewhere, the classes held here eventually led several Jews from various communities to join Mir after the war. Mir was the only East-European *yeshiva* to survive the war fully intact.

Original Cemetery

Originally known as the 'Israeli Cemetery' and later as the 'Mohawk Cemetery' (because it was on Mohawk Road), this was the first of four Jewish cemetaries in Shanghai; today, the site is a small park on the corner of Huangpi Beilu and Nanjing Lu. When opened in 1862, the area was the city's western edge; later, it would border the racecourse (today's Renmin

Square). All four Shanghai Jewish cemeteries were moved to the western suburbs in the 1950s, then destroyed during the Cultural Revolution, in the 1960s. There remain only two Kadoorie graves, in Soong Qingling Park in Hongqiao.

Stars of David on Building

Further down Nanjing Lu, turn right onto Xichang Lu, passing the racecourse tower on your right. Follow this narrow street one block. On your left, you will see a building decorated with Stars of David. This decorative motif was used by Sephardim throughout East Asia and can be seen in Singapore and elsewhere. Sir Silas Hardoon may have built this building as middle-class housing; he certainly owned a number of buildings of that type in this area.

Beth Aharon Synagogue

The Beth Aharon synagogue was located where a small office building stands today at No. 42 Huqiu Lu, off Beijing Lu near the Bund. It was built in 1927 by Sir Silas Hardoon in his father's memory and demolished in 1985. One large stone Menorah was saved and preserved by the Shanghai Museum. It was loaned to the United States Holocaust Museum in 2000 for an exhibit.

Hongkou

The central experience for most Shanghai Jews was the ghetto, in the district history called Hongkew (in Pinyin: Hongkou). Here, from 1943–1945, all but the wealthiest of the city's Jews were forced to live by Japanese occupiers seeking to appease their German allies.

The area had been badly damaged in the 1937 fighting between Japanese and Chinese forces. When the refugees came to Shanghai starting in 1938, many moved here because rents were significantly lower than elsewhere, since so much had to be rebuilt. When the Ghetto was established, this part of Shanghai was an obvious choice. Those that had built a life for themselves and even owned property in other parts of Shanghai were forced to move here, often at great economic loss.

Still, this was never a Ghetto in the European sense, as over 100,000 Chinese also lived in the area, and Jews with passes could leave to work in other parts of the city. Although ghetto conditions were desperate at times because of limited supplies, the Japanese never followed their German allies' requests to exterminate the Jews.

Today, Hongkou is a commercial, light industrial and residential district with a nearly 100 per cent Chinese middle- and working-class population. Local residents are still proudly aware of their district's history and of the role Shanghai played in saving more than 25,000 Jews from Hitler. Almost anyone will be happy to point you to the Jewish Museum or the Ghetto Memorial Statue.

Hongkou Walking Tour

The best way to see the district is to take a tour with local amateur historian and accomplished guide Wang Faliang. Call the Hongkou Jewish Museum in the historic Ohel Moishe Synagogue [tel: (021) 6512-0229] for an appointment. Wang Faliang lived in Hongkou during the war, and has been giving tours for many years.

Located at 62 Changyang Road (formerly Ward Road) in Hongkou district, Ohel Moishe marks the start of any Hongkou Ghetto tour. It's worth noting, though, that the synagogue itself predates the ghetto. It was originally constructed for the Russian immigrant community in 1927, led by Rabbi Ashkenazi, the city's most prominent rabbi of the late 1920s and 1930s. The 1927 building went up to house a rapidly expanding community that had started in an earlier building (also called Ohel Moishe), established on Hengsheng Road in the old French Concession in 1907. The headquarters of the Zionist youth organisation Brith Trumpeldor (Betar) was set up in this latter Ohel Moishe. Today, a small museum on the third floor of Ohel Moishe remembers the World War II refugees who found safety in Shanghai.

Make a right out of Ohel Moishe, then a sharp right down a narrow street of small stores and walk to Huoshan Road (history's Wayside Road). Cross Huoshan and walk left a few meters, to enter Huoshan Park. Roughly in the park's centre stands a memorial set up in 1994 to honour the city's role in saving refugees from the Holocaust.

There are many other vestiges of the community in Hongkou; check with Ohel Moishe and/or Wang Faliang for details. You can also check

http://www.chinajewish.org

for information on services and contact details for today's Shanghai Jewish community.

PUDONG

Pudong is, of course, the future of Shanghai writ large, etched high in the new skyline and flung out in kilometers of factories and residential districts. The Pudong New District (the former 'Pudong Development Zone') extends over a triangle of land 523 sq km (201.9 sq miles) in size, bounded by the Huangpu River on the east, the Yangtze's mouth to the south-west, and the Chuangyang River and East China Sea on the north, providing a good natural harbour that is currently being expanded.

For some 1,300 years after first settlement, Pudong was a fishing village and farmer's fields—some archaeologists believe the earliest Shanghai-area settlements were in Pudong. The site of a few riverfront warehouses and workshops in the Jazz Era, Pudong remained woefully underdeveloped until being blessed by late leader Deng Xiaoping in the early 1990s, when it became China's Miracle Mile.

Pudong New District is divided into five 'economic growth zones', each with a unique focus, all served by the new Shanghai Pudong International Airport:

- Waigaoqiao-Gaoqiao is a 10 sq km (3.9 sq miles) free trade zone with a modern harbour. Many firms have settled there, taking advantage of special tax and other benefits.
- Qingningsi-Jinqiao is a manufacturing zone focused on machinery
- Zhoujiadu-Liuli focuses on steel, iron and industrial glass
- Beicai-Zhangjiang encourages high-tech and emerging industry firms, and has attracted many computer hardware/software firms, education and R&D facilities

- Lujiazui-Huamu is Shanghai's Wall or Bond Street. Also called the 'New Bund', Lujiazui houses many banks, insurance houses and securities firms, as well as the stock exchange, Customs and many high-end apartment towers.

When most people speak of Pudong, they really mean the 28 sq km (10.8 sq miles) of Lujiazui, the 'miracle within the miracle', created by fiat when the government moved there not only the Stock Exchange, but also specialised exchanges in real estate, properties, human resources and diamonds. Today, Lujiazui is the heart of Pudong, and top Lujuazui real estate is now more expensive than Puxi. Sought-after residential developments are served by fine restaurants and by shopping/entertainment complexes like 'Super-Brand Mall', created by the team that designed 'Mall of America'.

Lujiazui includes several structures that are important, symbolically, to Shanghainese. Premier among these of course is the Oriental Pearl TV Tower (tallest in China and third in the Asia-Pacific Region), with 11 spherical areas that offer restaurants, discos and the fine new Museum of Shanghai History.

At the foot of the Pearl is the Shanghai International Convention Centre, a state-of-the-art meeting facility whose first major test was housing the first APEC regional meeting to which China had ever played host. Convention halls, function rooms, a media centre and the Oriental Riverside Hotel complete this 45,000-sq-m (484,376-sq-ft) facility, which also offers the chic new Seagull Restaurant, with excellent river views.

Just down the street is Jinmao Tower, China's tallest and —as of this writing—the third-tallest building in the world. The 420.5-m (1,379.6-ft) tower, designed in pagoda shape by SOM Design, includes a three-storey basement, 88 floors of offices, a scenic deck and the Grand Hyatt Hotel. It was financed by China's five top import-export companies.

This planned district, sprouted in little more than a decade from farm fields, can be overwhelming and almost alarming in its rapid-growth sanitised modernity: sort of Walt Disney meets the Blitzkrieg. But Pudong can also be enormously

Resembling a pagoda is China's tallest building, Jinma Tower.

pleasant. What it lacks in historical character compared with Puxi, it certainly makes up for in cleanliness and convenience, and it's hard not to admire the spirit that built it.

Three areas in Pudong particularly rate walking around:

- Waterfront Avenue (Binjiang Dadao), from the Seagull Restaurant down, makes a fine stroll on a warm day. You can catch breezes off the river, look at the old Bund and savour contrasts with the new. End at the Oriental Pearl, where you can (and should) tour the history museum for a longer term perspective, then zoom to the observation deck at the top and get a sense of the city as a whole.

- Century Avenue (Shiji Dadao), the so-called 'Champs Elysee' of Shanghai, links the Oriental Pearl with the Pudong New District Cultural Centre. The boulevard is 5 km (3.1 miles) long and some 100 m (328.1 ft) wide, and along the way are eight themed botanical gardens and special sculptures.

- Meantime, Century Park (Shiji Gongyuan) at 1001 Jinxiu Lu, is worth a wander as an excellent example of modern urban planning. In sight of the Jinmao and other Financial District skyscrapers, this 1.4 million sq m (about 15 million sq ft) park offers green fields, wooded areas, artificial lakes and meadows that offer picnic grounds for crowds to come and watch firework displays and laser shows above the river. Century Park is one of the places to catch a subway to and from Puxi. There are also two bridges and two tunnels linking the sides of the rivers, and taxis are not terribly expensive between the two. And at least once, you should ride the French-imported train through the 'Pujiang Tourist Tunnel', linking the Oriental Pearl with the statue of former Shanghai Mayor Chen Yi on the Bund side some 647 m (2,122.7 ft) away. The 5-minute ride includes computer-controlled laser light-and-sound shows, taking you on a 'time journey' between the Old Bund and the New.

PAST CITY LIMITS

For those who, at times, crave green and open spaces or quiet traditional culture, Shanghai's pleasures can at times feel a

TRIGG.

bit overwhelming. Fortunately, travel destinations—an easy day or weekend distance from the metropolis—offer far more idyllic settings; from the proverbially heavenly Suzhou and Hangzhou to such less travelled roads as the hiking trails of the Siming Mountains near Ningbo. The following sections summarise a few of the possibilities. The rest are limited only by your imagination and flexibility.

DAY TRIPS

All listings in this section are less than two hour's travel from central Shanghai (except in extraordinary traffic—which is, alas, not unknown on weekends). All make good 'escapes' from big-city bustle that are near enough to get back for dinner—or at least a jazz club nightcap.

Many day trips are easily accessible by suburban bus. The Tiyuguan (Shanghai Stadium) Bus Station has bilingual directions for day trips laid out so clearly it is nearly impossible to get lost; and if you show any confusion, attendants will personally escort you to your bus! A far cry from yesteryear's rattletraps, which left unwary passengers needing vacations from their vacations, today's buses are brand new, air-conditioned, come with DVD-fitted reclining seats, and go straight to tourist destinations. Bus tickets are usually under Rmb 100 round-trip, and include entrance fees to key tourist sites.

Another option if you don't have access to a long-term hire car, is to hire a taxi for the day. Rates for this service tend to hover between Rmb 400–800, depending on how far you want go, and the type of car. And a few sites below already are or will soon be accessible by subway. A few favourite day trips include:

Sheshan

A key Shanghai 'escape' for a century or more, Sheshan is one of few areas in the delta with some slant to the terrain. On the peak of She 'Mountain' (more of a hill, but welcome in these flatlands) is a major Catholic cathedral built by French Jesuit fathers in the 19th century. The next hill over is 'Jungle Park' (Senlin Gongyuan), a combination wilderness area and amusement zone. Both hills offer some lovely hiking and great views and, with very little effort, will take you off the crowded beaten paths and into some corners so secluded you'll hardly believe you're so near the Bund—though these are getting fewer as the new golf course and villa complex goes in!

Botanical Gardens

Technically inside city limits, this large park in the south-west corner of the city offers a breath of fresh air—as well as a lake, golf course, amusement park and collections of bonsais, roses and flowering trees that are each a pleasure in their season. Take a car directly to the gardens or ride Metro Line 1 to the end of the line at Xingzhuang and cab it from there; even on heavy traffic days, the subway makes the gardens accessible for a morning or afternoon stroll.

Qingpu

This 18th-century fishing village has an almost Dutch feel to the white-washed traditional houses, many set in fields of wheat or yellow rape flowers, surrounded by irrigation moats. The town features a lake where you can rent boats and fishing gear plus a silly but fun amusement park based on the theme of China's 'Monkey King' epics.

Zhouzhuang

A graceful town of canals and moon gates, half-moon bridges and curving old buildings, some of which date from the 12th century, Zhouzhuang has been 'discovered' by Shanghai intellectuals and, today, is a thriving arts colony. Many graceful ancient buildings are today full of trendy Internet cafés and boutiques, but the town remains a pleasant destination. And just keep walking. Past the 'touristicated' stretches remain lovely corners where you can still have tea in a traditional ceremony in someone's home, or watch little kids fishing the way their great-great-grandfathers did.

Songjiang

The 'latter day Zhouzhuang', Songjiang is in the process of being gentrified. For now, it offers many similar pleasures to Zhouzhuang, but is a little less touristy and built up, and a little closer to traditional lifeways.

Xitong

This 'undiscovered Zhouzhuang' is a lovely traditional fishing village at the meeting point of nine waterways where Zhejiang

Old wooden river waterboats ply the waterways of Xitong.

and Jiangsu Provinces border Greater Shanghai. Twisting alleys invite curious visitors into glimpses of ancient lifeways, while high arching bridges connect various sections of the town. A day in Xitong means relaxation: perhaps sitting at an alley corner playing Chinese checkers while kids play fantasy games nearby. Water fun is also available for hire in old wooden river rowboats, with lifejackets and paddles provided—though varying competence of renters can make the experience more like bumper-boats! The alleys abound with fresh seafood restaurants, most of which offer waterfront dining.

Jiaxing

Just a little past Xitong, the village of Jiaxing is surrounded by forested hills and old canals and other waterways. Be sure to try the famous *Jiaxing zongzi*, a traditional local snack of steamed sticky rice, red beans and pork wrapped in a lotus or sugar-cane leaf. *Zongzi* are famous throughout the Shanghai area, but connoisseurs say those of Jiaxing are the best.

Nanhui

Almost out to sea, the little fishing village of Nanhui has become a suburb of Shanghai and, indeed, some expats are choosing to commute to Shanghai from the garden villas that are springing up amidst the older architecture of the town. For more inner-city dwellers, a day trip to Nanhui offers some chances to wander down picturesque alleys that are relatively unchanged from the village's traditional days, as well as to get some fresh air where the village straggles toward the bay.

Chongming Island

The 'rice-basket' of Shanghai, Chongming Island is a farming and fishing area and nature reserve in the centre of the Yangtze, just a ferry boat ride away from the Bund. Once the new superhighway connecting the Port of Shanghai to parts north goes through on a series of massive planned bridges, Chongming will likely become a trucker's way-station of cheap restaurants and massage parlors. But for now, it is an unlikely haven of biking and walking trails, practically in the heart of Shanghai.

WEEKEND EXCURSIONS

A little further afield, the provinces neighbouring Greater Shanghai offer a surprising range of activities and venues easily accessible by car or train—or in some cases, by boat. Due east of Shanghai, offshore in the East China Sea, is the mountainous island of Putuoshan, holy to East Asian Buddhists and home to over 1,000 temples, large and small. There is a regular pilgrim's route on the island that gets as crowded as any street in Shanghai. But step just a little off the beaten path and you'll find many lovely views, secluded beaches, smaller and more intimate temples and other treasures. You can take a relaxing overnight ferry from the Bund to Putuoshan on a Friday evening, wander the island for a day and a half, then take a Sunday afternoon hydrofoil home.

Suzhou needs little introduction here, as it is the subject of long sections in virtually every tourist guidebook to China. Suffice it to say here that Suzhou is the city of canals and old walled gardens that Marco Polo is supposed to have called the 'Venice of the East'. Suzhou's ancient gardens and well-preserved architecture infuse the city with a calm often missing from Asian cities; several offer traditional tea ceremonies, concerts and other performances. Suzhou is easily reached by train: about 55 minutes from Shanghai North Station. You can also hire a car for the weekend, though it's hardly necessary, as the ancient city is really better seen on foot.

Not far past Suzhou is Taihu Lake, a shallow freshwater sea that covers some 2,200 sq km (850 sq miles) and includes several thousand islands. A bus or car will get you to Taihu from Suzhou or from the nearby Jiangsu Province town of Wuxi; and from anywhere on Taihu's edge, you can hire a boat to paddle about the islands, and/or a bicycle to peddle about once you're there.

To the south, in Zhejiang Province, another famous refuge for Shanghai urbanites is the mountain resort of Moganshan, built by 19th-century missionaries as a sanatorium, which later became one of the key retreats of the early Communist Party leaders. Today, Moganshan is a sleepy mountain town that offers excellent hiking, mountain biking and other outdoor sports, just a two-and-a-half to three hours' drive from Shanghai.

Past Moganshan is the other half of the famed heavenly duo, Hangzhou, home to West Lake (Xihu), with enough fabled islands and pavilions to keep a horde of painters busy for a lifetime. As with Suzhou, Hanghou is heavily written about in any good tourist guidebook. The one pleasant ramble the guidebooks often miss is a visit to the tea plantations of Longjing ('Dragon Well'), just to the north of the lake. Take a cab to Longjing Park, then basically meander downhill. All the paths lead through tea plantations and through little hamlets where quaint-looking tea farmers will invite you in to taste their crop and have a few snacks. The fees for fresh Longjing are high by local standards, but little enough in the absolute. Just keep walking downhill and eventually all paths lead back to the lake. Again like Suzhou, Hangzhou is easily reached by train (about two-and-a-half to three hours hours south-west of Shanghai), and you don't need a car.

A little further down from Hangzhou, the train line curves back east along the south rim of Hangzhou Bay, reaching the old wine-making town of Shaoxing, birthplace of famed writer Lu Xun. It's worth a visit to wander the Lu Xun Museum, enjoy the largely untouched traditional architecture and eat in any of several local restaurants that have been in business for two or three centuries, brewing the potent local rice wine and using it in distinctive dishes.

For the adventurous, there are charming country roads connecting Shaoxing with Hangzhou that make for a pleasant long day's bike ride.

Further along Hangzhou Bay is the old port town of Ningbo, home to some of China's most spectacular seafood and to several pleasantly sleepy oceanfront hotels. Ningbo is also a jumping-off point for a trek into the Siming Mountains, home to some of the wildest and loveliest countryside left in coastal China. The Siming range features excellent hiking, biking, fishing, birding and hunting. It was in a village in the Siming range, in fact, that one of the authors had one of her all-time favourite meals in China: wild boar, slow-cooked with bamboo shoots that were so freshly picked they were still sweet.

You can fly or take a relaxed overnight boat from Shanghai to Ningbo, and arrange to have a van bring mountain bikes around the bay. Have the van transport you to Xikou, a pretty village on the edge of the Siming that was birthplace to Chiang Kai Shek. From Xikou, you can start biking directly (or have your van bring you up the first, steep climb) to a picturesque monastery. From there, one dirt road criss-crossed by infinite foot-paths winds all the way through the range, allowing plenty of room for exploratory wanders. There will even be time to stay over in a village guesthouse before meeting your van, perhaps, where the road re-emerges from the mountains near Shangyu, for a Sunday evening drive back to Shanghai.

What we have described are just a small sampling of the excursions available near Shanghai. You can take quick trips to Nanjing, another major city, but one with a very different flavour from Shanghai. There are overnight trains (or quick flights) to Huangshan, China's justly famous 'Yellow Mountain', with some of the most spectacular scenery you will ever see. There are boat trips up the ancient Grand Canal to the town of Yangzhou, where Marco Polo claimed to have served as Mayor in the days of Kublai Khan. These trips are remarkably inexpensive by the standards of expat salaries in Shanghai, particularly if you enjoy trying local food, and don't insist on staying in foreign-owned hotels.

The limits are only in your imagination and your ability to get arrangements made in Chinese. Some non-bilingual expats tend to travel only in group trips arranged with bilingual guides, through the Shanghai Hiking Club, say, or the Hash House Harriers, and those trips are fun. You can have more flexibility at times, though, in a smaller group. Consider, for instance, offering to pay the way of an enthusiastic young Chinese student from a local university (you might easily find someone interested in such excursions in the 'English partner wanted' ads in expat magazines). Extra car seats and hotel rooms will not cost much relative to the experience and to the savings of not going through a formal tour agency.

You'll never have a better chance than your sojourn in Shanghai to explore the marvels of Eastern China. It's worth making more of at least some of your weekends than a chance to slob out in front of ESPN, watching other people have outdoor adventures!

VOLUNTEERING

Shanghai's siren call has proved irresistible not only to foreigners, but also to an estimated three million rural people who come seeking their fortunes without *hukou* residence permits that would guarantee minimum wage and other benefits. These bargain-basement workers fill the bottom tier of jobs: they are the street sweepers and construction hands and dishwashers who help make high living standards possible for more established Shanghainese. But their poverty strains Shanghai's social welfare system and, in response, the government has made many ineligible for welfare assistance or use of local hospitals or schools. Thus, while Shanghai has China's highest per capita income, it also has a large population of people living at subsistence levels. By China's own estimates, some 10 per cent of Shanghai's school-aged children have family per capita incomes under the Rmb 280 per month poverty level.

By dramatic contrast, many expatriates who were solidly middle class at home suddenly find themselves, by Shanghai standards, among the super-rich. Counting hardship allowances and other perks, they may make twice the money they did back home, on top of a company-paid luxury apartment with full-time maid, maybe even gardener and car-and-driver. Many expats in China find that enjoying such privilege carries a moral requirement to do a little more to give back to the local community than networking at the next cocktail party.

Poverty is relative. The gap between your disposable income and the poverty you'll see in Shanghai is likely greater than anything you'll see at home. In Shanghai, what you see as pocket change may make the difference between a child going to school or a sick breadwinner getting back to health or not. A few hours of your networking time may help destitute families find gainful employment. No matter what your skills may be, no matter how little time you can spare from your schedule or money you can eke out of the vacation allowance to share with those less fortunate, there is someone in Shanghai whose life can be changed forever by your generosity. Participating in charitable activities will also help shape the opinions that Chinese people have of foreigners, and will likely enrich your China experience as well.

Expatriates get involved in charitable activities at many levels, from Fortune 500 executives who write generous cheques to local charities, to individual expats who teach English in local schools at local salaries instead of in the far higher-pay international schools, in order to make a difference for local education.

Many 'trailing spouses' (typically wives who have given up careers to follow their husband's expat postings) have found charitable work instrumental in making their time in Shanghai rewarding. Many have traded in a life as a 'superwoman' career mom, and suddenly found themselves without a job, with full-time servants to take care of most daily household tasks, and frustrated or depressed for lack of feeling needed. One expat wife lamented, "I had a real career! I was in charge of lots of people! Here, I'm not even in charge of the laundry!" One solution is to step beyond the privileges of the expat enclave and join a charitable organisation where your skills, drive, and energy will help people who need you more than you may be able to imagine.

CHARITABLE GIVING IN CHINA

Expats have a long history of charitable activity in China that dates to the pre-revolutionary era, but virtually all foreign involvement in charity (and much else) in China disappeared between the Communist Revolution in 1949 and the Cultural Revolution between 1966–1976. During that period, the government was nominally responsible for taking care of society. Whether it fulfilled that responsibility or not is another question, but certainly there were none of the faith- or community-based organisations that Westerners call 'civil society'. Meantime, traditional Chinese culture favours families as the locus of social support in any case.

So the concept of non-governmental organisations (NGOs) seeking to systematically improve society was unfamiliar to most Chinese, and viewed with suspicion, when expats returned to China in large numbers following economic reform in 1979. Were these do-gooding foreigners trying to point out China's flaws? Acting as fronts for evangelism? Spying out weaknesses? In the late 1970s and early 1980s, foreigners had to do good works in China informally, through personal contacts, almost on the sly.

Gradually, however, reputable organisations and committed volunteers regained the trust of China's people and leaders. Groups such as Amity and the Red Cross became involved quite early, and eventually homegrown Chinese charitable organisations sprang up. Modern China's first charitable foundation was established in 1981; since that time, nearly

2,000 have come into being. It remains a challenge for charitable groups, in the words of one NGO report, to 'change centuries-old customs and beliefs... that an individual citizen's responsibilities stop at their front gate; and that it is up to the government to solve problems, not the citizens.' Acceptance of individual involvement in charity is growing rapidly, however, and many groups have found that once a new cause has been properly introduced, Chinese will embrace it with relish.

For instance, when Care for Children, a charity that places orphans with foster families, came to China in the late 1990s, the concept of foster care was so unheard of they had to invent a Chinese word. Yet the programme has seen incredible success, with foster families finding the experience so rewarding that China is now the world's only country with a waiting list of families wanting to foster a child.

The Byzantine intricacies of Chinese law still consider social and environmental welfare to be predominantly the domain of the government. It remains difficult to set up new charitable NGOs. Many that already exist are better described as GONGOs, or 'government-organised non-government organisations'; current law, for instance, requires all NGOs to be affiliated with a governmental agency.

The affiliation process is so difficult that only a handful of the global charities operating in Shanghai are officially recognised by the government. The rest are, technically, operating in a grey area, a form of strategic ambiguity quite common in China. The government is, in fact, happy to have these organisations in Shanghai, and often partners with and publicises their achievements. But the ambiguous legal situation lets leaders crack down on any groups perceived as behaving unacceptably. This conditional tolerance has the effect of making charitable groups in China careful to shy away from politically sensitive topics, a fact useful enough that the government is unlikely any time soon to rapidly increase room for more freewheeling global NGOs. The perception among many area experts is that an explosion in 'legitimised' civil society in China might unleash, in the

the words of one observer 'social forces [the government] cannot control'.

But on a day-to-day basis, the government is increasingly active in supporting these 'unofficial' charities. One sign of how far these groups have come appeared in 2002 when Tori Zwisler, American founder of the (not officially registered) Shanghai chapter of the global charity Roots and Shoots, became the first foreigner to be awarded the Shanghai government's Volunteer of the Year award.

Fund-raising also remains a grey area; officially, all fund-raising within China must be done in partnership with registered Chinese charities, and funds must be deposited in that organisation's account. Unrecognised charities do manage to get around this regulation on occasion, but the government has also been known to refuse permission for fund-raising efforts that are not funnelled through officially registered local NGOs.

CHARITABLE DUE DILIGENCE IN CHINA

In any community, people who want to participate in charitable activities should practise due diligence in evaluating options. Many countries offer independent organisations that vet charities and provide reports on such factors as 'flow-through', or the percentage of donations that reach charitable targets as opposed to being captured by organisational overhead. In China, while officially recognised NGOs must provide an annual report on their activities and finances to government monitoring agencies, those reports are rarely made available to private individuals. Given several past scandals involving misappropriation of funds within Chinese charities, individuals and organisations wishing to make charitable contributions in China must exercise caution.

The American Chamber of Commerce in Shanghai has created a vetting procedure for NGOs based on guidelines used by the Council of Better Business Bureaus (CBBB) in the United States. Their website (http://www.amcham-shanghai. org) gives an evaluation of the NGOs that have passed through their vetting procedure .

If investigating an NGO independently, ask:
- What percentage of funds raised by the organisation is used to support the programmes that are its core function?
- How much accountability is there in the use of organisation funds? Are donors allowed to earmark donations for specific purposes, and can they receive verification the funds were used as intended?
- Are the organisation's finances independently audited? Are audits available for donors to review?
- Is the organisation officially recognised in China? If not, does the organisation have official recognition as a charitable organisation by the government of another country? (Officially recognised organisations should be able to provide certificates of their status, regardless of country.)

CHARITABLE ORGANISATIONS THAT WELCOME FOREIGN INVOLVEMENT

There are innumerable opportunities for charitable donations of cash or goods in Shanghai and throughout China.

Expatriates interested primarily in cheque-writing should look into the very thoroughly researched (and, in web version, regularly revised) list created by the analyst group China Development Brief. Their guide, 250 Chinese NGOs (the updated version of which now contains profiles of 290 organisations), is probably the best single source of information on local agencies, and they also list nearly as many global NGOs with operations in China.

China Development Brief

You can view the regularly updated global NGO list at:
                http://www.chinadevelopmentbrief. com.
China Development Brief gives a very rough estimate of the number of international organisations active in China: 70 grant-making foundations, 70 advocacy groups, 150 religious charities and 200 humanitarian organisations. Their website also lists postings of (paid) job offers (both full- and part-time) with China-based charities.

Listed below are some of the most active charitable groups in Shanghai that welcome involvement by foreign volunteers. Most were established by or are operated by foreigners (often in partnership with government agencies). Most are registered internationally, though not all are registered in China. All will provide financial statements and flow-through data on request, and offer full accountability for donated funds. All of these organisations need financial assistance, and most can benefit from in-kind donations such as used computers or office equipment. (The contacts provided are current at the time of this writing. However, if they do change, there will be someone else in the organisation that will be able to help you.)

Care for Children
Care for Children is a ground-breaking programme that initiated the permanent foster care concept in China.

Their programmes have achieved placements at double typical US success rates. Many foster children have been identified as having special needs, but after placement with a family, develop normally. Care for Children focuses on capacity building, and partners the government on training programmes to elevate the level of care in China's orphanages and in foster care programmes. Care for Children has activities year-round which need volunteers. The organisation can also direct volunteers to local orphanages and schools that welcome volunteers. Officially recognised by the Chinese government, Care for Children is also a registered charity in the United States and the United Kingdom.

Contact person: Robert Glover
Tel: (021) 6288-1710
Email: robert@careforchildren.com.cn
Website: http://www.careforchildren.com.cn

Rotary Club of Shanghai (Provisional)

Rotary is an international organisation focused on humanitarian assistance and encouraging high ethical standards. Membership is by invitation only; however, they welcome all interested volunteers to participate in Friends of Rotary. Their primary community service activity is Gift of Life, an international Rotarian charity that sponsors heart surgeries for children in need. Other charitable activities include providing assistance to Inner Mongolia citizens and providing funds for the renovation of the Lu Wan District Old Folks Home.

Website: http://www.rotaryshanghai.org
          http://www.giftof lifeshanghai.com

Junior Achievement (JA)

JA is an international organisation that pairs knowledgeable professionals with students from high school to college level. JA programmes help students learn about four key concepts:

- the importance of market-driven economies
- the role of business in a global economy'
- the commitment of business to environmental and social issues
- the relevance of ethics and character development in business leaders.

In China, where these concepts are fairly new, businesspeople can help bring these ideas alive for students. Volunteers can help on a one-off or longer-term basis. The minimum commitment would be teaching a one-hour class on any business-related subject in your area of expertise. JA also seeks people willing to teach semester-long classes (one hour a week for 8–14 weeks), or mentor student teams participating in semester-long business-simulation exercises.

Contact person: Yaping Li
Tel: (021) 6415-9398 ext 2217
Email: yaping@jachina.org
Website: http://www.jachina.org

Operation Smile

An international organisation, Operation Smile organises missions that brings doctors from across the globe together to team with local surgeons. These doctors would then provide cleft palate surgery to children in need. The organisation works with the government and provides training for local doctors so that surgery can continue after the visiting doctors return home. Operation Smile welcomes volunteers interested in helping in their Shanghai office, or in helping one of their missions elsewhere in China. Operation Smile is a registered US charity.

Contact person: Clara Love
Tel: (021) 6391-0357
E-mail: clove@operationsmile.org
Website: http://www.operationsmilechina.org
           http://www. operationsmile.org

Project HOPE
(Health Opportunity for People Everywhere)

Project HOPE is an international group that provides health education and humanitarian assistance around the world. In Shanghai, Project HOPE partnered the Shanghai government to create China's first pediatric referral and teaching hospital. Project HOPE assists with training and education in the hospital on areas ranging from medical specialities and techniques to hospital management. Other projects include training and education in diabetes management and in the diagnosis and treatment of Gaucher disease.

A group called Friends of Hope Volunteers organises activities to support Project HOPE programmes. Activities include conversation sessions with Chinese doctors to help improve their English, and play sessions with children in the hospital.

Project HOPE
Contact person: C M Leung
Tel: (021) 6384-0609
E-mail: hopeshai@public.sta.net.cn
Website: http://www.projecthope.org/china
Friends of HOPE Volunteers
Contact person: Priscilla Ng
E-mail: hopeshai@public.sta.net.cn

Roots and Shoots

Roots and Shoots is a part of the Jane Goodall Institute, an international organisation encouraging 'children of all ages' to take action to make the world a better place. Dr Goodall's message—that the smallest positive act from any individual can make a difference—resonates with Chinese children. Twenty-eight schools in Shanghai currently run Roots and Shoots programmes, which are organised as hands-on environmental and humanitarian activities. Programmes have included cleaning up the Huangpu River, a research project on the sparrow population in Shanghai, recycling programmes in schools, and visiting the elderly in retirement homes. Older children lead activities for younger children, teaching them how to care for the environment, people and animals. Roots and Shoots welcomes all volunteers. The Jane Goodall Institute is a registered US charitable organisation.

Contact person: Tori Zwisler
Tel: (021) 6352-3580
E-mail: roots&shoots@zuelligpharma.com.cn
Website: http://www.jgi-shanghai.org
           http://www.janegoodall.org/rs

Shanghai Children's Discovery Museum

This organisation was founded by an expatriate mother who was surprised to learn there was no children's museum in Shanghai. Activities at the museum include displays and projects teaching science and nature, drama, art, music, practical life and international culture. The organisation welcomes all volunteers and has a particular need for early childhood educators, architects, lawyers, accountants, carpenters and people skilled in fund-raising. The Shanghai Children's Discovery Museum is a registered US charitable organisation.

Contact person: Nancy Wang
Tel: (1350) 180-3125; (021) 5688-0844
E-mail: info@shanghaidiscovery.org
Website: http://www.shanghaidiscovery.org

Shanghai Sunrise

Shanghai Sunrise helps provide a well-rounded education for underprivileged children in Shanghai and surrounding areas. An education in a Shanghai public school costs approximately Rmb 2,500 (US$ 305) per year, including school fees, books, school uniforms and other associated costs. All of the families of children sponsored by Shanghai Sunrise fall below the poverty line of monthly per capita incomes of less than Rmb 280 (under US$ 35). Shanghai Sunrise also builds libraries and provides computers to underfunded schools. The organisation welcomes volunteers to help with any aspect of their programmes. Shanghai Sunrise is officially recognised by the Shanghai Charity Foundation.

Contact person: Lori Burke
E-mail: director@shanghaisunrise.com;
              shanghaisunrise@hotmail.com
Website: http://www.shanghaisunrise.com

Special Olympics

Special Olympics helps people with mental retardation become physically fit, respected community members through participation in sports competitions. Their athletes' oath is: 'Let me win. But if I cannot win, let me be brave in the attempt'. Shanghai was awarded the 2007 Special Olympics World Summer Games, for which the Shanghai government has announced it needs to raise US$ 30 million, as well as recruit 40,000 volunteers. Preparations are in progress and the organisation is working to fulfill the government's promise that China will have 500,000 athletes participating in Special Olympics by the year 2005.

Website: http://www.specialolympics.org
          (international site)

Terry Fox Run

Terry Fox was a Canadian diagnosed with cancer at the age of 18, and later his right leg was amputated above the knee. While in hospital, touched by the suffering and spirit of the other cancer patients, he decided to raise money for cancer research by running across Canada. He ran for 143 days, covering over 5,000 km (3,000 miles) before he was forced to stop because his cancer had spread. He died at the age of 22, but his story has inspired people throughout the world. Today, the Terry Fox Marathon is run in over 50 countries, and has raised nearly US$ 200 million for cancer research. The Terry Fox Run has been held in Shanghai since 1998, and is typically held the third weekend in October. The organisers appreciate volunteers and encourage everyone to participate in the race. The Shanghai Charity Foundation is one of the main sponsors of the annual Terry Fox Run in Shanghai, and The Terry Fox Foundation is a recognised charity in Canada.

Contact person: Four Seasons Hotel Shanghai
Tel: (021) 6256-8888
E-mail: reservations.shg@fourseasons.com
Website: http://www.terryfoxrun.org (international site)

The Smile Train

The Smile Train provides medical equipment, training and financial assistance to enable local surgeons to perform cleft palate surgeries. When the Smile Train organises a training and surgery session, all surgeries are performed by local physicians. The organisation provides surgery for free to children who can't afford it and conducts research into finding a cure. Since the procedure to cure cleft palates is relatively simple and inexpensive, the Smile Train believes that the problem can be eradicated. The Smile Train is registered as a charitable organisation in the United States.

Contact person: Victoria Moy
Tel: (021) 6446-7213; (1367) 167-9518
Website: http://www.smiletrain.org

ADDITIONAL WAYS TO GET INVOLVED

Many other business and social organisations conduct charitable activities, sometimes in conjunction with existing charitable organisations, other times independently. Contact your country's consulate or chamber of commerce or look in the English-language magazines' community section for a group that interests you. The Rotary, the American Women's Club and the Shanghai Expatriate Professional Women's Society are all active in charitable activities.

GuideStar lists over 500 charities with some focus on China, and provides basic financial information for each one (http://www. guidestar.com). Charity Navigator lists a couple of charitable organisations with programmes in China, including several religious charities, providing comprehensive, independent comparative ratings and evaluations of each (http://www.charitynavigator. com).

'May it be permitted to a traveller to remark that if men were to give to the learning of Chinese and of Chinese requirements and methods of business a little of the time which is lavished on sport and other amusements, there might possibly be less occasion for the complaint that large fortunes are no longer to be made in Chinese business.'
—Isabella Bird, *The Yangtse River and Beyond* (1899); cited in the *Odyssey Illustrated Guide to Shanghai*

LIKE MANY OTHER CHINESE REGIONS, Shanghai has its own dialect—Shanghainese, or 'Shanghai Hua'. The term literally means 'Shanghai speech', perhaps reflecting the fact that in written form, there is little difference between Mandarin and Shanghainese. In spoken form, the two are as French is to Spanish: close enough to catch some words, but not mutually intelligible without study.

Of course, since Mandarin, the official 'state' dialect, is taught in all schools, virtually all Chinese under the age of 50 speak it. If you are learning Chinese for the first time, you will likely find Mandarin more broadly useful than Shanghainese.

The good news, though, is that for Mandarin speakers, Shanghainese is relatively easy to pick up, at least at a basic level. Even non-Chinese speakers can learn a few keywords and phrases, which will yield benefits in relations with Shanghainese colleagues, who generally appreciate the gesture.

ORIGINS OF SHANGHAINESE

Shanghainese belongs to the Wu dialect system, one of China's seven major dialects. Versions of Wu dialect are understood throughout southern Jiangsu Province, Shanghai, Zhejiang Province, north-east Jiangxi Province, north-west Fujian Province and southern Anhui. Altogether, some 70 million people in 110 cities and counties are native speakers of some form of Wu dialect.

As Shanghai became a city of immigrants (both foreign and Chinese) in the century and a half after the Opium Wars, the city developed a unique multiracial culture incorporating many different nationalities and backgrounds, a mélange Shanghainese call 'Haipai Wenhua', literally a 'culture arranged by the sea'. This multifaceted blending favoured the establishment of a dominant dialect as lingua franca, in an era before Mandarin had triumphed as China's official dialect. Thus English became the common language for the foreign community, and Shanghai's special version of the Wu dialect became the common tongue for the Chinese. The city's proud history makes it likely, even as peoples from throughout China continue to migrate to Shanghai, that Shanghainese will survive and remain the dominant conversational language in the area.

SHANGHAINESE AND 'IMMIGRANT CHINESE'

Shanghai's government releases no official statistics on immigration, so it is difficult to accurately state the number of Chinese moving to Shanghai from other cities. Waves of immigration have helped build Shanghai over the centuries; the current wave began with economic reform starting in the early 1980s. By any estimate, the numbers of such 'local expats' is large, probably in the millions, and they are key to the vital energy that keeps this city reinventing itself.

Almost every local expat will tell you that it is tough at first to get settled and make friends in Shanghai, and that language is perhaps the most central issue. While a foreigner who speaks no Chinese at all is tolerated and perhaps even accepted as status quo, a Chinese who speaks no Shanghainese is marked as an outsider, a recent arrival, not a 'real Shanghainese'. Outsiders are easily seen as targets for Shanghainese business 'cleverness', or outright rudeness.

The city is full of tales of non-Shanghainese Chinese getting the brush-off. The infamous joke about Li Peng is often also applied to the average Chinese. Why did the new sales-manager from Beijing get fired by the boss in Hong Kong? Because he didn't know what his job was. Why not? Because the staff meetings were held in Shanghainese.

The Difference of a Syllable

One native Beijinger, able to understand some Shanghainese since his family hailed originally from Jiangsu, experienced this when he first arrived in Shanghai. In a large state-owned store, he called to a sales lady at a food counter in Mandarin, to no avail; several salesgirls chatted on among themselves in Shanghainese, ignoring his existence. The Beijinger tried every polite form of address he could think of in Mandarin: *xiaojie* ('Young Miss'), *tongzhi* ('Comrade') and even *Ayi* ('Auntie' or 'Madam'). Failing to get anyone's attention, he left in anger. As he left, he heard another customer quickly get polite attention with the simple change of a syllable, from the Mandarin *xiaojie* to the Shanghainese *xiaojia*.

SHANGHAINESE TODAY

Of course, Shanghai is changing as the city gets ever more international, and sure of itself. The city government is now actively promoting Mandarin use. More and more people, especially those in the service sectors, use Mandarin as their working language. Still, Shanghainese remains the conversational language.

Shanghainese can be difficult to master. Each syllable in the dialect consists of three parts: an initial consonant, a simple or compound vowel, and a tone. Shanghainese has 28 initial consonants, 43 simple and compound vowel sounds, and five tones. The resulting combinations are subtle and complex, difficult for northern Chinese used to dialects that favour clear, strong pronunciations.

This fact plays at times into the rivalry between Shanghai and Beijing and other cities. Northern Chinese are given to claiming that Shanghainese sounds 'soft', and to denigrating Shanghainese men as 'singers when they speak', not like northern 'real men'. Of course, the Shanghainese happily return the compliment, dipping into the rich stock of curses in their dialect. What other language has so many words for 'fool'?

Few non-native Shanghainese master total fluency, but a smattering of Shanghainese comes easily, and can shift status for Chinese from 'outsider' to 'new Shanghainese'. Foreigners, too, will find more friendliness, more doors opening in return for the effort, and the face it gives to Shanghainese. Learning a few phrases requires only a basic feel for pronunciation, and for the sassy culture Shanghainese is rooted in. What other sports fans, for instance, razz officials so regularly at football matches that a Shanghai match in China's National Soccer League is almost not considered official without the crowd chanting '*sepu tsilou!*' ('the referee is a pig!').

PRONUNCIATION

Here is a pronunciation guide to Shanghai dialect Latinisation:

Shanghai Dialect Pinyin	Latin Phonemes	Pronounced as Equivalent English Phonemes
a	[a]	_ar_my
b	[b]	_b_ee
c	[ts']	le_t's_
d	[d]	_d_ay
e	[e]	—
f	[f]	_f_ive
g	[g]	_g_ate
h	[h]	_h_e
i	[i]	s_ee_
j	[tc]	—
k	[k]	s_k_ill
l	[l]	_l_ive
m	[m]	_m_ill
n	[n]	_n_ine
o	[o]	—
p	[p]	s_p_eak
q	[tc']	lun_ch_
r	—	—
s	[s]	_s_ee
t	[t]	s_t_ill
u	[u]	r_u_le
v	[v]	_v_ery

Shanghai Dialect Pinyin	Latin Phonemes	Pronounced as Equivalent English Phonemes
w	—	—
x	[c]	_sh_ine
y	—	—
z	[z]	_z_oo
ph	[p']	_p_en
th	[t']	_t_ime
ts	[ts]	—
dj	[dz]	—
ni	[n]	—
ny	—	—
zi	[z]	—
kh	[k']	s_k_ill
ng	[ŋ]	lo_ng_
oa	—	l_o_t
eu	—	—
oe	[Ø]	—
ia	[ia]	—
ioa	[io]	—
ieu	[iy]	—
ie	[iE]	—
ua	[ua]	—
ue	[uE]	—
uoe	[uØ]	—
yu	[y]	—
yuoe	[yØ]	—
el	[∂l]	—
ang	[ā]	enh_an_ce
ah	[a2]	—
oh	[o2]	—
eh	[∂2]	—

Shanghai Dialect Pinyin	Latin Phonemes	Pronounced as Equivalent English Phonemes
iang	[iā]	_yong_
ing	—	_in_k
iah	[ia2]	—
ioh	[io2]	—
ieh	[i∂2]	—
uang	[uā]	—
uah	[ua2]	—
ueh	[u∂2]	—
yueh	[y∂2]	—

COMMON PHRASES

The following lists common words and phrases in Shanghainese, including a few of the dialect's rich curses. This phonetic notation for Shanghainese was developed by Professor Tang Zhixiang of the Chinese University of Hong Kong. It's a solid system, but not self-evident: a 'real Shanghainese' should help you sort out your pronunciation.

Forms of Address

I	_ngu, or ala_
you	_nung_
he/ she/ it	_yi_
we	_ahlah_
you guys	_na_
they	_yila_
father	_papa_
mother	_mama_
kids	_xiaonoe_

Timing

time	_zengkuong_

What time is it now?	*Sa zengkuong?*
tomorrow	*mingtsoa*
afternoon	*wopoenieh*
Monday	*lipa yeh*
Tuesday	*lipa ni*
Wednesday	*lipa se*
Thursday	*lipa sy*
Friday	*lipa ng*
Saturday	*lipa loh*
Sunday	*lipa nieh*
Today is Monday	*Jingtsao lipa yeh*
January	*yeh yuehveng*
February	*liang yuehveng*
March	*se yueh*
April	*sy yueh*
May	*ng yueh*
June	*loh yueh*
July	*qieh yueh*
August	*pahyueh*
September	*jieu yueh*
October	*zeh yueh*
November	*zehyeh yueh*
December	*zehyni yueh*

Introduction and Greetings

My name is David.	*Ngu jiao David.*
Hello, Ms. Chen.	*Nung hoa, Zeng xiaojia!*
Hello, Mr. Lin.	*Nung hoa, Ling xisang!*
Hello, everybody.	*Daka hoa!*
How are you	*Nung hoa?*
Good morning.	*Nung tsoa!*
Welcome!	*Huoening*
Good bye!	*Tsewe!*

| See you tomorrow! | *Mingtsoa we!* |
| I am Shanghainese. | *Ahlah sang-heining.* |

Directions

I am staying at the Xin Jingjiang Hotel.	*Ngu zy leh Xing Jingkong Dajieuti.*
We will come by a taxi.	*Ahlah zyka ceng ceht.*
Beijing	*Pohjing*
Hong Kong	*Xiangkong*
Shanghai	*Zonghe*
The Bund	*Ngathe*
Oriental Pearl TV Tower	*Tungfong Mingzy*
Huaihai Road	*Wahe Lu*

Curses

Idiot	*gangdu*
Stupid fool	*tsedou kuanau, tsoudou kuachi*
Feebleminded/ crazy	*zeh-se di (literally, '13 o'clock')*
Shit	*tsena*
Bumpkin/ yokel	*hsiangwu ning*
Outsider	*ngadi ning*
Low-class rat	*hsiau chilau (from early Chinese Communist Party expression for Kuomintang traitors)*
Hooligan	*hsiau bi-sei*

Courting

| You are very pretty/ handsome. | *Nung lao hoa khoe.* |

As Shanghai booms, Shanghainese is increasing in popularity, throughout China and abroad. It's a fun dialect, and worth learning. If you learn just a few words each week, by the end of your stay you will have picked up enough to earn the joking-but-serious honorific, rare for foreigners, of 'half-Shanghainese'.

NON-VERBAL COMMUNICATION

Shanghainese talk more with their hands than the average Chinese, but not at the level of New York Jews, or Southern Italians. Like most Asians, Shanghainese are relatively conservative about touch and other forms of physical expression. Expect plenty of fun and sass from Shanghainese slang and humour, but Shanghai humour tends to be physically understated, unlikely to be delivered with backslapping or huge belly-laughs.

A handshake has become a standard (but not universal) greeting among Shanghainese, especially when dealing with Westerners, though typical Chinese grips may be less firm than Westerners are used to (unless a given Shanghainese is really trying to offer a 'true Western handshake'). Bone-crushing is frowned upon. A heavily physical, arms on the shoulder approach may also make your Shanghai friends and colleagues uncomfortable. When in doubt, follow local leads.

That said, in terms of personal space, Shanghainese tend to be comfortable with shorter distances between speakers than is the norm for Americans and other Westerners, perhaps as a result of growing up in such crowded cities. This can result in almost comical interactions wherein Shanghainese strive to stand as close to Western colleagues as feels natural to the Shanghainese, while the Westerners keep trying to back up to create a Western-sized personal space, and the two chase each other across the room!

CHAPTER 9

BUSINESS UNUSUAL

'The truth is not that the cleverest people in the world
come from Shanghai, but that the cleverest people in
the world come TO Shanghai.'
—Attributed to former Shanghai Mayor Xu Kuangdi

DOING BUSINESS IN CHINA is the subject of many fine books, and this chapter does not attempt to reproduce them. The 'Further Reading' section lists several favourites, including our former colleague Scott Seligman's *Chinese Business Etiquette*, which offers a thorough and sensitive discussion of the crucial cultural side of China business. The US-China Business Council (http://www. uscbc.org) and Economist Intelligence Unit (http://www.eiu.com) offer excellent publications and other guidance, much of it specialised by industry.

This chapter focuses on tips especially crucial in Shanghai, for with apologies to Tolstoy, we might say that all business in China is challenging alike, but each Shanghai business is challenging in its own special way. Following are some ground rules.

THINK LOCAL: BE AWARE OF SHANGHAI'S 'SPECIAL STATUS'

Shanghainese are proud of their city—government leaders and top corporate executives probably more so than average. A little flattery goes a long way; that translates in the business world into preference for doing business with those who show appreciation for the city. Take the time to visit the Old City and Museum, to try traditional Shanghainese food and go up the Oriental Pearl. Sharing with Shanghainese counterparts/colleagues the pleasure you take in their hometown will more likely win you business—and collaboration—than any other simple act you could perform.

It also never hurts to position business projects in terms of how they will help Shanghai regain its status as the 'Pearl of the Orient'. Will that cell phone system you want to sell just be 'fast'? Or will it 'make Shanghai the communications hub of Asia'? How sexy are those shoes? Are they vogue enough that 'Paris will imitate Shanghai'? You get the idea. Sometimes such messages need to be subtle, sometimes not (though, at all times, Shanghai marketers must take care not to contradict global corporate messages). The point is to work wherever possible with Shanghainese pride, not against it.

Three other aspects of Shanghai's 'special status' deserve particular mention.

Language

Shanghai is surely one of the few cities in the world that boasts its own language. As Chapter 8: Learning Shanghainese points out, Shanghainese can be difficult to master, but with a little effort you can memorise a few phrases or colourful bits of slang. Almost any Shanghainese will happily spend a few minutes helping you hone your pronunciation. Sprinkling a little Shanghainese into conversation will bring out many smiles, and help break business ice.

Shanghai as China's Business Leader

As China's most industrialised city, Shanghai has a love-hate relationship with the government in Beijing, and with China's hinterlands alike. The communist government has never been sure quite how to treat the embarrassing success of this quintessentially capitalist city. Through the years, leadership responses have ranged from making Shanghai the target of purges to levying taxes at the highest rate in the nation. Similarly, poorer Chinese often both resent, and seek to emulate—or move to—Shanghai.

Then too, even as the Shanghai Gang in Beijing has given the city unprecedented power, Shanghai Gang leaders have often felt themselves to be walking tightropes. They could not be seen granting special privileges to their wealthy hometown, and could not maintain their own grip on power without demonstrating loyalty to the regime.

As a result of all this, Shanghai can be in some ways China's most conservative city—a surprise to many who focus on her business acumen. Compared with freewheeling Guangzhou, which looks to Hong Kong as a model, Shanghai always seems to operate with one eye on Beijing. Business may be businesslike, but comes with a veneer of attention to the values of the central government leadership and of some imagined—and easily offended —'average Chinese' in the provinces.

Thus, Shanghai newspapers will often be first to print bad news about a foreign company, and last to print anything good. Shanghai bankers are notoriously cautious with loan guarantees. Shanghai import brokers are the greatest sticklers to the letter of the customs law—and so on and so forth. Foreign businesspeople in Shanghai must learn to moderate expectations accordingly and not demand benefits they received in Guangzhou which may be impossible in Shanghai. Successful businesses find ways to push the envelope of acceptability by helping Shanghainese counterparts position projects as supporting the goals of Beijing, and 'good for China'.

Shanghai First

To some extent this is true across China, but nowhere more so than in Shanghai. One cosmetics manufacturer, for instance, was able to arrange favourable terms for building a plant by promising linkages with a famed Shanghai cosmetology school, which in turn attracted senior cosmetologists from across China (some training of which the firm agreed to fund). It was a stroke of genius: appealing to Shanghai's special status as leader and demonstrating Shanghai's commitment to the provinces at once.

Shanghai and Hong Kong

Economists will debate for decades the degree to which Hong Kong's fabled 20th-century growth rates were due exclusively to the city's role as entrepôt for China's mainland. Certainly in the years when China was essentially closed, Hong Kong was the premier if not only gateway to her markets and a generation of managers there specialised in getting things done in China for firms from countries whose citizens could not visit China themselves. Even after economic reform began, Hong Kong remained the site where managers who had 'special knowledge' and who 'held the China keys' lived.

But as reform gained traction, global firms could operate directly in China. Then when the financial crisis took the bloom off many Asian economies while China escaped nearly unscathed, many looked at the mainland with renewed interest. When Hong Kong returned to China in 1997, special privileges for Western residents largely disappeared. Even without the erosion of Hong Kong's rule-of-law since China took control (a topic of rancorous debate), Hong Kong's attractions as entrepôt and China's headquarters had already dimmed. One needn't take a position in the debates on which factor is most responsible to recognise that Hong Kong's growth rates have plummeted in recent years, while Shanghai's have risen.

A great deal more could obviously be said about this set of topics, and has been said, in many books and articles, documentaries and speeches. For here, suffice it to say that the question of Shanghai's status vis à vis Hong Kong remains a sensitive one, around which successful Shanghai businesspeople tread lightly.

Most Shanghainese believe Shanghai has succeeded Hong Kong as principal gateway to the markets of China and is on schedule to re-emerge as Asia's trade and financial centre, a role it held when Hong Kong was a mudflat. An understanding of that perspective, and a care about contradicting it, are as useful in Shanghai business as is avoiding politics and religion at cocktail parties. At the same time, global firms that operate throughout the region must be wary of taking public stances for Shanghai audiences that would play poorly in Hong Kong. The more global firms move their Asian headquarters to Shanghai, the more sensitive this issue is likely to become.

BE FLEXIBLE, IN THIS CITY OF RAPID CHANGE

As Shanghai continues to grow and change with seeming meteoric speed, business must shift with it. Just think of the changing needs of Pudong as it erupted from farm fields to the world's most active construction zone, to real-estate crash, to retrenched but still-growing financial centre, all inside 15 years. Your business may well need as rapid a set of changes and a strategy to be ready for them.

Again, this chapter does not try to recreate the wealth of knowledge available on doing business at times of rapid change. Rather, it summarises a few principles that seem particularly important in Shanghai, including:

- Having broad and varied sources of information.
- Keeping a clear channel between local Shanghai operations and global headquarters.
- Building strong cross-cultural teams capable of rapid response.

Each of these is discussed in more detail below. The bottom line is, successful firms in Shanghai need a management committed to keeping its finger on the pulse of the city's growth, so corporate knees can stay bent to go wherever the market veers next.

Broad Sources of Information

Keeping a managerial finger on the pulse requires knowing how to read the signals, and that means enough sources of local information to give a sense of context. Some key factors include:

Wide Reading of News Media, Chinese and Foreign

Many Shanghai expats avidly read the *Asian Wall Street Journal* (AWSJ), and *International Herald Tribune* (IHT, or the 'Trib'), and consider themselves well informed about Shanghai. (The *Far Eastern Economic Review* (FEER) was also very popular until recently when it ceased publication.) Of course, relative to headquarter counterparts, they are right. But relative to Shanghainese who get news from a wider range of sources, such expats can be woefully behind the times.

Consider, for instance, the *Shanghai Ribao* (Shanghai Daily), one of two English newspapers in the city, which publishes seven days a week with a circulation topping 250,000. Think about Shanghai TV's 30-minute news feature, which broadcasts nightly at 6:30, to a viewership topping 800,000. Then there are specialised trade publications, thought-leader journals, radio stations and much more. National media also impact Shanghai audiences; for instance, the Documentary Channel of Beijing's China Central TV is very popular in Shanghai. Other local TV stations also land in Shanghai through the city's cable TV network, via satellite transmission. Today, the average Shanghainese family will have some 20 TV stations to choose from, and families with access to a satellite dish many more—this on top of several local dailies and a host of national newspapers, and some 9,000 Chinese-language news weeklies and other magazines.

These local media have far more immediate and lasting impact on average Shanghainese than anything in FEER or the Trib. They report local news faster (often articles on Shanghai in the English-language press are spurred belatedly by news appearing first in Chinese), and in a form more accessible to and influential over local audiences. And that means if you're relying on FEER or the Trib for all you need to know about the local market, your market may get away from you before you know there's a problem.

More than one foreign firm has basked contentedly in positive coverage from English-language media, for instance, even as problems heated up in local coverage. The resulting disparity can be tragicomic. One direct sales firm was targeted by massive negative coverage in Shanghai media after some salespeople were charged with unethical tactics (high-pressure sales to shut-ins, etc.). But the firm's management kept lionising salespeople with high sales records—apparently unaware of either the growing media frenzy, or the unethical behaviour that caused it (while also building sales).

The low point arrived when a previously written article celebrating a particularly high-flying salesman appeared in the company's employee journal—the same week the salesman in question was arrested for fraud. The media attacks on this and related incidents lost the company 50 per cent of its Shanghai sales before it reorganised to fix the problem.

Needless to say, the time needed to intelligently read all key articles on Shanghai in the local and the global media is beyond that available to most managers, even those who read Chinese fluently.

Information Industries

Fortunately, a whole industry has grown, offering media clipping/summary services to busy businesspeople. These range from simple clippings provided by local agencies (many staffed inexpensively by students), to sophisticated analytical reports from global consulting firms, with every permutation in between. Ask at AmCham, BritCham or other groups for recommendations suited to your business. Some firms also assign junior staffers to do clipping, which can work well if staffers are well-trained on what to look for, and given time to look.

Whatever route you take, make sure you have regular access to the news in Shanghai that affects your business and industry. It's a worthwhile investment. Like so many seemingly simple but surprisingly complex business maintenance activities, active media monitoring can prevent many problems and reveal many opportunities.

Internet

Among the various media available for research, the Internet deserves special mention. Web use is exploding in coastal

China. Analysts counted over 371,000 Chinese-language websites by end-2002, with more than 10 per cent of all Chinese-language sites worldwide coming from Shanghai. Chinese-language web content and applications are both expanding exponentially; some analysts claim that if current trends continue, Chinese will eventually succeed English as the main language of web content. China's much-discussed efforts to censor electronic information available to average Chinese may have had some effect on political news, but has little affect on business information.

Unlike traditional media, the Internet—with all its meandering byways for browsing—is not well-suited to simple monitoring or clipping summaries. Yet web discussions, and website-based information, can be useful if not crucial for your business. The answer is to keep Internet browsing for business purposes in-house. Many (especially younger) Shanghainese are highly technically literate. With little trouble, in any but the lowest-tech industries, you should find at least one junior staffer who is a web-literate native speaker of Chinese. Try assigning that person (or those people) a few hours a week to check websites key to your business, lurk in on relevant discussion groups, and bring useful points to your attention. The junior staffer(s) will likely be flattered and diligent; and you may well be happily surprised with what they come up with.

Networking
Shanghai (as noted in Chapter 3: Shanghai's People) is a city of networkers, to the point that most social interactions are coloured by it. In a rapidly changing business environment where information comes at a premium, networking can be a great way to stay in-the-know.

Shanghai offers dozens of business organisations devoted to networking and to sharing information/ideas on the evolving business environment. There are also many key groups based in other cities which many Shanghai businesspeople find worthwhile to belong to (or at least be in touch with). Following are some of the best-regarded:

- **The American Chamber of Commerce in Shanghai**
  The Portman Ritz-Carlton Hotel
  4/F, 1376 Nanjing Xi Lu, Shanghai 200040
  Tel: (021) 6279-7119; fax: (021) 6279-7643
  E-mail: amcham@amcham-shanghai.org
  Website: http://www.amcham-shanghai.org
  Tom Gougarty, Executive Director

- **Asia Pacific Council of American Chambers of Commerce (APCAC)**
  No 4501 Trade Tower, 159-1 Samsung-dong, Kangnam-gu, Seoul 135-731, Korea
  Tel: (82-02) 564-2040; fax: (82-02) 564-2050
  Website: http://www.apcac.org
  George M Drysdale, Chairman & CEO

- **Australian Trade Commission (Austrade) Shanghai**
  Australian Consulate-General
  Suite 4710-4712, Plaza 66, 1266 Nanjing Road (West), Shanghai 200004
  Tel: (021) 6321-1333; fax: (021) 6321-1222
  Website: http://www.austemb.org.cn
  http://www.austrade.gov.au
  Dr Dan Sun, Senior Trade Commissioner

- **British Chamber of Commerce, Shanghai**
  Unit 1701-2, Westgate Tower 1038 Nanjing Xilu Shanghai 200040
  Tel: (021) 6218-5022/(021) 6218-5183; fax: (021) 6218-5066/(021) 6218-5193
  Email: britcham-sh@online.sh.cn
  Jan Robertson, General Manager

- **Canada China Business Council**
  Suite 912, Central Plaza 227 Huang Pi Bei Lu, Shanghai, 200003
  Tel: (021) 6359-8908/ 6359-8909; fax: (021) 6375-9361
  Email: ccbcsh@ccbc.com.cn
  Website: http://www.ccbc.com
  Tina Chen, Shanghai Office Manager

- **China Australia Chamber of Commerce, Shanghai**
  1440 Yan'an Zhong Lu, Apollo Building, Suite 531, Shanghai 200040
  Tel: (021) 6248-8301; fax: (021) 6248-5580
  Email: caccsha@uninet.com.cn
  Kate Dunmore McLean, Chair

- **China Chamber of International Commerce (CCOIT) China Council for the Promotion of International Trade (CCPIT)**
  No 1 Fuxingmenwai Jie, Beijing 100860
  Tel: (010) 6801-3344/ (010) 6803-4830; fax: (010) 6801-1370/ (010) 6803-0747
  E-mail: ccpit@ccpit.org
  Website: http://www.ccpit.org

- **The Economist Group**
  No 9 Villa, Ruijin Guesthouse, 118 Ruijin Er Lu, Shanghai 200020
  Tel: (021) 6473-7128; fax: (021) 6473-9268
  Email: shanghai_customerservice@economist.com
  Website: http://www.economistcorporatenetwork.com
  Sean McDermott, Business Development Manager

- **European Union Chamber of Commerce in Shanghai**
  Suite 1709-1710, Building No.1, Corporate Avenue, No 222 Hu Bin Road, Shanghai 200021
  Tel: (021) 6385-2023 / (021) 6385-2133; fax: (021) 6385-2381
  Email: shanghai@euccc.com.cn
  Website: http://www.europeanchamber.com.cn
  Dr Ioana Kraft, Business Manager

- **Finland Trade Centre (Finpro China, Shanghai)**
  Consulate General of Finland, Room 401, Building 2, 690 Bi Bo Road, Zhangjiang Hi-Tech Park, Shanghai 201203
  Tel: (021) 6104-2280; fax: (021) 6104-2289
  Email: shanghai@finpro.fi
  Website: http://www.finpro.fi/shanghai
  Matti Niemela, Head of Trade Centre

- **French Chamber of Commerce and Industry in China (CCIFC)**
  586 Pan Yu Lu, Shanghai 200052, China
  Tel: (021) 6281-3618; fax: (021) 6281-3611
  Email: ccifc-shanghai@ccif.org
  Website: http://www.ccifc.org
  Béatrice Guerin-Coutansais, CCIFC Shanghai Manage

- **French Trade Commission**
  Jinling Building Block 1/11 Floor, 28 Jinling Xi Lu, Shanghai 200021
  Tel: (021) 5306-1100 / (021) 5606-4031; fax: (021) 5306-3637
  Website: http://www.tresor-dree.org/chine
  Isabelle Fernandez, Trade Commissioner
  E-mail: isabelle.fernandez@dree.org

- **Delegation of German Industry & Commerce (AHK)**
  German Industry and Commerce, Shanghai Branch (GIC)
  29/F Pos Plaza, 1600 Shiji Dajie, Pudong, Shanghai 200122
  Tel: (021) 5081-2266 (AHK) / (021) 6875-8536 ; fax: (021) 5081-2009 (AHK) / (021) 6875-8573
  Email: office@sh.china.ahk.de
  Website: http://www.china-net.de
  Dr. Klaus Grimm, President & CEO (GIC)

- **Hong Kong Chamber of Commerce in China**
  Room 817, Shui On Plaza, 333 Huaihai Lu, Shanghai 200021
  Tel: (021) 5306-9533; fax: (021) 5306-9532
  Richard Tam, Secretary General
  Email: richard.tam@tdc.org.hk

- **Italian Trade Commission**
  Room 404, Office Building, Hotel Equatorial, 65 Yan'an Xi Lu, Shanghai 200040
  Tel: (021) 6248-8600 / (021) 6248-0081; fax: (021) 6248-2169
  Email: shanghai@shanghai.ice.it
  Website: http://www.ice.it/estero/shanghai
  Carlo Addis, Trade Commissioner

- **Japanese Chamber of Commerce**
  Room 2001, International Trade Building, 2200 Yan'an Xi Lu, Shanghai 200335
  Tel: (021) 6275-2001; fax: (021) 6270-1579
  Saki Oka, Director

- **Korean Chamber of Commerce**
  Room 303, Li Ang Garden, 60 Lane, Rong Hua Dong Dao, Gubei, Shanghai 201103
  Tel: (021) 6209-5175; fax: (021) 6208-1743
  Email: my2china@chollian.net
  Han Ying Ji, Chairman

- **Quality Brands Protection Committee**
  APCO Associates Inc.
  2005 China World Tower 2, 1 Jianguomenwai Dajie, Beijing, 100004
  Tel: (010) 6505-5127; fax: (010) 6505-5257
  Email: qbpc@apcochina.com
  Website: http://www.qbpc.org.cn/
  Secretariat: Ms Rachel Ding/ Ms Mimi Chang

- **Swiss Chamber of Commerce**
  21-C, 1078 Jiangning Lu, Shanghai
  Tel: (021) 6266-0844; fax: (021) 6276-0856
  Website: http://www.swisscenters.com
  Phillippe Zwahlen, General Manager
  Email: p.zwahlen@swisscenters.com

- **The United States Chamber of Commerce**
  1615 H Street, NW, Washington, DC 20062-2000, USA
  Tel: (1-202) 659 6000
  Email: intl@uschamber.com
  Website: http://www.uschamber.org

- **The United States-China Business Council**
  Room 1301, 1701 Beijing Xi Lu, Shanghai 200040
  Tel: (021) 6288-3840; fax: (021) 6288-3841
  E-mail: info@uschina.org.cn

Website: http://www.uschina.org
Iain K McDaniels, Deputy Director of China Operations
and Chief Representative, Shanghai Office
Email: imcdaniels@uschina.org.cn

In addition, virtually every key industry in Shanghai
offers industry-specific organisations, either as subsets
of the umbrella groups listed above, or independently.
The organisations listed above will be able to help direct
you to appropriate networking opportunities specific to
your business.

Finally, most consulates have a commercial section
which can also be worthwhile getting to know. Consular
resources are typically limited and available only to
firms headquartered in the countries they represent, but
they can be excellent channels for getting messages to
government officials in face-saving ways, and for hearing
about recent leadership shifts. The US and UK consulates are
particularly active.

MAINTAINING A CLEAR CHANNEL WITH HQ

Large ships have trouble turning quickly, and small ships
tethered to large ships can have trouble turning at all. The
flexibility inherently possible in the structure of a global
firm with local offices in Shanghai too easily turns to brittle
restrictiveness without mutual understanding.

Too junior a senior-most executive in Shanghai, or one
without strong headquarters ties, can make it impossible
to get support for key projects, or the operating freedom
needed to respond to Shanghai's rapid changes. One
Shanghai-based manufacturer found this to its cost, when
it took three years for HQ to permit changes to a product
label that local market research showed would be better
received in Shanghai than the global standards. By the
time the corporate Leviathan gave the nod, the market had
moved on and new standards were needed. "In the end,"
said one local executive, "we just gave up market share to
competitors, because customers understood what those guys
had to sell."

Office towers in the Lujiazui
Financial Centre district.

At the same time, manoeuvres designed by local executives to respond to local needs, taken without informing headquarters, can be equally if not more disastrous. The Shanghai branch of a manufacturing firm took a happy video of their Chinese New Year festivities, attended by local government officials, and flushed with pride, sent copies of the video off to global media without stopping to ask higher-ups. The result, from several key media which HQ could have told the branch were poorly disposed to China, was a spate of articles on how this firm was 'sucking up to Beijing'.

At best, failures to communicate lead to friction, lost opportunities and setbacks. One technology firm's local branch, after years of struggle, finally came up with a business model that made the Shanghai firm's operations, though small, one of the most profitable on a percentage basis of the firm worldwide. Profitable, that is, until a hapless global executive, in a meeting with a Shanghai vice-mayor, happily bragged about his firm's local profitability. Within days, the branch was audited by the Shanghai Tax Bureau, which found an excuse to levy higher taxes. In this case, the Shanghai team told HQ just enough to make HQ very dangerous.

There is no shortcut to solid ties and clear communication between headquarters and the local branch, the sort that build shared understandings, mutual trust and a willingness to defer to each other's wisdom when appropriate. Some useful tools include:

Share General News
If you subscribe to a clipping or summary service, think about sharing it with select members of the HQ team, perhaps with a 'summary of the summary' that you draft yourself.

Share Company News
Make HQ part of your 'brag board' for local business wins, new hires, and other good news that highlight local growth.

Make the Pilgrimage

Unless you have world-class video-conferencing—and even if you have—there's no substitute for sending Shanghai executives to headquarters for training, exchanges, to give lectures on local conditions, to attend meetings with the global HQ of your key Shanghai customers, and so forth. There's no better way to let headquarters 'press the flesh' and get to know and trust the local team.

Invite Visitors

Conversely, one of the best ways to strengthen the local team is to bring in HQ visitors regularly via conference call, videoconference, and at least occasionally, in person. But don't just give HQ visitors wine and dine tours—put them to work answering questions from junior staffers, providing training, meeting with customers. This will help build pride and a sense of belonging to the global firm among local staff, and help the global team understand the local talent you have available. And making sure HQ visitors have to sing a bit for their suppers also helps avoid 'junket' types who just want to see Suzhou and figure that poking their heads in the Shanghai office for 30 minutes justifies having the company foot the bill for their trip.

Offer Solid Briefings

When HQ visitors do come, especially when they will meet local customers and/or government officials, make sure they are well-briefed. At minimum, they need to have general background material on China, on the state of play in your industry, on your local offices, and on the personal backgrounds of anyone senior they'll meet, including goals and key messages for the meetings. They need to know both what to say and what not to say. Again, local and global communications firms can help with professional briefing materials.

Build a Strong Cross-cultural Team

This is the key to success in many aspects of Shanghai business, and the subject of the next section.

BUILDING STRONG CROSS-CULTURAL TEAMS IN SHANGHAI

Much has been written on Human Resources (HR) in Shanghai and in China, on the advantages and perils of 'localisation' and/or 'globalisation' of staff, and on finding, motivating and keeping good local staff. Two US-China Business Council publications offer excellent summaries: *Human Resources in Foreign-Invested Enterprises in China: Strategies and Solutions*; and *Beyond the Rhetoric: A New Look at Localisation*. You can find out more at the Council's website:

http://www.uschina.org

We won't, in this short section try to summarise those book-length reports. But it would be remiss in a chapter on Shanghai business to not touch on HR matters, for in this proud and complex city, more firms flounder due to poor relations between expat and local managers than for any other single reason. And tension between Hong Kong and Shanghai makes the common fallback strategy of bringing in a Hong Kong manager to 'fix the local Chinese problem' particularly fraught.

The bottom line, and key to successful business growth in Shanghai, as in most other markets, is motivated local employees. Replacing disgruntled or non-performing expats is expensive, unsettling and devoutly to be avoided if other paths present themselves. But ultimately, it can be done fairly quickly, with limits to the cost.

But replacing or rebuilding an entire team of disgruntled, demoralised or dysfunctional local employees is a far longer process in which costs, both direct and to business reputation, can be nearly limitless. One financial organisation had to fire its entire Shanghai team after a global audit found corruption and widespread fraud. Despite swift action, the firm became the target of several lawsuits that were expensive to settle. Altogether, it took more than a decade to get the company's local offices back on track.

So how does one find and motivate and keep a strong team of local talent? It requires a full range of thoughtful HR programmes that touch, at minimum, on:

- Salary and benefits
- Training opportunities
- Challenging work
- Respectful work environment
- Career paths and opportunities for advancement

Again, books can be—and have been—written on each of these subjects: the USCBC publications provide a useful overview. The sections below touch on a few points of particular concern in Shanghai.

Listening for Local Knowledge

Decades of extremist policies, combined with traditional Confucian respect for authority, have led to a degree of caution among Chinese employees about speaking out or contradicting superiors that can be difficult for individualistic Westerners to understand. In conservative Shanghai, Ground Zero for Cultural Revolution 'struggle sessions', this can be even more true than in Beijing. Suffice it to say that, unless encouraged, Shanghainese will tend not to share information and ideas that seem in any way to contradict superiors, even when they know superiors are dead wrong.

This means that managers who assert their own opinions too strongly, and fail to give local employees sufficient time or invitation to speak out, may find themselves 'flying blind', cut off from the 'human radar' that the intimate local knowledge of their Shanghainese employees could offer.

In the Nick of Time

One expat manager, trying to organise a posh corporate event in a prestigious local venue, got almost to the event's launch-date before learning by accident that the venue he had selected could only hold less than half the number of people planned. Confronting the staffer responsible for venue liaison, the manager found her distraught: "But you told me you absolutely wanted to hold it there; I assumed you must have made some other arrangement about the people."

The key is to not just leave room for opinions, but actively invite them—both individually and in groups—understanding that the Chinese are more comfortable with conversational pauses than Westerners, and can take some time to start speaking. You as manager must also be willing to publicly change your mind, and perhaps to share tales of your own past mistakes. It's also crucial to not punish or ridicule employee contributions. Poor ideas can be glossed over with 'even better ideas', but if employees are laughed at, their timid willingness to offer a suggestion won't be repeated when they have something better to share. And a bit of humour never hurts.

Over time, a corporate culture of 'speaking out' and sharing ideas can be developed in a given office, but that takes time, dedication and a certain amount of ongoing feeding and watering. Some offices that have been very open and good at sharing ideas under one manager, have deteriorated into fiefdoms of hoarded information when a change of management brought an environment less friendly to sharing.

Maintaining Communication Over Goals

One management consultant helped diagnose the ills of a Shanghai-based manufacturing firm with several joint ventures (JVs). Intensive interviews revealed the JVs were each, in essence, three firms in one: expat managers seeking to build market share and make money; local partner managers seeking to maximise investment flows; and local line employees seeking to hold onto jobs. These goals were not necessarily mutually exclusive, but at best they were less than fully parallel, and communications breakdowns had put them increasingly at odds.

At fault in that and many similar situations in Shanghai was a failure to establish big-picture trust and open communication. At the micro level, strong communication involves active, patient listening as discussed above. At the mid-level, trust requires the full range of hiring policies, training and advancement opportunities, and career paths that let Shanghai employees understand that there is no glass ceiling, that they can safely identify their future with the company's.

At the macro level, firms need to communicate about goals, in ways that engage and motivate local employees. With rapid growth and easy job mobility (not what it was in the boom years, but still far easier than nationwide), establishing this long-term bond is particularly important in Shanghai. Some key tools include career development plans with regular written reviews, regular staff meetings discussing progress on local and global goals, employee newsletters, web-based information and plain old-fashioned availability by management when employees need a friendly ear.

Creating Cross-fertilisation

The best expatriate executives in Shanghai see themselves as educators, bringing global knowledge to help burnish the strengths of the local team. Such educational activities can be encouraged and formalised via training sessions, mentoring programmes, shadowing opportunities, and the like.

At the same time, more junior international employees, hired perhaps out of one of China's growing number of international training/educational programmes, can help strengthen the local team practically. Role modeling is all very well, but it is also useful for mid-level Chinese managers to get real practice, cutting global managerial teeth by managing junior-level foreigners. Such arrangements provide needed cross-cultural experience and practice to local managers, and also helps combat any image of a glass ceiling. Also, when the junior-level foreigners hail from various countries, they can help create a learning culture, in which everyone is more open to learning from everyone else.

Similarly, regional expats from Hong Kong, Taiwan or Singapore, and/or 'returnee' Chinese coming home after study and/or work abroad can be an extremely valuable part of the mix—so long as they are not viewed as 'silver bullets'. Shanghainese pride makes local employees highly sensitive to any real or imagined slight, perhaps more so from a regional expat or returnee than from a Westerner, so the 'fellow Chinese' need to take exquisite care not to appear arrogant. But incorporated properly into the team, they can add significant value, with unmatched depth of understanding of the need to balance Chinese tradition with global norms.

Cross-cultural training can help, especially if given to ALL employees, and not presented as something that the Chinese need to learn and foreigners don't (or vice versa). Several Shanghai-based firms offer strong training programmes, though many firms prefer to develop internal programmes specific to their business.

Sending local employees overseas for training and developmental assignments can also help groom future leaders and combat 'glass ceiling' rumours. The key is maintaining the channels with other offices, to ensure that cross-office assignments offer valuable learning opportunities and are not just make-work, and so returning employees are reintegrated smoothly, at levels that reflect the new experience.

This is, of course, only the merest top-line summary of a complex set of topics worth exploring in all their rich depths. In Shanghai, the old cliché about best managers constantly grooming their own replacements is not only true, but comes with an additional twist. The best managers in Shanghai are constantly creating a culture in which their replacements will have a richer experience and broader perspective than they, in a firm that is ever broader and more cross-cultural in its operations.

THINK BROADLY: CONSIDER ALL YOUR MARKETS AND AUDIENCES

When considering market opportunities in Shanghai, how to develop them, and who you need to be speaking with, it is crucial to keep your vision as broad as possible. This is not always as easy as it sounds. In the rarefied atmosphere of AmCham dinners, charity balls and seeing everyone you know at Starbucks in Shanghai Centre, it can be easy to start imagining that everyone you need to know, or might need to sell to, can be met at charity balls or at Starbucks.

And it is true that elite Shanghainese, who live not so very differently from most expats, are a key audience for many Shanghai businesses. By some estimates, the top 10–15 per cent of local income earners hold more than 50 per cent of the city's disposable income. These are the people upgrading computers, arranging car purchases and renovating old mansions in the old French Concession; for the luxury trades, they are the ONLY customers.

But for most businesses, the vast middle class of office workers, the vaster working class of factory workers, and the still more numerous rural poor, offer far larger markets. Yet astonishingly few, among the shark-pool of firms competing in crowded Shanghai, look seriously at those bigger-pond markets. One consumer products firm estimated that of 80–90 shampoo brands competing in the high-end hair care market in Shanghai, fewer than ten had any brand extensions or sister brands aimed at the middle class.

Many fine articles have been written and many consulting careers are being made looking beyond the so-called 'Tier-1 Consumers'. It is worth your while to start researching them, to think about the possibility of tiered marketing strategies, and to look beyond Shanghai Centre and the Bund when thinking about your market.

Similarly, when thinking about the target audiences you must work with, think more broadly than AmCham and your immediate customers. At minimum, your outreach efforts should include:

- Senior leaders within Chinese organisations and government bodies that regulate your industry
- Mid-level managers in those same organisations, with day-to-day responsibility over your business
- Media, as channels to influencing other audiences
- Industry associations relevant to your industry
- Academia (as researchers into your industry, and as sources of potential future employees)
- Consumer associations, which have increasing influence and regulatory power

Again, the broader your perspective, the bigger your market and the more secure the base of relationships that will help keep your company stable in changing times.

KEEP A TIGHT LID ON COSTS

It is a truism that China has lured many firms with the promises of low-cost operations, only to prove one of the world's more expensive investment destinations. Nowhere is this more true than in Shanghai, where office space can run over US$ 200 per sq m, and housing can top US$ 15,000 per month, and where wages can run several times national norms.

Many firms have found themselves in the queer position of making higher gross revenues than predicted in Shanghai, and still falling short on budgeted profits. Such gaps occur whenever firms fail to rein in expenses. Millions in revenue can disappear like desert rainfall when managers all have cars and drivers and live in expensive compounds. Also, junior staffers, seeing lavish habits at the top, feel less inclined toward thriftiness in small matters—even 'small' computer purchases and office supply choices can add up rapidly in Shanghai. The compounded results of unrestrained spending can pummel almost any gross revenues into the red.

The better choice is to encourage a culture of thriftiness appropriate to your business and stage of development. Obviously a well-established Mercedes dealership needs to spend more on plush sales room space than a new discount Santana parts dealer needs. But both can—and should—be careful with any expense that is unnecessary for their business.

Attention to thriftiness starts from the top. Choices in housing and transportation, office sites, decorative materials, IT connections, and other matters can save millions of Rmb. Earlier chapters have offered some guidance in these areas, and more resources can be found at the business associations listed in this chapter, and by asking local employees to help with research. Doing so is a worthwhile effort, as thrifty versus spendthrift corporate budgets can easily make the difference between profit and loss, between team members getting raises and bonuses, and having to cut jobs.

And therein lies perhaps the core reason for thriftiness, particularly surrounding the too-often-out-of-control cost of high-end expat benefits. Thriftiness in Shanghai is not just a virtue, but a powerful business tool, because it helps build strong teams that in turn help build a more and more profitable company: the beneficent cycle of good management.

On the whole, Shanghainese tend not to question salary differentials. After all, they are used to earning more than the China average, and to great gaps between top and bottom Shanghainese earners. Especially when an expat is seen as bringing special talents, helping to rain-make new business, educating junior staffers, or otherwise helping the company grow, local employees are unlikely to be upset by high expat salaries, even when details get leaked (as, unfortunately, they too often are).

Non-salary benefits, however, are a different story, especially with benefits that (as is often the case) are limited to expats. If a local manager knows her salary will increase over time, but she'll never get a housing allowance no matter what, she will naturally look skeptically at expat housing costs, particularly when expats choose compounds that effectively exclude nearly all Chinese by price. And unlike salaries, addresses cannot be kept secret, even in the best-managed firms.

If a company is failing to make healthy profits, rightly or wrongly, expat benefits are the first thing local employees will point at. Pity the expat manager living in a US$ 10,000 per month apartment at Shanghai Centre, or a US$ 15,000 per month garden villa, trying to maintain team motivation while explaining that failing profits mean no Chinese New Year bonus. He may as well pack it in. And if his successor wants to avoid a vicious spiral of top employees quitting for greener pastures elsewhere, leading to declining sales and even poorer profits, he or she will wisely return to the values of thriftiness.

THINK GLOBALLY: HELP SHANGHAI MOVE TO GLOBALLY-ACCEPTED NORMS

Finally, it is worth considering what steps you can personally take during your Shanghai sojourn to help move forward Shanghai's 10,000-mile journey toward full transparency.

The cynics would say: 'Nothing. China is China and will go its own way as it has for 5,000 years, so don't waste breath.' Such cynics can certainly look around on any given day and find plenty of fodder for their views. But the trouble with cynicism, of course, is that it too often breeds self-fulfilling prophecy, where a more optimistic outlook might have a more positive effect. And so it seems useful to outline a few suggestions on being a cautious optimist with regards to China's long journey toward rule of law.

What NOT To Do…

The first point is that businesses could do worse than borrow from the medical ethic of 'at least do no harm'. In order not to harm progress toward transparency, you should:

Follow Transparent Ethical Procedures in Your Own Business

There is plenty of corruption in Shanghai, and foreign firms have certainly gotten involved; but few have profited by it long term. This is not some Pollyanna prediction of evil begetting evil. Rather, it's a cold fact of business life in China that anti-corruption campaigns are often hijacked for political/competitive aims, and foreign firms found tainted are first to be pilloried by media and government. Deals have been lost, offices closed and foreign managers sent to Chinese prisons for corruption. It's just not worth it. For every shady character who swears Shanghai business requires payoffs, others clinch deals BECAUSE of their ethical record, because anti-corruption campaigns make working with a company 'known to be clean' politically safe. By sticking to the straight and narrow, you may lose some deals in the short term, but you'll build a stronger business over time—as market-leading firms like DuPont, BP, Intel, and others have found.

To help achieve ethical behaviour, ensure your firm has a written corporate Code of Conduct. Make it available and understandable to employees, vendors and contractors; and enforce it. Make sure it contains enough flexibility to allow normal business entertaining, token gifts and other common Shanghai business practices that fall within the guidelines of the US Foreign Corrupt Practices Act. Such normal business practices, for instance (as in the West), commonly include business entertaining, seminars and study tours organised around desirable trips, and the like. There are grey areas, but there are also lines that should not be crossed, and you should organise internal seminars or discussion groups, and make senior management available, to help junior staffers sort out what is and isn't acceptable.

Resist the 'Run to Daddy' Urge

Not every negotiating setback is a WTO (World Trade Organisation) compliance issue, and not every disagreement is best resolved by pounding the doors of the US Trade

Representative (USTR) or the British Commercial attaché. Chinese appreciate business partners who work with them toward creative, win-win resolutions of conflicts; firms that learn to do so generally fare best over time. Several IT firms once got caught in an inter-ministerial regulatory 'turf war' that ended in a government crackdown on businesses that had been operating in a regulatory 'grey area'. Some firms fought the crackdown in public, taking complaints to the USTR, the WTO and the media. Others sat and negotiated carefully with Chinese counterparts, seeking a win-win resolution. It's a no-brainer that the quiet negotiators came away from the table happier. In at least one case the authors were involved with, investors were happy enough with returns they ended up with to reinvest in a new, slightly less-grey, project.

Be Wary about Hanging Dirty Laundry in Public

Chinese in general and Shanghainese in particular are emotionally allergic to scandal. The loss of face involved tends to rebound against the party that brought the issues to light. It's much better, where possible, to resolve issues quietly. The threat of going to the media or to senior government leaders can occasionally work as a threat, but generally to the detriment of the long-term relationship. And once such a threat is carried out, the leverage is gone, and that business relationship is generally pretty much over.

Be a Little Humble about Pointing Fingers

The Chinese are fond of the old saying that when you point a finger at someone else, three fingers are pointing back at you. After all, it took 300 years of free-market development in the Americas for the United States to produce Enron. Chinese who were lectured ad nauseum by Westerners on corruption, transparency and ethics in China's first 20 years of reform took a certain delight in the US market meltdown that resulted from Enron and ensuing scandals. Be a bit careful about lecturing, if you don't want to simply be lectured in return.

Be Careful Playing the WTO Card

China worked for 15 years to join the WTO, and the commitments made as part of her accession were vast, far-reaching and not universally agreed to by all parties. Progress toward compliance has certainly been uneven: tariff adjustments have proceeded quickly, for instance, while some administrative barriers have remained or even grown. Confusion abounds as to exactly what was agreed to, on what time frame, in which geographies. Before running to your government to complain about WTO compliance, you should first be very sure of your legal grounds, and also attempt to resolve the issue quietly via education and negotiation.

What TO do...

All that said, there are times and places and venues appropriate for action:

- DO raise WTO issues when you're sure of your grounds, and have exhausted other methods. Global businesses investing in China have a right to insist on compliance with WTO accession agreements. If efforts at education and negotiation have failed, and it's clear a given regulatory or other body is in deliberate violation, then the time has come to appeal to the WTO for support.
- DO raise issues through appropriate channels. Wherever possible, intervention on WTO compliance or other 'big-picture' issues should be raised not by individual firms, but via multilateral bodies. An industry association making a complaint is FAR stronger than an individual company, particularly if there are Chinese members of the association.
- DO seek win-win solutions. Get creative in your discussions with the Chinese. Can payment issues be resolved with compensatory trade? Can collection issues be prevented by shipping product cash on delivery? Can a dispute over intellectual property be resolved with joint branding? Such creative solutions will not always work, but in Shanghai, you should always be thinking more in terms of negotiating disputes, than litigating them.

- DO maintain quiet dialogues on global norms. To say that one shouldn't lecture does not mean that one shouldn't ask for change. The key is how the request is presented. There is a world of difference between discussing how Enron has damaged the US economy, and the lessons that may offer for Shanghai; and simply lecturing Shanghainese on accounting standards.
- DO praise progress and celebrate successes. If the Chinese are allergic to negative publicity, they are also responsive to praise. You can catch a lot more flies with honey than with vinegar, and in Shanghai that translates into the value of congratulatory ads, positive media placements, stirring speeches, and the like.

Shanghai, like much of China, seems to be at something of a crossroads. In 20 years of reform policies, the nation has made tremendous strides: a quick comparison with Russia or Indonesia is all that is needed, despite all the problems, to reinforce the accomplishments that have been made. The new generation of leadership seems poised to take China to the next level of reform, if all goes well, and every effort that can help move Shanghai and China in the direction of openness, transparency and rule-of-law should be made. The alternative is for reforms to languish in a stew of corruption that could eventually give China the worst of both Russian-style mafia chaos and Indonesian-style cronyism.

You can, and should, do your bit to help the rule-of-law forward. It is good business for you in the long run, and the right thing to do. To paraphrase Margaret Mead, never doubt that a small group of thoughtful, committed businesspeople can help change the world. Indeed, it's one of the only things that ever really does.

FAST FACTS
ABOUT SHANGHAI

CHAPTER 10

'Paris of the East, Whore of China, Queen of the Orient;
city of bums, adventurers, pimps, swindlers, gamblers,
sailors, socialites... Trend-setter, snob, leader...
a hybrid of Paris and New York in the 1930s with
millions trampling the streets where millionaires once trod.''
—*Lonely Planet: China*

Official Name
Shanghai Municipality

Flag of China
Red with a large, yellow five-pointed star and four smaller yellow five-pointed stars (arranged in a vertical arc toward the middle of the flag) in the upper left-hand corner

Time Difference
Greenwich Mean Time plus 8 hours (GMT + 0800)

Telephone Country Code
Country Code for China   86
Area Code for Shanghai   021

Climate
The climate in Shanghai is quite extreme. Summer is hot and humid, with temperatures reaching up to 40°C (104°F). Rainy season starts in June and autumn is relatively mild. In winter, temperatures can go below freezing and spring begins in March.

Population
China   1,306,313,812 (July 2005 est.)
Shanghai   over 20 million

Language and Dialects

The official language is Mandarin, however, Shanghainese is also widely spoken by the locals. English is not so common.

Religion

In China, religion consists of Taoism, Buddhism, Islam, Christian and Judaism.

Government Type

Communist State

Currency

The renminbi (Rmb), also referred to as the yuan (CNY), is the official currency in China.

Industries

Shanghai's major industries are in coal, crude oil and manufacturing of footwear, garments, household electrical appliances, general metalwares, pharmaceuticals, sports goods, steel products, telecommunication equipment, textiles and toys.

Exports

Electronics, telecommunications, biomedical supplies, footwear, garments

Ethnic Groups

China consists of Han Chinese (91.9 per cent), Zhuang, Uygur, Hui, Yi, Tibetan, Miao, Manchu, Mongol, Buyi and Korean. Other nationalities make up about 8.1 per cent. There is also a large long-term foreign population but their exact numbers are not known as the statistics are not readily available.

Airport

The main airport is now at Pudong, newly constructed in the Pudong new district, far from the city centre but connected by a network of buses, taxis and the new high-speed magnetic levitation train system (very fast, but expensive and not always available at convenient hours at the moment). The old Hongqiao Airport is now reserved for short-distance domestic flights.

Electricity
220 volts

Famous People
Lu Xun (1881–1936)
Famous Chinese writer of the early 20th century. His most famous works include *The True Story of Ah Q* and *The Diary of a Madman*. On his death in 1936, he was buried in the Shanghai Municipal Council's Foreigner's Cemetary. It was only in 1956 when his remains were finally moved to their final (and current) resting place in Hongkou Park where he lived when he was alive.

Zhou Enlai (1898–1976)
This former premier of China once live in the French Concession in 1946 as head of the Communist Party's Shanghai office.

Sun Yat Sen (1866–1925)
Famous for leading the republican forces which overthrew the Manchu Empire in 1912, his house is still open to the public today.

Soong Qingling (1893–1981)
Wife of Sun Yat Sen who led the democratic party her husband's name after his premture death in 1925. She was made honorary president of the People's Re[ublic of China on 29 May 1981, as she lay almost comatose two weeks before her death.

Places of Interest
The Bund (Wai Tan)
Situated along the Huangpu River, this waterfront promenade is packed with tourists and locals alike.

Shanghai Museum (Shanghai Bowuguan)

Opened in 1995, this museum focuses on the pre-1911 period of China's history. It is located in the middle of People's Square and houses jade, Ming and Qing dynasty furniture and multiple paintings, sculptures and ceramics. It also has an excellent bookstore.

Garden of Contentment (Yu Yuan Garden)

First built during the Ming dynasty, this garden now covers 2 hectares (about 4.9 acres) and is said to have six main scenic areas. These are centred around certain structures and known as Three Ears of Corn Hall (San Sui Tang), Ten Thousand Flowers Chamber (Yi Wan Hua Lou), Hall of Heralding Spring (Dian Chun Tang), Scenery Gathering Tower (Hui Jing Ge) Hall facing the Jade Rock (Yu Hua Tang) and the Inner Garden (Nei Yuan).

Jade Buddha Temple (Yu Fo Si)

Located at the corner of An Yuan Lu and Jiang Ning Lu, this religious site is home to two Buhhda statues that are carved entirely out of single blocks of jade. One of these is an usual reclining Buddha.

Xintiandi

Formerly a neighbourhood of *shikumen*, this district has been renovated with fine restaurants, bars and clubs.

CULTURE QUIZ

SITUATION 1

You have just arrived in Shanghai with your six-month-old son. You sit down in a restaurant and the waitress swoops over, coos at your child in Chinese, then picks him up and trots off to show him to a gaggle of other waitresses. You should:

A Scream for the cops.

B Step in front of the waitress, explain politely but firmly (using hand signals if necessary) that you don't want your son touched by strangers, and take your son back.

C Relax and let the waitresses baby-sit your son while you enjoy your meal.

D Smile, stand and follow the waitress, letting her understand that you're happy she shares your joy in your son, and you are also available to keep an eye on him.

Comments

This common situation is one of the most jarring for new parents in Shanghai, whose instinct often tells them to do **A**.

The trouble is, of course, that the waitress almost certainly intended no harm. **❸** is less damaging, but will still brand you as rather cold and untrusting. **❹** is probably the best balance, at least at first—although after a time, if you have a good view of him just in case he becomes upset, particularly on repeat visits to the same restaurant, you may well find you can relax into **❸**!

SITUATION 2

You are volunteer-teaching English to children of migrant workers in a community-run school. One of your students plagiarises an essay from the textbook. You ask a Shanghainese friend for advice, and the friend says: "Well, that just goes to show you those migrant kids are stupid. It's a waste of time trying to teach them." You should:

❹ Tell the friend politely but firmly that you disagree with such prejudice. Return to class, and praise the child for effort in order to avoid hurting fragile self-esteem.

❸ Agree with the friend. Quit teaching and turn your volunteer efforts elsewhere.

❸ Thank the friend for input, but resolve to try pushing the child to succeed. Give a poor grade, explain why, and say "try harder next time."

❹ Ask several Chinese friends how well Chinese kids understand plagiarism. Consider discussing the issue with the class, and re-assigning a new essay to the offender.

Comments

China's education system tends to emphasise memorisation over creativity. Looking up the most apt commentary by the most recognised master on a given topic, and copying it out, is considered to be valuable scholarship, often more so than having 'mere' students express personal opinions as an academic exercise. The Chinese are taught that they should cite attribution, but do not in general have the visceral revulsion toward plagiarism that is so central to teaching in the West. Your response to your plagiarising student (or for that matter, employee) needs to take this background into account.

That said, China's leadership does want to increase creativity in its educational process, while also gradually overcoming the urban-rural prejudice displayed by the 'Shanghainese friend' in this example. Both of these laudable objectives illustrate why either

Ⓐ or **Ⓑ** would be wrong. **Ⓒ** is a possibility, especially with repeat offenders, and/or after you have already explained your stance on plagiarism to the class. If this is a first-time situation, however, and especially if you think the problem may be more general than the one student, **Ⓓ** is your best choice.

SITUATION 3

One week into your new job, you are responsible for a major event. Preparations seem smooth, but the day of the event the caterer fails to show. A quick investigation reveals the deposit payment was never made, so the caterer took another job; your predecessor, it seems, left without signing the payment authorisation. You arrange last-minute hotel catering. When you rush authorisation for that bill into Accounting, the bookkeeper shrugs, "You seemed awfully busy this week. I didn't want to disturb you." The event goes well, but catering cost twice what it should have due to last minute charges. You:

Ⓐ Shrug and accept the higher bill as part of the price of your learning curve.

Ⓑ Call the team together for a post-event debriefing, thanking them for all that went well, and discussing all that could be improved, including admitting your own fault for not following up on details, and ask that everyone feel free to come to you with any question at any time in the future. Make time after the meeting to talk with team members individually.

Ⓒ Scream at and threaten to fire the bookkeeper for costing the company so much.

❶ Privately criticise the bookkeeper for failing to follow through, but do not drag other employees into the conversation.

Comments

Employees worldwide often take wait-and-see attitudes toward new bosses, watching how 'new management' behaves under pressure and handles employee mistakes before deciding how much to trust it going forward. Chinese staffers often raise this scrutiny to a high art, in ways Westerners sometimes find passive-aggressive. The bookkeeper's snippy comment about the boss seeming 'awfully busy' is a backhanded way of saying he or she felt snubbed, since the new boss didn't bother checking in with him or her. No matter how busy you are in a new Shanghai job, it's important to find time in the first days to meet with all your direct reports—ideally first in a group and then one by one. Find out what they have on their plates, and what they need and expect of you.

Given the above, it should be obvious why **❸** won't do. It would, in fact, likely make a mortal enemy of the bookkeeper, especially if the screaming happened in public and made him or her 'lose face'. If you fired this person, his or her teammates might decide you deliberately entrapped him or her, distrust you, and find ways to undermine you over time. **❶** is neutral, offends nobody, solves nothing, and leaves you seeming ineffective. **❶** might work, but its long-term effects are dependent on how the bookkeeper describes your private conversation (as this person will) to the others. **❷** is your best choice. A little humility (don't overdo it) goes a long way to establishing trust, and the bookkeeper will understand your implied criticism. You can also follow up in a private conversation, in a way that doesn't make him or her lose face.

SITUATION 4

At a morning language lesson, you ask your Chinese tutor for help correctly pronouncing the name of a Taiwanese client. You hand him the piece of paper on which you have carefully copied out the client's name: Lin Cheng. But the tutor shakes his head, saying that without the Chinese characters, he's not sure how to pronounce the name. You decide:

Ⓐ There's something you don't understand about Chinese names; better bring the business card to your next lesson—or to a Chinese colleague.

Ⓑ The teacher is trying to sneak a look at the business card to steal client information.

Ⓒ The teacher is a bit dim.

Ⓓ Taiwanese Chinese language is different from Mainland Chinese language.

Comments

Chinese names are traditionally written family name first (almost always one character), given name second (usually two characters). Thus Mao Zedong was 'Chairman Mao'. When writing in Chinese characters, whether traditional complex characters (as in Taiwan) or simplified characters (as in the Mainland), family name is always first. But when writing out a Romanised version of the name using English letters, Westernised Chinese sometimes reverse order and put given name first 'for the convenience of Western friends'. This can cause confusion, especially with two-character names.

Adding to the confusion, Taiwan and the Mainland use different Romanisation systems. Taiwan uses the Wade-Giles system (developed by 19th century missionaries), while the Mainland uses the Hanyu Pinyin system (developed by Russian sinologists—which is why *pinyin* pronunciations are closer to Cyrillic than to English; **c** for instance is pronounced *ts*). This might lead you to suspect the answer is **Ⓓ**. But in fact, though Wade-Giles and *pinyin* spellings look quite different, they are just two ways of trying to express in English letters the pronunciation of the same character. Give or take minor differences of accent, Taiwanese Chinese and Mainland Chinese are the same (at least when people are speaking Mandarin Chinese and not local dialects, which are another story). **Ⓐ** is the answer. Seeing the characters, your Shanghai tutor will be able to correctly pronounce your Taiwanese client's name.

SITUATION 5

Your children's wonderful Beijing *Ayi* ('Auntie'/nanny) has followed you when the company transferred you from Beijing to Shanghai. But somehow she seems less wonderful here. She seems to have trouble doing the shopping, she often seems confused, and the kids say that when she tried to take them to the park she got lost, and couldn't even understand when people tried gave her directions. You conclude:

Ⓐ She is homesick. You should send her back to Beijing and find a local nanny.

Ⓑ She is having trouble adjusting to Shanghai. You should have a heart-to-heart about whether she wants to stay, and if she does, about what support she needs.

Ⓒ It's just a phase. Everyone has down times. Ignore it and she'll get better.

Ⓓ The kids have been too hard on her. Have a heart-to-heart with them about not picking on the nanny, and being more understanding of her difficulties.

Comments

Many foreigners, focused on their own cross-cultural adjustment to China, make the mistake of assuming that all Chinese are comfortable throughout China. In fact, local differences between cities like Beijing and Shanghai are significant, and Chinese people—traditionally less mobile than Westerners—can find them disturbing. Add to that the unfamiliarity of places and people that afflict any move, perhaps especially for poorly-educated and less well-travelled people, and you begin to understand the *Ayi*'s discomfort. Finally, the local Shanghai dialect, commonly spoken on the streets, is different enough from Mandarin (the official language throughout China, close to the Beijing regional accent) to not be mutually comprehensible without study, making your Beiing Ayi almost as 'foreign' in Shanghai as you are. While most Shanghainese speak Mandarin, some, jealous of Beijingers 'taking jobs from locals', may deliberately speak Shanghainese only around a hapless Beijinger wandering 'their' streets in charge of foreign kids.

You should think long and hard before transferring an *Ayi* (or any other employee) from one Chinese city to another. And if, as in this case, the move proves difficult, you have a problem that needs to be dealt with. Ignore it (**C**), and she might adjust on her own or might not, and fall into depression. On the other hand, having brought her, it is not right to just cut bait and send her home to Beijing (**A**) without giving her a choice. Your best bet is **B**. If she wants to make a go of it, consider funding lessons in Shanghainese which she, as a native Mandarin speaker, should be able to pick up quickly with some support. Meantime, encouraging extra understanding from the kids (**D**) wouldn't hurt.

SITUATION 6

You and your spouse will be out of town for the weekend. Your teenaged son asks permission to hold a party for friends while you're gone. You agree, on condition that the *Ayi* chaperones, and you instruct the *Ayi* not to allow liquor. But on return, you find an empty liquor cabinet, the *Ayi* cleaning and your son nursing a giant headache. You:

A Replace the *Ayi* for being too stupid or weak to follow instructions.

B Apologise to the *Ayi* for putting too much responsibility on her, ground your son and announce there will be no more parties in your absence until he's more mature.

C Decide to resign your expat position and go home; your son is obviously getting into a bad crowd in Shanghai, and your job isn't worth threatening his health.

D Repeat your instructions to the *Ayi* 'for next time', louder.

Comments

Living with *Ayis* is wonderful—they can take many day-to-day burdens off parents, and make hectic modern life civilised. But expecting *Ayis* to wholesale take over disciplining and inculcating a sense of responsibility into your children is expecting too much. *Ayis* know that while you pay their salary, they must work every day with your kids, and they generally bend over backwards to please their young charges. Also, since most come from poorer, less educated families, they tend to be vulnerable to spoiled kids who enjoy playing 'young master' or 'young mistress', and lording it over 'the servants'. Leaving an *Ayi* in charge of a houseful of foreign teenagers is asking for trouble.

In the case above, having learned their mistake, the parents should apologise (**❸**), and take steps to make sure it doesn't happen again. If it does happen again, without permission, parents who care about the welfare of their children should consider more drastic steps, like **❸**. There is far more heavy drinking, drug use and other abuses in the teenaged expat community in Shanghai than is readily admitted, too often because parents excited about their careers, deliberately ignore the effect that career focus may be having on the family as a whole. Some reflection on fundamental values may be needed.

SITUATION 7

Invited to a fancy Canton-style restaurant, you are presented with an unfamiliar dish arranged beautifully on a golden plate. Enquiring politely, you hear it is *xiaozi xiongmao*, a name you don't know. Your hosts give you to understand it is a rare and wonderful treat, an honour for you and hint it was very expensive. You flip through a dictionary and find you're being served Lesser Panda, an endangered species. You:

Ⓐ Vomit and run screaming from the restaurant.
Ⓑ Politely explain you are a strong environmentalist, and so have difficulty eating endangered animals. But thank your hosts deeply for the honour, and eat heartily of other foods.
Ⓒ Grin and eat it. An honour is an honour, this is an important business deal; and the panda is already dead.
Ⓓ Pretend to taste, smile politely, push it around your plate and focus on other foods.

Comments

Chinese, in general, are adventurous eaters, a result of millennia of culinary experimentation. Even among Chinese, the Cantonese have a reputation for eating, as the saying goes, 'everything with legs but the table, everything that flies but airplanes, and everything that swims but boats'. In many cases, this adventurousness has uncovered wonderful delicacies that Western cooking profligately throws away. If you try them with an open mind, for instance, you may come to agree that specialities like fish cheeks, chicken claws, seaweed and eels are both thrifty and delicious. And in an absolute sense, there's nothing stranger about eating pig blood or fermented tofu than there is about eating, say, blue cheese—a Western delicacy many Chinese find strange ('milk so curdled and moldy that it's gone solid? EEEEEWW!').

A special problem arises in the case of edible items which Westerners find not just weird but morally repugnant, such as animals considered house pets in the West (like dogs and cats), and endangered species. Increasingly, as Chinese become wealthier, better-educated and better-travelled, begin to afford having house pets of their own and become more aware of environmental issues, these tastes are changing. Today, many Chinese also avoid eating dogs, cats and endangered animals—and the impact of Severe Acute Respiratory Syndrome (SARS), which is suspected to have originated with the eating of exotic animals, is expected to push this change further. But, unfortunately, as of this writing, the fact that a species is endangered still means for some Chinese (as indeed for some Westerners) that they had better taste it while there is still some to be tasted.

A is clearly unacceptable since, after all, the panda was intended as an honour. **C** is probably equally unacceptable for most Westerners. Whether you choose **D** or **B** will depend on your personality, your relationship with your hosts and your sense of the situation. If you do it with a light touch, describing your own environmentalism as if you yourself find it a tad extreme, you may be able to get the point across, and help push forward the change described above, without causing any loss of face for your host. **D** is the safer bet, however. Your hosts will note that you aren't exactly digging in, and most will be polite enough to not put any more on your plate. If they do, you can push that around also. Eventually, they'll get the point, and the message will get across, without anyone having to lose face.

SITUATION 8

You've been brought to Shanghai to shore up a division in financial trouble. The China CEO suggests you rely on a manager newly transferred from Hong Kong: "Great guy," the CEO says, "really turned things around when I worked with him down there." The Hong Kong manager says the Shanghai staff is incompetent. Local staff seem wary of you, and you hear they think the Hong Kong manager is 'arrogant'. You should:

Ⓐ Accept that there may be some staff competency issues, and seek to improve matters with skills training and, if necessary, by replacing the weakest links.

Ⓑ Accept that there may be issues with management arrogance. Try improving matters with sensitivity training and, if need be by replacing poor-performing managers.

Ⓒ Accept that cross-cultural issues are a problem for the company and seek ways through training, staff outings and other tools to improve understanding and morale.

Ⓓ Work with both staff and managers to seek root causes of the financial trouble—lost sales, high costs, whatever. Work together to attack the root causes.

Comments

Foreign-invested enterprises fail in China for many reasons—poorly conceived business plans, improper pricing strategies, inflexible policies that make it impossible for the company to respond nimbly to market shifts, and so on. But in many, many cases, at the base of this seeming plethora of problems is a single root cause: failed communication and trust between Chinese employees and foreign managers that makes joint problem-solving impossible. Many firms respond to this breakdown by bringing in so-called 'regional expats' from Hong Kong, Singapore or Taiwan, seen as a 'bridge' to local staff since 'at least they speak the same language'. Sometimes such appointments prove astute. But too often, such transfers carry baggage of their own in perceived 'glass ceilings' for local-born Chinese and traditional jealousies between 'overseas Chinese' and their mainland 'compatriots' that complicates matters even further.

Training of various forms and a focus on sensitivity and improved morale are important tools for turning around a company or division that has gotten stuck in the cross-cultural divide. **A**, **B** and **C** may all be useful steps, particularly in combination, so everyone sees that no one group has been targeted as 'the cause of the problem'. But training and morale-building are not ends in themselves. You will best gain respect for and buy-in to your turnaround efforts by focusing on identifying and solving fundamental problems (**D**). Do you need to add salespeople? Reduce overhead? Improve collections? In the first months of your appointment, you will have something of a 'honeymoon' in which you can try fairly radical changes—and these will be most effective if any belt-tightening that you recommend affects you too. Have you found that expat cars and drivers have become an unhealthy expense? Sell all the cars and dismiss all the drivers, including your own, and the team will follow you anywhere.

DO'S AND DON'TS

DO'S

- Explore and get to know Shanghai and China.
- Try to learn Mandarin Chinese, and/or at least a few words of Shanghainese.
- Be as adventurous as you feel able to in trying new foods and other experiences.
- Expect to have guests, in your office and home, and lay in a stock of tea, sodas and simple snacks.
- Learn how to 'give face', and how to avoid making people 'lose face'.
- Prepare business cards in Chinese, and always carry a good stock with you.
- Always carry tissues, toilet paper and bottled water when travelling away from hotels or expat enclaves.
- Exercise caution when crossing streets.
- Politely ignore strangers, unless you want to invite interaction ("May I practise my English with you?").
- Shake hands when introduced; though Chinese handshakes are rarely firm.
- Learn to enjoy the art of small talk, especially with older Chinese associates/ clients.
- Reciprocate hospitality.
- Bring small gifts when invited to a private home: a treat from home is always appreciated, or some wine or nice fruit.
- Offer compliments that err on the side of being effusive, if you mean them, and polite mutterings even if not (unless you mean to be insulting).
- Observe and provide appropriate token gifts for Chinese holidays like the Mid-Autumn Festival.
- Accept that 'business is personal' in China, and encourage friendly relations among staff and clients.
- Clarify expectations for household and business staff.
- Adopt a 'show-and-tell' attitude: demonstrate wishes as much as possible to improve clarity.

- Do feel free to share your perspectives on Chinese culture, in appropriate circumstances, in a way that demonstrates respect and avoids face loss.

DON'TS

- Don't be one of those expats who lives in an expat enclave and never tries to enjoy China.
- Don't give up easily on Chinese: you can learn at least enough to get around if you try.
- Don't wrinkle your nose in disgust if a Chinese host presents you with a 'delicacy' like sea slug.
- Don't feel you MUST eat something you find morally repugnant; you can politely push it around your plate, while continuing to eat other things.
- Don't be impatient with small talk—it is often a prelude to more important things
- Don't crush anyone's hand in a shake, or hug a Chinese person unless they hug first.
- Don't interpret a token gift as implying anything overly much.
- Don't accept anything more than a token gift without understanding clearly what's being implicitly 'asked for' in return,
- Don't bring cut flowers as a gift, unless you want them to be interpreted as romantic (or, if they are white, as a condolence gift for mourning).
- Don't give a clock as a gift: it's considered unlucky—the Chinese term for 'to give a clock' (*song zhong*) is homophonous to a phrase meaning 'to wish someone death'.
- Don't fail to compliment a host, or to offer food and drink when you are a host, potentially more than once (since Chinese often make polite refusals to avoid being seen as greedy).
- Don't make negative comments about China gratuitously, or in situations that make people lose face.

GLOSSARY

THE BASICS

English	Shanghai Dialect Pinyin	Simplified Characters
hello	*nung hoa*	你好
thank you	*ziazia*	谢谢
goodbye	*tsewe*	再见
man	*noening*	男人
woman	*niuning*	女人
no problem	*nmeh vengdi*	没问答
take care	*xiaoxing ti*	小心点
Is that right?	*ahzy*	是不是
Do you want it?	*ah yoa*	要不要
sorry	*boaqi*	抱歉
long time no see	*zangyuoe veh ji*	很久不见
not bad	*he hoa*	还可以

NUMBERS

English	Shanghai Dialect Pinyin	Simplified Characters
zero	*ling*	零
one	*yeh*	一
two	*ni*	二
three	*se*	三
four	*sy*	四
five	*wu*	五
six	*loh*	六
seven	*qieh*	七
eight	*pah*	八
nine	*jieu*	九
ten	*zeh*	十

PLACE NAMES AND TERMS—SHANGHAI

English	Shanghai Dialect Pinyin	Simplified Characters
Beijing	Pohjing	北京
Shanghai	Zonghe	上海
Guangzhou	Kuongtseu	广州
Nanjing	Noejing	南京
Xiamen	Womeng	厦门
Shandong	Setung	山东
Zhejiang	Tsehkong	浙江
Anhui	Oehue	安徽
Guangdong	Kuongtung	广东
Taiwan	Dewe	台湾
Hong Kong	Xiangkong	香港
Harbin	Ha'elping	哈尔滨
Xi'an	Xu'oe	西安
Guilin	Kueling	桂林
Hangzhou	Hongtseu	杭州
Suzhou	Sutseu	苏州
Qingdao	Qingtoa	青岛
Dalian	Dali	大连
Tibet	Xizong	西藏
Singapore	Xingkapu	新加坡
Korea	Hoekoh	韩国
Japan	Zehpeng	日本
Australia	Oadaliya	澳大利亚
US–Canada	Me–Ka	美国–加拿大
Bund	Ngathe	外滩
Hongqiao Airport	Hungdjioa Jizang	虹桥机场
Oriental Pearl TV Tower	Tungfong Mingtsy	东方明珠
Lujiazui Financial District	Lohkatsy	陆家嘴

English	Shanghai Dialect Pinyin	Simplified Characters
Jingjiang Park	Jingkong Lohyuoe	锦江乐园
Nanpu Bridge	Noephu Dadjioa	南浦大桥
People's Park	Zengming Kungyuoe	人民公园
Xujiahui (shopping area)	Zikawe	徐家汇
gate	*meng*	门
outside	*ngami*	外面
inside	*lixiang*	里面
east	*tung*	东
west	*xi*	西
north	*po*	北
south	*noe*	南
lane	*lilung*	里弄
avenue	*ka*	街
road	*lu*	路
taxi	*cehtsuco*	出租车

NAMES AND TITLES

English	Shanghai Dialect Pinyin	Simplified Characters
Mister (Mr)	*xisang*	先生
Miss (Ms)	*xioajia*	小姐
Mistress (Mrs)	*thatha*	夫人
colleague	*dungzy*	同事

Some common Chinese family names (surnames) in Shanghai are:

English	Shanghai Dialect Pinyin	Simplified Characters
Zhang	Tsang	张
Wang	Wong	王

English	Shanghai Dialect Pinyin	Simplified Characters
Li	Li	李
Liu	Lieu	刘
Huang	Wong	黄
Chen	Zeng	陈
Lin	Ling	林
Wu	Wu	吴
Zhou	Taeu	周
Zhu	Tsy	朱
Yang	Yang	杨
Gu	Ku	顾
Deng	Deng	邓
Ding	Ting	丁
Dong	Tung	董
Fang	Fong	方
Guo	Koh	郭
He	Wu	何
Jiang	Kong	江
Ma	Mo	马
Qian	Zi	钱
Tian	Di	田
Xia	Wo	夏
Yan	Ni	严
Yu	Yu	于
Zhao	Zoa	赵

FOOD

English	Shanghai Dialect Pinyin	Simplified Characters
fish	*ng*	鱼
meat	*nioh*	肉

English	Shanghai Dialect Pinyin	Simplified Characters
chicken	*ji*	鸡
egg	*de*	蛋
beef	*nieunioh*	牛肉
lamb	*yangnioh*	羊肉
crab	*ha*	蟹
seafood	*hexi*	海鲜
mineral water	*khuongdjyuoesy*	矿泉水
tea	*zo*	茶
rice	*mi*	米
tofu (bean curd)	*deuwu*	豆腐
vegetables	*suce*	疏菜
water	*sy*	水

MISCELLANEOUS

English	Shanghai Dialect Pinyin	Simplified Characters
close enough	*cavehtu*	差不多
correct	*te*	对
foreigner	*ngakoh ning*	外国人
friend	*bangyeu*	朋友
Mandarin	Phuthungwo	普通话
outsider	*ngadi ning*	外地人
relationship	*kueyi*	关系
subway	*dithieh*	地铁
work unit	*tewe*	单位
English	*Yingveng*	英文
the day before yesterday	*ziniehtsy*	前天
yesterday	*zohnietsy*	昨天
today	*jingtsoa*	今天

English	Shanghai Dialect Pinyin	Simplified Characters
tomorrow	*mingtsoa*	明天
the day after tomorrow	*heunieh*	后天
last year	*djieunitsy*	去年
this year	*jingnitsy*	今年
next year	*mingnitsy*	明年
morning	*tsoalong (deu)*	早上
noon	*tsunglong (deu)*	中午
afternoon	*wopoenieh*	下午
night	*yadeu*	晚上
massage	*oemo*	按摩

RESOURCE GUIDE

All the telephone numbers in this section are Shanghai numbers unless otherwise stated.

EMERGENCIES

Ambulance	120
Fire	119
Police/PSB	110
Weather	121
Directory Inquires	114
Speaking Clock	117
Traffic Police	(021) 5631-7000
Harbour Emergency	(021) 6519-1710
Electricity Hotline	(021) 6329-2222
Gas Emergency	(021) 6350-7777
Water Problems	(021) 6509-0015

Shanghai Public Security Buearu (Exit-Entry Management Department for Foreigners)
333 Wusong Lu
Tel: (021) 6357-6666

MEDICAL SERVICES
Emergencies

- **International SOS**
  11C Guangdong Development Bank Tower, 555 Xujiahui Lu
  Tel: (021) 6295-9951; fax: (021) 6390-1428
  Website: http://www.internationalsos.com
- **Hua Shan Hospital**
  15/F, Foreigner's Clinic, Zonghe Lu, 12 Wulumuqi Lu
  Tel: (021) 6248-3686 / (021) 6248-9999 ext 2531
- **Hua Dong Hospital**
  2/F, Foreigner's Clinic, 221 Yanan Xi Lu
  Tel: (021) 6248-4867; after hours—(021) 6248-3018 ext 3160
- **The First People's Hospital**
  International Medical Care Centre, 585 Jiulong Lu (near the Bund)
  Tel: (021) 6324-3852

- **Rui Jin Hospital**
  197 Ruijin Er Lu
  Tel: (021) 6437-0045 ext 668101; after hours—
  (021) 6437-0045 ext 668202

General

- **Shanghai United Family Hospital**
  1111 Xianxia Lu
  Tel: (021) 6433-3963; fax: (021) 6291-1637
  Website: http://www.shanghai united.com.cn
- **World Link Clinic, Hong Qiao**
  Mandarine City Unit 30, 788 Hongxu Lu
  Tel: (021) 6405-5788; fax: (021) 6405-3587
- **World Link Clinic, Portman Clinic**.
  Shanghai Centre #203 W, 1367 Nanjing Xi Lu
  Tel: (021) 6279-7688, appointments (021) 6279-8678;
  fax: (021) 6279-7698

Dental

- **World Link Clinic, Hong Qiao**
  Mandarine City Unit 30, 788 Hongxu Lu
  Tel: (021) 6405-5788; fax: (021) 6405-3587
- **Dr. Harriet Jin's Dental Surgery**
  Rm 17C Sun Tong Infoport Plaza, No 55 Huaihai Xi Lu;
  Tel: (021) 5298-9799; fax: (021) 5298-9799
- **No 9 People's Hospital 7th Floor/ Sino-Canadian Joint Venture**
  Shanghai Dental Medical Centre Cooperative Co, Out
  Patient Service Building, 639 Zhizaoju Lu
  Tel: (021) 6313 3174

Maternity and Gynecology

- **International Peace Maternity Hospital**
  910 Hengsha Lu
  Tel: (021) 6407-0434
- **The First Maternity and Child Hospital**
  536 Changle Lu
  Tel: (021) 5403-5335

Pediatrics

- **Shanghai Children's Medical Centre**
  1678 Dongfeng Lu (by appointment only)
  Tel: (021) 5873-2020
- **Pediactic Hospital, Foreigner's Clinic**
  Shanghai Medical University, 2/F, 183 Fenglin Lu
  Tel: (021) 6403-7371

Veterinary Hospital

- **Companion Animal Hospital**
  Yanggao Lu and Fujian Lu
  Tel: (021) 6385 5905
- **Naughty Family Pets, Hong Qiao**
  2293 Hongqiao Lu
  Tel: (021) 6268-9501
- **Naughty Family Pets, Pudong**
  1529-1531 Dongfang Lu
  Tel: (021) 5875-0999
- **Shanghai PAW Veterinary Surgeons**
  1367 Gubei Lu
  Tel: (021) 3223-1498
  Email: Shanghai_paw@yahoo.com.au

ACCOMMODATION
Higher End

- **Crowne Plaza Shanghai**
  400 Panyu Lu
  Tel: (021) 6280-8888; fax: (021) 6280-6408
  Website: http://www.shanghai.crowneplaza.com
- **Forty One Hengshan Road**
  41 Hengshan Lu
  Tel: (021) 6473-1818; fax: (021) 6467-3366
- **Four Seasons Hotel Shanghai**
  500 Weihai Lu
  Tel: (021) 6256-8888; fax: (021) 6256-5678
  Website: http://www.fourseasons.com/shanghai

- **Grand Hyatt Shanghai**
  Jin Mao Tower, 88 Century Blvd
  Tel: (021) 5049-1234; fax: (021) 5049-1111
  Website: http://www.shanghai.grand. hyatt.com
- **Hilton Shanghai Hotel**
  250 Huashan
  Tel: (021) 6248-0000; fax: (021) 6248-2007
  Website: http://www.hiltonshanghai.com.cn
- **Howard Johnson Int'l (PRC)**
  C5, 20/F, Jiangsu Bldg, 528 Laoshan Dong Lu
  Tel: (021) 6886-8840; fax: (021) 6867-0173
  Website: http://www. hojochina.com
- **JW Marriott Hotel Shanghai**
  12A, Eastern Tower, 689 Beijing Dong Lu
  Tel: (021) 6360-0503; fax: (021) 6360 0510
  Website: http://www. marriotthotels.com
- **Mafair Hotel Shanghai**
  1525 Ding Xi Lu
  Tel: (021) 6240-2288; fax: (021) 6210-5500
  Website: http://www.mayfairshanghai.com
- **Okura Garden Hotel Shanghai**
  58 Maoming Nan Lu
  Tel: (021) 6415-1111; fax: (021) 6415-8899
  Website: http://www.gardenhoTel: (021) shanghai.com
- **Portman Ritz-Carlton Shanghai**
  1376 Nanjing Xi Lu
  Tel: (021) 6279-8888; fax: (021) 6279-8282
  Website: http://www.ritzcarlton.com
- **Pudong Shangri-La Hotel**
  33 Fucheng Lu
  Tel: (021) 6882-8888; fax: (021) 6882-0120
  Wbesite: http://www.shangri-la.com
- **Radisson Plaza / Xing Guo Hotel Shanghai**
  78 Xingguo Lu
  Tel: (021) 6212-9998; fax: (021) 6212-9996
  Website: http://www.radissonasia pacific.com
- **Regal International East Asia Hoyrl**
  516 Hengshan Lu

Tel: (021) 6415-5588; fax: (021) 6445-2755
Website: http://www.regal-eastasia.com

- **Renaissance Yangtze Shanghai Hotel:**
2099 Yanan Xi Lu
Tel: (021) 6275-0000; fax: (021) 6275 0750
Website: http://www.renaissancehotels.com
- **Shanghai JC Mandarin**
1225 Nanjing Xi Lu
Tel: (021) 6279-1888; fax: (021) 6279-2314
Website: http://www.jcmandarin.com
- **Shanghai Marriott Hotel Hongqiao**
2270 Hongqiao Lu
Tel: (021) 6237-6000; fax: (021) 6237-6275
Website: http:// www.marriott.com/shaqi
- **Shanghai Sino Glory Properties**
2000 Jianhe Lu;
Tel: (021) 6262-2020; fax: (021) 6261-3770
Website: http:// www.le-chateau.com
- **Sheraton Grand Tai Ping Yang, Shanghai**
5 Zunyi Nan Lu
Tel: (021) 6275-8888; fax: (021) 6275-5420
Website: http://www.sheratongrand. com.cn
- **Sofitel Hyland Shanghai**
505 Nanjing Dong Lu
Tel: (021) 6351-5888; fax: (021) 6351-4088
Website: http://www.accorhotels-china.com
- **The Westin Shanghai**
88 Henan Zhong Lu
Tel: (021) 6335-1888; fax: (021) 6335-2888
Website: http://www.starwood.com

Budget Hotels

- **Changyang Hotel**
1800 Changyang Lu
Tel: (021) 6543-4890
- **Lao Zhengxing Hotel**
556 Fuzhou Lu
Tel: (021) 6351-5496

- **Linglong Hotel**
  939 Yanan Xi Lu
  Tel: (021) 6225-0360; fax: (021) 6252-2714
- **Pujiang Hotel**
  15 Huangpu Lu
  Tel: (021) 6324-6388
- **Music Conservatiory**
  20 Fenyang Lu
  Tel: (021) 6437-2577
- **Wugong Hotel**
  431 Fuzhou Lu
  Tel: (021) 6326-0303; fax: (021) 6328-2820

INTERNATIONAL SCHOOLS

- **The British International School**
  600 Cambridge Forest New Town, No 2729 Hunan Lu
  Tel: (021) 5812-7455; fax: (021) 5812-7465
  Email: enquires@bisshanghai.com
  Website: http://www.bisshanghai.com
- **Concordia International School Shanghai**
  999 Mingyue Lu
  Tel: (021) 5899-0380; fax: (021) 5899-1685
  Email: registrar@ciss.com.cn
  Website: http:// www.ciss.com.cn
- **Shanghai American School**
  Website: http://www.saschina.org
  Puxi Branch
  258 Jinfeng Lu, Zhu Di Town Minhang District, 201107
  Shanghai Links Executive Community
  Tel: (021) 6221-1445; fax: (021) 6221-1269
  Pudong Branch
  Sanjia Gang, Pudong New Area
  Fax: (021) 5897-0011
- **Yew Chung Shanghai International School**.
  1 Shuicheng Lu
  Tel: (021) 6242-3243; fax: (021) 6242-7331
  Email: inquiry@ycef.com
  Website: http://www.ycef.com

- **French School of Shanghai**
  437 Jinhui Lu
  Tel: (021) 6405-9220 ext 105; fax: (021) 6405-9227
  Email: meunier@guomai.sh.cn
- **German School of Shanghai**
  437 Jinhui Lu
  Tel: (021) 6405 9220; fax: (021) 6405 9235
  Email: info@ds-shanghai.org.cn
  Website: http://www.ds-shanghai.org.cn
- **Shanghai Changning International School**
  79 Lane, 261 Jiangsu Lu
  Tel: (021) 6252-3688; fax: (021) 6212-2330
  Email: info@ scischina.org
- **Shanghai Singapore International School**
  288 Jidi Lu, Zhudi Town, Minhang District
  Tel: (021) 6221-9288; fax: (021) 6221-9188
  Email: info@ssischool.com

Kindergartens

- **Tiny Tots**
  43 Fuxing Lu, 7888 Humin Lu;
  Tel: (021) 6431-3788; fax: (021) 6433-2468
  Email: infoiaso@ tinytotschina.com
  Website: http://www.tinytotschina.com
- **Bingchangtian Kindergarten**
  1178 Lane, 38 Shangcheng Lu
  Tel: (021) 6876-2010
- **Dasong Kindergarten**
  5/F, 645 Changping Lu
  Tel: (021) 6215-7502
- **Elizabeth Boarding**
  31 Lane, 500 Wuzhong Dong Lu
  Tel: (021) 6270-2098
- **Fortune Kindergarten**
  1361 Dongfang Lu (Pudong), or
  2151 Lianhua Lu (Hong Qiao)
  Tel: (021) 5875-1212/ (021) 5458-0508; fax: (021) 5458-0598
  Email: fortunek@online. sh.cn
  Website: http://www.fkis.com.cn

- **Golden Bean**
  Lane 501, 25 Gauquan Lu
  Tel: (021) 5661-2872
- **KinderWorld International Kindergarten**
  2/F, Somerset Grand Shanghai, 8 Jianan Lu
  Tel: (021) 6386-7880; fax: (021) 6387-7131
  Email: kinderworld_sh@yahoo.com
  Website: http://www.kinderworld.net
- **IPP Longbai Kindergarten**
  2461 Hongqiao Lu
  Tel: (021) 62680-8320/ (021) 6268-8728
  Email: lsasha@online.sh.cn
- **New Century Kindergarten**
  181 Guilin Dong Jie, Guilin Lu
  Tel: (021) 6475-2305; fax: (021) 6268-2921
- **Shanghai Rainbow Bridge International Kindergarten**
  2381 Hongqiao Lu
  Tel: (021) 6269-0913; fax: (021) 6269-1294
  Email: rbik@public1.sta.net.cn
  Website: http://www.rbik. com
- **Shanghai Utsukushi Gaoka Montessori Kindergarten**
  24 Lane, 788 Dajie, Hongxu Lu
  Tel: (021) 6405-6318
- **Small White Pigeon (Private) Kindergarten**
  58 Lane, 301 Hongshan Lu
  Tel: (021) 5874-3772; fax: (021) 5886-7515
- **Wunang Kindergarten**
  14 Wulumuqi Nan Lu
  Tel: (021) 6433-7993

MAIDS

- **Unique Nanny Service (Shanghai) Corporation**
  A/4F, 608 Zhaojiabang Lu
  Tel: (021) 6431-7572/ (021) 6431-7573
  Website: http://www.china-nanny.com
- **Shanghai Ejll Home Economics Service Co Ltd**
  4E 982#, Changning Lu

Tel: (021) 6226-5355/ 56/ 57; fax: (021) 5239-4292
Email: info@ejll.com
Website: http://www.ejll.com

FINANCE
Insurance

- **AIU Insurance Company, Shanghai Branch**
  7/F, Novel Plaza, 128 Nanjing Xi Lu
  Tel: (021) 6350-8180; fax: (021) 6350-8182
  Website: http://www. aiush.com.cn
- **American International Assurance Co Ltd, Shanghai Branch**
  AIA Building, 17 Zhongshan No 1 Dong Lu
  Tel: (021) 6321-6698; fax: (021) 5396-2010
- **China Life-CMG Life Assurance Company Ltd**
  Level 21, China Insurance Building, 166 Lujiazui Dong Lu
  Tel: (021) 6887-6304; fax: (021) 5882-5245
  Website: http://www.chinalifecmg.com
- **Chubb Group of Insurance Companies**
  32/F, HSBC Tower, 101 Yincheng Dong Lu
  Tel: (021) 6841-5188; fax: (021) 6841-1866
  Website: http://www.chubb.com/china
- **Continental Insurance Co Shanghai Representative**
  Rm 2003, Overseas Chinese Mansion, 129 Yanan Xi Lu
  Tel: (021) 6249-7511; fax: (021) 6249-7512
  Website: http://www.cna.com
- **General Reinsurance Corporation**
  Rm 1803, China Merchants Tower, 161 Lujiazui Dong Lu
  Tel: (021) 5876-1100; fax: (021) 5878-4018
  Website: http://www.gcr.com
- **Liberty International Holdings Inc, Shanghai Office**
  Suite C, 17/F, New Shanghai International Tower, 360
  Pudong Nan Lu
  Tel: (021) 6886-2626; fax: (021) 6886-2080.
- **Winterthur Insurance (Asia) Ltd, Shanghai Branch**
  Rm 2405-2409, 24/F, Shanghai Stock Exchange Building
  North Tower, No 528 Pudong Nan Lu
  Tel: (021) 6882-3351; fax: (021) 6882-5603
  Website: http://www.winterthur.com.cn

Banking

- **Bank of America**
  18/F, South Tower, Shanghai Stock Exchange Building, 528 Pudong Nan Lu
  Tel: (021) 6881-8686; fax: (021) 6881-9200
- **BNP Paribas, Shanghai Branch**
  Rm 1002, 10/F, China Merchants Tower, 161 Lujiazui Xi Lu
  Tel: (021) 5879-7725; fax: (021) 5879-5636
  Website: http://www.bnpparibas.com.cn
- **Citibank**
  20/F, Marine Tower, 1 Pudong Dadao
  Tel: (021) 5879-1200; fax: (021) 5879-5933
  Website: http://www.citi.com
- **Credit Lyonnais Shanghai**
  36/F, China Merchants Tower, 161 Lujiazui Xi Lu
  Tel: (021) 5887-0770; fax: (021) 5887-7037
- **Deutsche Bank AG, Shanghai Branch**
  29/F, 101 Yincheng Xi Lu
  Tel: (021) 6841-0808; fax: (021) 6841-2277
- **Rabobank Netherlands (China) Ltd**
  33/F, China Merchants Tower, 161 Lujiazui Dong Lu
  Tel: (021) 5888-9888; fax: (021) 5876-8088
  Website: http://www.rabobank.com
- **Standard Chartered Bank, Shanghai**
  35/F, China Merchants Tower, 161 Lujiazui Xi Lu
  Tel: (021) 5887-1230; fax: (021) 5876-4237
- **American Express International Inc.
  Shanghai Representative Office**
  Rm 455, East Tower, Shanghai Centre, 1376 Nanjing Xi Lu
  Tel: (021) 6279-7072; fax: (021) 6279-7193

LEISURE AND ENTERTAINMENT
Cafés

- **Moonbeam Coffee Company**
  1/F, Central Plaza Central Plaza, 283 Huaihai Zhong Lu
  Tel: (021) 6390-6951
- **Monte Carol Bar and Restaurant**
  2F, Central Plaza, 381 Huaihai Zhong Lu
  Tel: (021) 6391-6891

- **Discovery Coffee**
  344 Shanxi Nan Lu (corner of Nanchang Lu)
  Tel: (021) 6467-1082
- **Starbucks Coffee**
  Rm 109, 222 Huaihai Zhong Lu
  Tel: (021) 5396-6379
- **Delifrance**
  Rm 125, Central Plaza, 381 Huaihai Lu
  Tel: (021) 5382-5171
- **Espresso Americano**
  Rm 105, Shanghai Centre, 1376 Nanjing Xi Lu
  Tel: (021) 6279-8888
- **Espresso Monica**
  1399 Nanjing Xi Lu
  Tel: (021) 6247-8707
- **Java Jive**
  18 Xianxia Lu
  Tel: (021) 6278-8534
- **Old China Hand Reading Room**
  27 Shaoxing Lu
  Tel: (021) 6473-2526
- **Sparkice**
  Rm 105, Central Plaza, 381 Huaihai Lu
  Tel: (021) 6391-5582
- **Coffee Club**
  8 Jinan Lu
  Tel: (021) 5382-8370
- **Coffee Oasis**
  Rm 102, Kerry Centre, 1515 Nanjing Xi Lu
  Tel: (021) 6298-6009
- **Bonami Cafe I**
  Rm 226, Bund, 12 Zhongshan Dong Yi Lu
  Tel: (021) 6329-7505
  and
  5F, Exhibition Hall, 50 Renmin Square / Basement,
  Exhibition Hall, 50 Renmin Square
- **Kent Cafe**
  969 Nanjing Xi Lu (at Maoming Lu)
  Tel: (021) 6272-6704

- **Passion Flower Cafe Bar**
  1110 Huaihai Dong Lu
  Tel: (021) 6415-8158 ext 70198
- **Cafe Fifi**
  No 65, Lane 405, Zhenning Lu
  Tel: (021) 6240-5860
- **Vis-a-Vis**
  103,Golden Bridge Garden, Dongzhu An Bang Lu
  Tel: (021) 6211-6857
- **Xiao Xuan Feng**
  132 Anting Lu
  Tel: (021) 6433-7995

Shopping Districts and Size Conversions

- **Yuyuan**
  On Renmin Lu, east of Henan Lu
- **Garment Market**
  999 Huaihai Zhong Lu
- **Huating Lu**
  Located off Huaihai Lu by the Changshu Lu Subway Station
- **Flower Market**
  225 Shanxi Nan Lu
- **Xizhimen Bird and Flower Market**
  Xizang Nan Lu, opposite entrance to Dongtai Lu
  Antique Market
- **Junk Market**
  Fuxing Dong Lu, at intersection with Zhonghua Lu

Cinemas

- **Shanghai Film Art Centre**
  160 Xinhua Lu
  Tel: (021) 6280-6088
- **Grand Theatre**
  216 Nanjing Xi Lu
  Tel: (021) 6327-2223
- **Cathay Theatre**
  870 Huaihai Lu
  Tel: (021) 6473-2592

- **Heng Shan Cinema**
  838 Hengshan Lu;
  Tel: (021) 6431-3740
- **Tian Shan Cinema**
  888 Tianshan Lu
  Tel: (021) 6229-9570
- **Guo Ji Cinema**
  330 Haining Lu
  Tel: (021) 6324-0778
- **Xiang Ying Cinema**
  1111 Xiangyang Lu
  Tel: (021) 6511-3356
- **Liao Yuan Film Centre**
  600 Changshou Lu
  Tel: (021) 6277-4022
- **Paradise Palace**
  308 Anfu Lu
  Tel: (021) 6433-6291
- **Shanghai International Broadcasting Centre**
  651 Nanjing Xi Lu
  Tel: (021) 6256-5899

Theatres

- **Shanghai Grand Theatre**
  300 Renmin Dajie
  Tel: (021) 6386-868; fax: (021) 6318-4478
- **Shanghai Centre Theatre**
  1376 Nanjing Xi Lu
  Tel: (021) 6279-8600
- **Majestic Theatre**
  66 Jiangning Lu
  Tel: (021) 6258-6493
- **Shanghai Acrobatic Theatre**
  400 Nanjing Xi Lu
  Tel: (021) 6327-7182
- **Shanghai Concert Hall**
  523 Yan'an Dong Lu
  Tel: (021) 6327-5694

- **Changjiang Theatre**
  21 Huanghe Lu
  Tel: (021) 6327-6008
- **Huangpu Theatre**
  780 Beijing Dong Lu
  Tel: (021) 6320-6598
- **People's Grand Stage**
  663 Jiujiang Lu
  Tel: (021) 6322-1242
- **Shanghai Artistic Theatre**
  57 Maoming Nan Lu
  Tel: (021) 6253-0788

Bookshops

- **Shanghai Hong Kong Joint Publishing Co Ltd**
  624 Huaihai Lu (M)
  Tel: (021) 5306-4393/ (021) 5306-8170; fax: (021) 5306-0848
- **Shanghai Foreign Language Bookshop**
  390 Fuzhou Lu
  Tel: (021) 6322-3200
- **Shanghai Bookmall**
  465 Fuzhou Lu
  Tel: (021) 6391-4778/ (021) 6350-8763; fax: (021) 6391-4778
  Website: http://www.bookmall.com.cn
- **Shanghai Tourism Bookshop**
  68 San Pai Lou Lu
  Tel: (021) 6328-2534

Libraries

- **Shanghai Library**
  1555 Huaihai Zhong Lu
  Tel: (021) 6445-5555; fax: (021) 6445-5001
  Website: http://www.library.sh.cn

Cultural and Social Organisations

- **Abundance Club**
  Email: frdemmer@netscape.net
- **Active Kidz Shanghai**
  2/F, The Clubhouse, Nice Year Villas, 333 Hongmei Lu

Tel: (021) 6406-6757; fax: (021) 5458-1402
Website: http://www. activekidz.org

- **Australian Women's Shanghai Group**
  Tel: (021) 5458-0247
- **Belgium Night**
  Tel: (021) 6474-6166
- **Busy But Single Club**
  Email: Chinasingleclub@yahoo.com
- **Cambridge and Oxford Society**
  Tel: (021) 6360-7029 ext 101
  Email: ian.riley@asialink.com.cn
- **Cascade Club**
  Tel: (021) 6252-3688
  Email: mwilliams@scischina.org
- **CEIBS Alumni Relations**
  Tel: (021) 2890-5121
  Website: http://www.ceibs.edu
- **Cercle Francophone de Shanghai**
  Tel: (021) 6262-4732
  Email: michelle@uninet.com.cn
- **Chatterboxes**
  Email: simona62mk@yahoo.com
- **China Volunteers United**
  Website: http://www.cvu.org.cn
- **China -Italy Exchange Centre**
  Tel: (021) 6410-3937; fax: (021) 6469-0753
- **Chinese Antique Furniture Society**
  Suite 24 D E 28 Caoxi Bei Lu
  Tel: (021) 6438-2200; fax: (021) 6427-9520
  Email: gwang@public4.sta.net.cn
- **Club Italia**
  Website: http://www.clubitaliashanghai.com
- **Colombians in Shanghai**
  Tel: 138-0199-7032
  Email: colesh2003 @hotmail.com
- **Cornell Club of Shanghai**
  Tel: (021) 6258-2582 ext 5311
  Email: Dean.Ho@ubssh.com

- **CultureXChina**
  Email: events@cluturexchina.com
- **Designers' Group**
  Email: marcarsenault@raffles-lasalle.com
- **Dutch Community**
  Website: http://nvsdss.nease.net
- **Elites Club of Shanghai**
  Email: ChinaShanghaiMBA@ hotmail.com
- **English Conversation Club**
  Tel: (021) 6279-3348 ext 16
  Email: forfast@ssbg.com.cn
- **English & More Club**
  Website: http://www.englishandmore.com
- **Expatriate Professional Women's Society**
  Email: epws2001@yahoo.com
- **Filipino Community in Shanghai**
  Tel: 136-2191-2016
  Email: filcomsha@hotmail.com
- **Finnish Society**
  Tel: (021) 6474 4533
- **Fourth Way Group**
  Website: http://www.4thway.vip.sina.com
- **Futune Cookies Club**
  Website: http://www.fcclub.com
- **German Centre**
  Tel: (021) 6501-5100 ext 4001
- **German Club Shanghai**
  Tel: (021) 6262-8226
- **Health Professionals Organisation**
  Tel: (021) 6433-6880 ext 2244
- **Here International Club**
  Suite 711, Zi An Building, 309 Yuyuan Lu
  Tel: (021) 6248-6806
- **Holiday Leisure Club**
  Tel: (021) 6230-7011
  Website: http://www.s-holiday.com
- **Inter-asia International Club**
  Email: sweety_angie@sohu.com

- **International Fashion Club**
  Tel: (021) 6208-9320
- **Jewish Community of Shanghai**
  Villa No 2, Shangmira Garden, 1720 Hongqiao Lu
  Tel: (021) 6278-0225; fax: (021) 6278-0223
  Website: http://www.chinajewish.org
- **La Leche League Shanghai**
  Tel: (021) 6431-9424
- **New Zealanders Group**
  Email: ShanghaiNZ@hotmail.com
- **Princeton Club of Shanghai**
  Email: mdroslyn@yahoo.com
- **Russian Club**
  Tel: 139-0181-4942
  Website: http://www.russian shanghai.com
- **Shanghai American Club**
  Tel: (021) 6393-2880 ext 3228; fax: (021) 6393-6766;
  Email: membership@sh.americanclubs.org
- **Shanghai Health Club**
  Email: daviddai123@hotmail.com
- **Swiss Club Shanghai**
  Tel: (021) 6266-0844; fax: (021) 6276-0856
  Website: http://www.swissclubshanghai.com
- **Talking China Languages Exchange Club**
  Tel: (021) 6289-4308
  Website: http://www.talkingchina.net
- **Toastmasters Clubs in Shanghai**
  Website: http://www.shanghai-biz.com/atm
- **UCLA Shanghai Club**
  Website: http://www.UCLACLUB.com
- **University of Chicago Club**
  Tel: (021) 6248-7677
  Email: benjamin.morgan@afp.com
- **Wellesley Club of Shanghai**
  Email: gkzee@hotmail.com
- **Young Entrepreneurs' Organisation Shanghai Chapter**
  Email: Shanghai2003s@yeo.org

- **Wharton Club of Shanghai**
  Tel: 139-1734-4848
  Website: http://www. whartonshanghai.org

Bars & Clubs

- **Libra**
  880 Henshan Lu
  Tel: (021) 6483-8441
- **Long Bar**
  Level 2, Retail Plaza, Shanghai Centre, 1376 Nanjing Xi Lu
  Tel: (021) 6279-8268
- **Malone's**
  255 Tongren Lu
  Tel: (021) 6247-2400
- **Mandy's**
  9 Dongping Lu
  Tel: (021) 6474-6628
- **Manhattan Bar**
  905 Julu Lu
  Tel: (021) 6247-7787
  Website: http://www. manhattanbar.com
- **Noble Single**
  980 Xiangying Lu
  Tel: (021) 6548-6676
- **O'Malley's Irish Pub**
  42 Taojiang Lu
  Tel: (021) 6437-0667
- **O'Richard's Bar & Restaurant**
  . 2/F Pu Jiang Hotel, 15 Huangpu Lu
  Tel: (021) 6324-6338
- **Paulaner German Beerhouse**
  50 Fenyang Lu
  Tel: (021) 6474-5700
- **Peace Hotel Bar**
  Peace Hotel, 20 Nanjing Dong Lu
  Tel: (021) 6321-6888
- **Penthouse Bar**
  39/F, Hilton Shanghai, 250 Huashan Lu
  Tel: (021) 6248-0000 ext 8640

- **POP**
  45 Yueyang Lu
  Tel: (021) 6437-2949
- **Shanghai Jin-Chuan**
  158 Han Zhong Lu
  Tel: (021) 6353-5988
- **Shanghai Sally's**
  4 Xingshan Lu
  Tel: (021) 6358-0738/ (021) 6327-1859
- **Stock Bar**
  17 Maoming Nan Lu
  Tel: (021) 6256-5337
- **Super Star Country Pub**
  No 1 Alley, 155 Xinhua Lu
  Tel: (021) 6280-3557
- **Tequila Mama**
  Basement 24A Ruijin Lu
  Tel: (021) 6433-5086
- **Time Passage**
  100 Huashan Lu
  Tel: (021) 6252-2901
- **Y.Y's (Yin Yang)**
  125 Nanchang Lu
  Tel: (021) 6431-2668/ (021) 6466-4098
- **Zoo Bar**
  593 Fuxing Zhong Lu
  Tel: (021) 6415-1583
- **D&K Bar**
  758 Julu Lu
  Tel: (021) 6247-3943
- **Sophia's Teahouse**
  480 Huashan Lu
  Tel: (021) 6249-9917
- **99 Disco**
  928 Xikang Lu
  Tel: (021) 6266-9999
- **H J H Club**
  878 Julu Lu
  Tel: (021) 6249-5535/ (021) 6249-5536

- **Aero Pit**
  Regal Stadium Hotel, Tianyao Qiao Lu
  Tel: (021) 6426-6888
- **Buff Disco**
  1088 Liyang Lu (near Hong Kou, McDonalds)
  Tel: (021) 5671-4936
- **Club de Mako**
  409-456 Nanjing Dong Lu
  Tel: (021) 6360-2449/ (021) 6352-0535 ext 118
- **D D's**
  298 Xinfu Lu
  Tel: (021) 6280-8670
  Website; http:// www.ddsclub.com
- **Groove**
  308 Hengshan Lu
  Tel: (021) 6471-8154.
- **Galaxy Hotel Entertainment Centre**
  888 Zhongshan Xi Lu
  Tel: (021) 6275-2999 ext 2380
- **Hit House**
  2069 Siping Lu (near Guoding Lu)
  Tel: (021) 6548-1001
- **Judy's Too**
  176 Maoming Nan Lu
  Tel: (021) 6473-1417
  Website: http://www.judysco.com
- **Mars Disco Pub**
  88 Changshu Lu
  Tel: (021) 6249-3028/ (021) 6249-3228
- **MGM**
  141 Shanxi Nan Road
  Tel: (021) 6467-3353
- **New York New York**
  146 Huqiu Lu
  Tel: (021) 6321-6097
- **Passion**
  288 Panyu Lu
  Tel: (021) 6283-3575

- **Time Disco**
  5/F, 550 Huaihai Lu
  Tel: (021) 6359-8951
- **Tong Tong Disco**
  80 Xingchang Lu
  Tel: (021) 6359-1636
- **Tribesman Pub**
  2150 Siping Lu
- **Bar Twist**
  Jinmao Building, 2 Shi Ji Boulevard, Pudong District, 53/F
  Grand Hyatt Hotel Shanghai
  Tel: (021) 5047-1234 ext 8764
- **101 Bar**
  98 Xinle Lu
  Tel: (021) 5404-7719
- **1931 Cafe Pub**
  112 Maoming Nan Lu
  Tel: (021) 6472-5264
- **Zoo Bar**
  180 Maoming Nan Lu
  Tel: (021) 6445-2330; fax: (021) 6445-2330
- **BJ Bar**
  18 Chongqing Nan Lu
  Tel: (021) 6372-3476
- **Blues & Jazz Bar**.
  4, Sinan Lu (near Xiangshan Lu)

Physical Fitness Centres & Sports Facilities

- **Regal International Hotel Fitness Centre**
  516 Hengshan Lu
  Tel: (021) 6415-5588; fax: (021) 6445-8899
- **Kerry Centre Gym**
  2/F, Kerry Centre, 1515 Nanjing Xi Lu
  Tel: (021) 6279-4625; fax: (021) 6279-0182
- **Body Tech**
  387 Fanyu Lu
  Tel: (021) 6281-5639/ (021) 6281-9587

- **Citigym**
  8/F 333 Huaihai Zhong Lu and
  333 Linpin Bei Lu, Rei Hong Xin Cheng
  Tel: (021) 5306-6868; fax: (021) 5306-6000
- **Clark Hatch Fitness Centre**
  Radisson Plaza Xing Guo Hotel, 78 Xingguo Lu
  Tel: (021) 6212-9998; fax: (021) 6212-9996
- **Dynamic Recreation Club**
  1011 Zhongshan Xi Lu
  Tel: (021) 6219- 9199; fax: (021) 6295-2868.
- **Fitness First At Plaza 66**
  B1, 1266 Nanjing Xi Lu
  Tel: (021) 6288-0152
  Website: http://www.fitnessfirst.com
- **Gold's Gym**
  2/F, Jiu An Plaza, 258 Tongren Lu
  Tel: (021) 6279-2000
- **Lan Shen Gym**
  5/F, 8 Huaihai Zhong Lu
  Tel: (021) 6386-2262
- **Megafit**
  1/F, Zhong Hai Building, 398 Huaihai Zhong Lu
  Tel: (021) 5383-6633
- **Mina International Health Centre**
  4/F, Tai Hao Building, 3211 Hongmei Lu
  Tel: (021) 6401-5155
- **Shanghai Gubei Gym Club**
  59 Ronghua Xi Dao
  Tel: (021) 6219-5818 ext 152
- **Shanghai International Tennis Centre**
  3/F, 516 Hengshan Lu, Regal International East Asia Hotel
  Tel: (021) 6415-5588 ext 82
- **Shanghai Jia Bao Tennis Club**
  Jia Ding Sports Centre, 118 Xincheng Lu
  Tel: (021) 5999-7151
- **Shanghai Racquet Club**
  555 Jinfeng Lu, Hua Cao Town, Min Hang District
  Tel: (021) 2201-0088; fax: (021) 2201-0909
  Website: http://www.src.com.cn

- **Spa at Club Oasis of Grand Hyatt Shanghai**
  57/F, Jin Mao Tower, Grand Hyatt Shanghai, 88 Shiji Dadao
  Tel: (021) 5047-1234 ext 8948
- **The Spa at the Hilton**
  4/F, Jing'an Hilton Hotel, 250 Huashan Lu
  Tel: (021) 6248-0000 ext 2600
- **Total Fitness Club**
  5-6/F, Zhong Chuang Plaza, No 819 Nanjing Xi Lu
  Tel: (021) 6255-3535
  and
  4/F, Lu Heng Da Plaza, No 285 Changshu Lu
  Tel: (021) 6276-2922
- **Weider-Tera International Gym**
  4/F, 231 Wuning Lu
  Tel: (021) 6243-6069/ (021) 6254-9870
- **Xian Xia Tennis Centre**
  1885 Hongqiao Lu
  Tel: (021) 6262-6720

FURTHER READING

Selecting from the literally thousands of books on China is a daunting task. A few of our favourites follow.

CHINESE LANGUAGE STUDY

A Chinese-English Dictionary and *An English-Chinese Dictionary.* Both Beijing: Commercial Press, 1988.

Chinese for Today. Beijing Language Institute. San Francisco: China Books & Periodicals Inc, 1986.

Business Chinese 500. Beijing Language Institute. San Francisco: China Books & Periodicals Inc, 1982.

Continental's English-Chinese Dictionary. Hong Kong: Hong Kong Press, n.d.
- Good pocket-sized dictionary.

English-Chinese Lexicon of Business Terms. Compiled by Andrew C Chang. Boston: Cheng & Tsui Company, 2002.
- An excellent and useful guide.

Spoken Standard Chinese (3 Volumes). Hugh M Stimson and Parker Po-Fei Huang. New Haven, CT: Yale Far Eastern Publications, 1976.

Matthew's Chinese-English Dictionary. Taipei: Dunhuang Press, 1975 (13th ed).
- A simple introduction to classical characters, useful for introductory *wenyan* study.

Rosetta Stone CD-ROM Web-based Chinese Program (http://www.rosettastone.com).

Barron's Chinese at a Glance. Scott D Seligman and I-Chuan Chen. Hauppage, NY: Barron's Educational Series, 2001.

Xinhua Zidian. Beijing: Xinhua Press, 1975.
- Excellent pocket-sized Chinese-Chinese dictionary including both complex and simplified characters.

BUSINESS GUIDES/ECONOMIC OVERVIEWS

Wen and the Art of Doing Business in China. Daniel R Joseph. Pittsburgh, PA: Cultural Dragon Publishing, 2001.
- Not without flaws, but a useful cautionary tale.

Internationalizing China. David Zweig. Ithaca, New York: Cornell University Press, 2002.
- Useful 20,000-foot survey of the forces transforming China, and underlying much of current business change.

Back-Alley Banking: Private Entrepreneurs in China. Kellee Tsai. Ithaca, NY: Cornell University Press, 2002.
- A good explanation of China's growing small and medium enterprises.

Success Secrets to Maximize Business in China. Larry T Luah. Portland, OR, USA: Graphic Arts; Singapore: Marshall Cavendish Business, 2001.

Strategy, Structure and Performance of MNCs in China. Luo Yadong. Westport, Connecticut: Quorum Books, 2001.
- Less analytical than it could be, but still a useful survey of why some foreign-invested businesses succeed, and others fail.

Chinese Intellectual Property Law and Practice. Ed. Mark A Cohen. A Elizabeth Bang and Stephanie J Mitchell. The Hague: Kluwer Law International, 1999.

Integrating China into the Global Economy. Nicholas R Lardy. Washington, DC: Brookings Institution, 2002.
- An excellent analysis of the impact of WTO accession.

Chinese Business Etiquette. Scott D Seligman. New York: Warner Books, 1999.
- One of the best summaries of the cultural aspects of business in China.

The China Dream:The Elusive Quest for the Last Great Untapped Market on Earth. Joe Studwell. London: Profile Books, 2002.
- Thoughtful summary of many of the pitfalls in pursuing those 'two billion feet'.

The authors also strongly recommend membership in at least one or two of the business associations listed in *Chapter 9: Business Unusual*, with special mention of the US-China Business Council, and its publications: *China Market Intelligence* and *China Business Review.*

CULTURE-RELATED ISSUES

Culture Shock! China. Kevin Sinclair with Iris Wong Po-Yee. Portland, OR, USA: Graphic Arts; London, UK: Kuperard; Singapore: Times Books International, 2003.

Two Years in the Melting Pot. Liu Zongren. San Fancisco: China Books and Periodicals, Inc, 1988.
- A good turnabout: a Chinese perspective on the difficulties of adjusting to US culture.

Iron and Silk. Mark Salzman. New York: Vintage, 1987.

The Traveler's Guide to Asian Customs & Manners. Nancy L Braganti and Elizabeth Devine. New York: St. Martin's Press, 1988.

Living in China. Rebecca Weiner, Margaret Murphy and Albert Li. San Francisco: China Books & Periodicals, Inc, 1991/1997.

SHANGHAI HISTORY AND CULTURE
Shanghai Longtang. Ed. Luo Xiaowei and Wu Jiang. Shanghai: Shanghai People's Fine Art's Publishing, 1997.

Shanghai: A Century of Change in Photographs. Lynn Pan with Xue Liyong and Qian Zonghao. Shanghai: Haifeng Publishing, 1995.

Life and Death in Shanghai. Nien Cheng. Penguin, 1988.

The Jews in Shanghai. Ed. Pan Guang. Shanghai: Shanghai Pictorial Publishing House, 1995.

In Search of Old Shanghai. Pan Ling. Hong Kong: Joint Publishing Co, 1982.

Odyssey Illustrated Guide to Shanghai. Peter Hibbard, Lynn Pan, May Holdsworth and Jill Hunt. Hong Kong: The Guidebook Company. Ltd, 1995.

A Last Look: Western Architecture in Old Shanghai. Tess Johnston and Deke Erh. Hong Kong: Old China Hand Press, 1993.

Shanghai '37. Vicki Baum. London: Oxford University Press, 1939/1986.

Shanghai and the Yangzi Delta. (The Yangzi River Trilogy series). Eric N Danielson. Singapore: Times Editions, 2004.

CHINESE HISTORY/CULTURE
Good Deeds & Gunboats. Hugh Deane. China Books & Periodicals Ltd, 1990.

Confucian China and Its Modern Fate: A Trilogy. Joseph R Levenson. University of California Press, 1965.

Chinese Shadows. Simon Leys. Penguin Books, 1978.

Son of The Revolution. Liang Heng & Judith Shapiro. Vintage Books, 1984.

Roses and Thorns: The Second Blooming of the Hundred Flowers in Chinese Fiction, 1979-80. Perry Link. University of California Press, 1984.

Bird in a Cage: Legal Reform in China After Mao. Stanley B Lubman. Stanford University Press, 1999.

The Soong Dynasty. Sterling Seagrave. Harper & Row, 1986.

The Gate of Heavenly Peace. Jonathan D Spence. Penguin Books, 1982.

Mooncakes and Hungry Ghosts: Festivals of China. Carol Stepanchuk and Charles Wong. China Books & Periodicals Ltd, 1991.

Sharks Fins and Millet. Ilona Ralf Sues. Garden City Publishing, 1945.

China Chic. Vivienne Tam with Martha Huang. Regan Books, 2000.

Riding the Iron Rooster. Paul Theroux. Ivy Books, 1988.

250 Chinese NGOs. Ed. Nick Young. China Development Brief, 2001.

ABOUT THE AUTHORS

Rebecca has lived 11 of the last 15 years in China, including five years in Shanghai. She's now returned to the United States to live with her husband Mike Rastelli and their daughter Sarah, but is always up for return visits to the land of *zongzi* and jazz.

Angie, like many long-term residents, came to Shanghai 'on a three week trip' in 1995, and has lived and worked in the city since. Deeply involved with the community, she served two years as Chairman of the Board of the American Chamber of Commerce in Shanghai (AmCham), and has supported non-profit initiatives like Special Olympics, Roots & Shoots, and a charity race in Outer Mongolia (http://www.ultramongolia. com) that was started by Shanghai runners. Angie is now a Managing Director at Burson-Marsteller in China.

Xu Jun was born in Beijing and relocated to Shanghai eight years ago—among the first group of post-economic reform 'local expats'—for global consulting firm Burson-Marsteller (for which he was the first local hire). He is now with DuPont China Holding Company in Shanghai. He has also worked in Hong Kong, Singapore and Australia. Xu Jun is proud to bring his first--hand knowledge of working in cross-cultural environments in Shanghai and throughout the Asia-Pacific region to readers of this book.

INDEX

A

American Chamber of Commerce (AmCham) 10, 32, 33, 112, 224, 251, 253, 266, 267

Ayi 48, 72, 84–86, 96, 123, 124, 126, 127, 237

B

Bund 2, 3, 4, 11, 13, 14, 15, 24, 56, 59, 92, 112, 118, 133, 156, 160, 165, 169, 172, 173, 176, 181–182, 184, 191, 202, 207, 210, 212, 214, 216, 217, 242, 267, 278

business 245–274
  business leader 246–247
  communication 257–261
  costs 268–270
  cross-cultural teams 262–266
  Hong Kong 247–249
  networking 252–257
  staying informed 249–252
  think local 245–246, 270–274

C

charitable activities 222–232
  charitable organisations 225–232
  donating money 221–224
  NGOs 224–225
  volunteering 220, 225–233
children 70–73
  baby-sitter 72
  baby supplies 73–74

E

education
  adult 86–88
  arts 88
  Chinese language 86–87
  Chinese public schools 75–76
  cost 75–76
  day care 72–73
  extra-curricular activities 76–77
  international schools 74–75
  pre-school 72–73
  universities 87–88
entertaining guests 130–132
  traditional Chinese guests 131–132
excursions
  day trips 213–217
  walking tours 180–181, 182, 184–188, 192–194, 195–199, 200–202, 208–209
  weekend 217–220

F

family activities 77–83
  during summer 82–83
  for a rainy day 81–82
  outings 77–80
festivals 174–176
  Chinese New Year 175–176
food 132–158
  Benbang cai *See* Shanghainese
  Chinese 133–134, 142–146, 147–150
  dim-sim 152–154
  fusion 136–137, 156–157
  international 154–156
  Muslim 146–147
  restaurant listing 137–157
  Shanghainese 134–136, 138–142
  tea food 151–152
  vegetarian 150

G

geography 6

H

health care 101–110
  concerns 106–108
  hospitals and facilities 102–105
  insurance 105–106
  tips 108–110
history 6–16
housing 56–70
  downtown 68
  garden villas 62–64
  golf course living 67–68
  non-serviced apartments 60–62
  purchasing 69–70
  serviced apartments 58–60
  Shangurbia 64–67

J

Jews 11, 19, 19–20, 20, 21, 25, 26, 27, 31, 203–209, 243

L

language 235–243, 246
  common phrases 240–242
  Mandarin 236–237
  origins 235–236
  pronunciation guide 238–240
life cycle 47–53
  birth 47–48
  childhood and beyond 48–51
  death 52
  marriage 51
  retirement 52
Lu, Xun 21–22, 128, 194, 195, 199, 218, 278
Lujiazui 3, 14, 15, 67, 140, 210, 258

M

money matters 99–100

N

non-verbal communication 243

O

Old City 178–180

P

politics
  Chiang, Kai Shek 9, 10, 196, 219
  Chinese Communist Party (CCP) 8–10, 194, 196, 197, 198, 199, 200, 201
  Gang of Four 12
  Kuomintang (KMT) 9, 12, 194, 196, 199, 200, 201, 242
  Mao, Zedong 12, 21, 26, 40, 89, 91, 148, 193, 194, 195, 197, 199
  Shanghai Gang 13, 27–28, 28, 246
  Sun, Yat Sen 74, 194, 195, 196, 199, 278
Pudong 14, 15, 56, 59, 65, 66, 67, 80, 81, 111, 161, 167, 202, 209–212, 249

R

recreation
  cultural activities 166–167
  intellectual clubs 163–164
  karaoke 173
  massage 165–166
  morning walks 165
  night life 167–173
  sporting activities 161–162
relocation
  to China 120–122
  to home 122

S

safety & security 124–127
  home 126–127
  office 127
Shanghainese *See* language
Shanghai particularities 37–43
  alternative lifestyles 42
  business focus 38
  competition 42
  cosmopolitanism and pride 37–38
  education and opportunity 38–39
  multinationalism 37
  strong women 39–42
shopping 89–99
  antiques 95–96
  books 95
  fakes 90–91
  groceries 96–97
  sundries 98–99
  tailors 91
  toys 93–94
Soong, Qingling 74, 199, 207, 278

T

teenagers 83
telecommunications 123–124
transportation 110–117
  bicycles 115–116
  cars 112–113
  driver's licence 116–117
  feet 118
  subway and buses 113–114
  taxis 111–112

V

visa 119–120

Titles in the CULTURE**SHOCK**! series:

Argentina	Hong Kong	Paris
Australia	Hungary	Philippines
Austria	India	Portugal
Bahrain	Indonesia	San Francisco
Barcelona	Iran	Saudi Arabia
Beijing	Ireland	Scotland
Belgium	Israel	Sri Lanka
Bolivia	Italy	Shanghai
Borneo	Jakarta	Singapore
Brazil	Japan	South Africa
Britain	Korea	Spain
Cambodia	Laos	Sweden
Canada	London	Switzerland
Chicago	Malaysia	Syria
Chile	Mauritius	Taiwan
China	Mexico	Thailand
Costa Rica	Morocco	Tokyo
Cuba	Moscow	Turkey
Czech Republic	Munich	Ukraine
Denmark	Myanmar	United Arab
Ecuador	Nepal	Emirates
Egypt	Netherlands	USA
Finland	New York	Vancouver
France	New Zealand	Venezuela
Germany	Norway	Vietnam
Greece	Pakistan	

For more information about any of these titles, please contact any of our Marshall Cavendish offices around the world (listed on page ii) or visit our website at:

www.marshallcavendish.com/genref